P9-CEO-010

Also by William Poundstone

Big Secrets (1983)

The Recursive Universe (1984)

Bigger Secrets (1986)

Labyrinths of Reason (1988)

The Ultimate (1990)

Prisoner's Dilemma (1992)

Biggest Secrets (1993)

Carl Sagan: A Life in the Cosmos (1999)

How Would You Move Mount Fuji? (2003)

Fortune's Formula (2005)

GAMING THE VOTE

GAMING

THE

VOTE

Why Elections Aren't Fair

(and What We Can Do About It)

WILLIAM

POUNDSTONE

Hill and Wang

A division of Farrar, Straus and Giroux

New York

Hill and Wang
A division of Farrar, Straus and Giroux
18 West 18th Street, New York 10011

Library of Congress Cataloging-in-Publication Data
Poundstone, William.
    Gaming the vote : why elections aren't fair (and what we can do about it) / by William
Poundstone.—1st ed.
        p.   cm.
    Includes bibliographical references.
    ISBN-13: 978-0-8090-4893-9 (hardcover : alk. paper)
    ISBN-10: 0-8090-4893-0 (hardcover : alk. paper)
    1. Elections—United States. 2. Voting—United States. 3. Politics, Practical—
United States. 4. Game theory. 5. United States—Politics and government. I. Title.

JK1976.P68 2008
324.973—dc22

                                                                    2007036770

Designed by Maggie Goodman

www.fsgbooks.com

1   3   5   7   9   10   8   6   4   2

Frontispiece: Clifford Berryman's 1912 cartoon exposes the dark side of voting. Despite the smiling faces, presidential contenders Teddy Roosevelt, Woodrow Wilson, and William Howard Taft well knew that elections can be unfair when there are three or more candidates.
(U.S. Senate Collection, Center for Legislative Archives)

To Scott

Contents

6. Year of the Spoiler 120

THE SOLUTION

7. Trouble in Kiribati 133

8. The New Belfry 149

9. Instant Runoff 162

▪ Lord Salisbury ▪ H. G. Wells ▪ instant-runoff voting ▪ one-stop shopping ▪ the winner-turns-loser paradox

Contents

17. Blue Man Coup   279

Karma ▪ George Allen ▪ YouTube ▪ Glenda Parker's vacation money ▪ the Blue Man from Bozeman ▪ Y2K ▪ the Heimlich maneuver ▪ Smurfs ▪ little microchips inserted in our brains ▪ conspiracy theories

GAMING THE VOTE

Prologue:

The Wizard and the Lizard

Even when he was Grand Wizard of the Ku Klux Klan, David Duke felt he was destined for something bigger. The Klan was just one of a number of organizations that Duke had joined, been actively involved with, and discarded when they no longer fit his purpose.

As a student at Louisiana State University, Duke had studied German so that he could read *Mein Kampf* in the original. Each April 20, he celebrated Hitler's birthday with a party. He draped his dorm room with swastika flags and wore a Nazi uniform around campus.

Duke was equally comfortable in the uniform of an ROTC cadet. One of his instructors praised Duke's "outstanding leadership potential." But then "we started receiving information on him from the Department of Defense . . . Here was a 19-year-old kid getting money from Germany."

The money was for American Nazi activities. The Pentagon rejected Duke's application for an advanced-training program and refused to commission him as an officer. That rebuff caused Duke to channel his leadership potential into the Ku Klux Klan. In just a couple of years, he rose to the Klan's highest post, Grand Wizard, in 1975. This meteoric ascent was a matter of his being in the right place at the right time. The previous Wizard had just been gunned down in a motel parking lot.

Duke stood out in the Klan almost as much as he had at LSU. He preferred to appear in a crisp business suit and tie rather than a hood and robe. He adopted the corporate-sounding title "National Director." One of his more surprising actions as Klansman was to write a book called *African Atto* (1973), under the pseudonym Mohammed X. He sold it by mail order, taking out ads in black newspapers with the heading WHEN WAS THE LAST TIME WHITEY CALLED YOU *NIGGER*? The book was a martial arts manual. Duke told people that its real purpose was to compile the names and addresses of the blacks who ordered it—for Ku Klux Klan records.

In 1980 Duke abruptly left the organization. His story is that he realized the Klan would never be taken seriously as a political force. It was time for the defenders of the white race to get out of the cow pastures and into the hotel suites. People who knew Duke in the Klan have a different story. "We had to get David out," explained Karl Hand, formerly Duke's lieutenant. "He was seducing all the wives . . . He had no qualms about putting the make on anybody's wife or girlfriend, and the flak always came back to me, because I was his national organizer."

The immediate cause of Duke's departure was his attempt to pocket a quick thirty-five thousand dollars by selling the top-secret Klan membership list to an enigmatic character named Bill Wilkinson. Wilkinson presented himself to Duke as a Klansman intending to set up his own splinter organization. In fact, he was secretly an FBI informant. Wilkinson videotaped Duke dickering over the price, then threatened to play the tape at a KKK meeting. Possibly the whole thing was an FBI sting—or possibly Wilkinson saw a freelance opportunity. Duke left the Klan after that.

Duke had never held a regular job and was not keen to start. Naturally, he turned to politics. Plastic surgery and a blow-dryer transformed him into something resembling a game show host. Starting in 1975, he began running for local offices in Louisiana. In 1980 he founded his own organization, the National Association for the Advancement of White People. He discovered that there was good money to be made in fringe nonprofits. After Duke and some Klansmen were arrested at a demonstration in Forsythe County, Georgia, he raised nineteen thousand dollars from white supremacists nationwide to pay a fifty-five-dollar fine.

In 1988 Duke ran for president of the United States, entering several primaries as a Democrat. No one took him seriously except for writers of offbeat feature articles. He then ran as a Populist and got 47,047 votes.

In 1989, Duke downsized his ambitions to run for the Louisiana legislature. Not only did he win, but he won against former Republican governor Dave Treen. This coup encouraged Duke to run for the U.S. Senate in 1990. He lost. Then in 1991, he decided it was time to try for governor of Louisiana.

Edwin Edwards "plays the system like a violin. He had an uncanny knack of charging headlong to the brink and knowing exactly where to stop . . . and he doesn't even try to cover his trail, he's that cocky." These were the words of U.S. Attorney Stanford Bardwell, Jr., one of the many prosecutors who indicted Edwards and saw him wriggle off the hook. Some called Edwards the most corrupt politician in a corrupt state.

Edwards was born dirt-poor in an cypress-wood farmhouse his father built with his own hands. He attended Louisiana State University and became a successful trial lawyer in Cajun country. Entering politics as a populist Democrat, he made a successful run for governor in 1972, winning on an alliance of the Cajun and black vote. In the governor's mansion, so close to the flow of money and power (the two great aphrodisiacs), he was like a kid in a candy store.

His plump patrician face, ruddy nose and cheeks, graying hair, and salacious wit perfectly fit the part of an aging roué. "Two out of ten women will go to bed with you," ran one of Edwards's maxims, "but you've got to ask the other eight." Edwards inherited the Louisiana tradition of influence peddling and used it to live lavishly. His most expensive habit was gambling. The New Orleans *Times-Picayune* reported that Edwards

> is granted up to $200,000 casino credit at the stroke of his pen . . . He is classified by his favorite hotel-casino—Caesars Palace—among the 0.25 percent of its customers whose importance as gamblers makes the company unwilling to share credit information with other casinos. Caesars even waives its maximum bet limit when Edwards steps to the table . . . He eats his meals on the casinos' tab in the Strip's poshest restaurants. He sunbathes on casino-owned yachts at Lake Tahoe. He glides around town in casino limousines, and he and his entourage stay at luxury suites in the most popular hotels. All for free.
>
> What can Edwards get from the Vegas casinos? "Anything he wants," a former Caesars Palace employee said.

"I like to gamble," Edwards admitted. He was able to get away with all he did because of a good ol' boy charisma that charmed journalists, voters, and grand juries alike. A reporter once asked Edwards if it wasn't illegal for him to accept a reported twenty-thousand-dollar bribe from South Korean lobbyist Tongsun Park. Edwards replied, "It was illegal for them to give, but not for me to receive." Or as Edwards asked another time: "What's wrong with making money?"

One of Edwards's most puzzling contributions to Louisiana politics was the open primary, more evocatively known as the jungle primary.

Candidates of all parties run against one another in a no-holds-barred primordial contest. The two candidates with the most votes go on to a runoff election for the office.

The open primary, proponents say, gives more power to voters and less to decision makers in smoke-filled back rooms. *That* was the part that mystified the pundits. It defied belief that such a consummate player as Edwin Edwards would have backed a high-minded reform without considering what was in it for him.

In 1972, Louisiana's registered Democrats outnumbered Republicans twenty to one. That made the primary system used in other states ludicrous. The real fight was for the Democratic nomination. The final Democrat-versus-Republican election was a formality, a waste of time and money. With the open primary, both the primary and the runoff were meaningful, hard-fought elections.

No one believed that this rationale was sufficient to outweigh an obvious negative: Edwards was a Democrat, and his jungle primary would help the Republican Party.

A slew of Democrats would run in each primary. There would probably be only one Republican. The Republican would automatically corner the conservative vote, while each Democrat would have to scratch and claw for a scrap of the liberal vote (and for liberal campaign money). That would almost guarantee that the Republican made it to the runoff. The Republican could spend his campaign dollars where they counted—on the runoff election.

So what was in it for Edwards, a liberal Democrat? The only theory that made sense was worthy of Machiavelli. Under Louisiana law, the governor cannot run for a third consecutive term. Edwards, who was reelected in 1976, was out of the game when his second term expired in 1980. The law did not preclude a third term (or more), as long as it wasn't three in a row.

According to this theory, by backing the open primary Edwards was looking several moves ahead, to 1984. Believing it would be easier to beat an incumbent Republican than a younger, less baggage-encumbered

Democrat, Edwards knew (made sure?) that there would be no heir apparent in the Democratic Party. With the open primary, the Democratic vote would be more fragmented than usual, and Edwards could
therefore count on the split Democratic vote to lead to the election of
a Republican—someone to house-sit the governor's mansion for him.
Then, in 1983, he would reunify the Democrats and sail to an easy
third victory.

If this really was Edwards's plan, it was a bigger gamble than the
ones he was making at the craps tables. No Republican had been
elected governor of Louisiana since Reconstruction.

This "theory" describes exactly what happened. In 1979, five Democrats ran, and only one Republican. The front-running Democrat,
Louis Lambert, was the most liberal of the group. Under the old, party-
controlled system, the Democrats surely would have chosen someone
more moderate than Lambert. As it was, Lambert ran in the runoff
against Republican David Treen, and Treen won. He became Louisiana's
first Republican governor since 1877.

And in 1983, Edwin Edwards had no problem making sure that
Treen's first term would be his last. He told the press that Treen was
"so slow it takes him an hour and a half to watch *60 Minutes*." As Election Day approached, Edwards boasted that he couldn't lose unless he
was caught "in bed with a dead girl or a live boy." He won the runoff
with 63 percent of the vote.

Is it possible that Edwards planned all this, back when he launched
the open primary? Columnist John Maginnis recalls an enigmatic comment Edwards made in 1978 to a Republican Women's Club. The club
members were pleased that the then-new open primary was helping
Republicans get elected. Edwards said, "You are happy with the open
primary now, but there will come a day when you will not be." Without
explaining the statement, he left the room.

Edwards celebrated his victory over Treen by flying six hundred supporters to Paris for a week of gourmandizing. At ten thousand dollars a head, the trip paid off Edwards's four-million-dollar campaign debt. To top it off, Edwards won fifteen thousand dollars at Monte Carlo's craps tables. "Give me a wheel barrow for my money," he told the croupier.

The *bon temps* quickly passed. The petroleum taxes that had subsidized Louisiana state government in the 1970s were no longer enough to keep personal taxes low and enrich Edwards's cronies. With the Louisiana economy tanking, the voters were less forgiving of Edwards's indiscretions. Federal prosecutors began nipping at his heels.

In 1981, before Edwards's return to power, the government indicted one of his closest associates, Charles Roemer II. An FBI sting revealed that Roemer was taking bribes from New Orleans mob boss Carlos Marcello. At the trial, prosecutors played covert tapes of Marcello bragging about his ties to the Edwards administration. "He's the strongest sonofabitchin' governor we ever had," Marcello said of Edwards. "He fucks with women and plays dice, but won't drink. How you like dat?"

Edwards escaped prosecution. It was Roemer who took the fall. During his fifteen months in prison, FBI agents plied him with offers of release if only he would deliver the goods on Edwards. Roemer served his time in silence.

In 1985, Governor Edwards himself went on trial. According to indictments, he had shaken down four hospitals for $1.9 million in bribes in order to secure licenses. He needed the money badly. He had racked up two million dollars in debts to Nevada casinos. A Caesars Palace executive told the court of making trips to the governor's mansion to collect suitcases full of cash.

The trial ended in a hung jury. The prosecutors tried again, and Edwards was acquitted.

In 1986, Governor Edwards advanced a plan for jump-starting Louisiana's economy by bringing in casino gambling. The legislature rolled their collective eyes and rejected it.

When Edwards ran for his fourth term, in 1987, he discovered how thin his Teflon had worn. "A $100,000 contribution to Edwards was once considered an investment," wrote John Maginnis. "Now it's an open invitation to the grand jury."

Edwards's jungle primary turned cruelly against him. He came in second to a young Democratic challenger who happened to be the son of the man who had gone to prison for him. Charles "Buddy" Roemer III got 33 percent of the vote, versus 28 for Edwards. Seeing the handwriting on the wall, Edwards dropped out of the race. Most believed that his political career was finished. *Shreveport Journal* columnist Lanny Keller declared, "The only way Edwards can ever be reelected is to run against Adolf Hitler."

Keller had no way of knowing how prophetic those words would be.

The man who defeated Edwards was handsome, Harvard-educated, and sixteen years his junior. Buddy Roemer knew a lot about politics. He had even worked on Edwards's first campaign for governor. In the mid-1970s, Roemer was one of the state's most successful political consultants. He then served four terms in Congress. In the 1987 race for governor, Roemer took on one of the best political strategists, Raymond Strother, to manage his own campaign. Strother deftly distanced Roemer from the crimes of his father and of Edwards. "The choice is between Edwin Edwards, who's gone corrupt," went one of the 1987 TV ads, "and Buddy Roemer, who's trying to start a revolution."

The voters favored the revolution over Edwards's ethically challenged status quo. Roemer delivered on most of his promises. He cleaned up state government to a degree many Louisianans hadn't thought possible, and he made measured cutbacks suited to a time of austerity. Of all the candidates Strother had managed, only one compared in his estimation—Arkansas governor Bill Clinton. "I was representing them both at the same time, shuffling back and forth between

Baton Rouge and Little Rock," Strother remembered. "Roemer had all the equipment, more so than Clinton. He was at least as smart as Clinton, maybe smarter . . . But as far as skill, intelligence, vision—Roemer was better than Clinton. The ingredient missing in Clinton is not his intellect, not his memory, but his creativity. Clinton is not creative. Roemer is creative."

In October 1989, Roemer's wife, Patti, left him, taking their nine-year-old son, Dakota. Roemer had what the media called a midlife crisis. With the governor's mansion suddenly empty, he took to wearing a rubber band around his wrist. When he felt tense or hostile, he snapped the rubber band against his pulse point, murmuring, "Cancel, cancel." The personal soul-searching found echo in his political life. On March 11, 1991, Roemer had one of his "creative" ideas. He announced that he was becoming a Republican.

The once solidly Democratic South was edging right. Roemer was aware that Edwards's jungle primary squeezed candidates in the middle. "I felt the Republicans almost had to put up somebody," he explained, "and that somebody gets 15 percent of the vote. My 15 percent." He reasoned that it was smarter to run as a Republican, locking in the conservative vote while preserving his moderate base.

Another reason to turn Republican: Roemer had presidential ambitions. He confided his calculations to friends. George H. W. Bush would win reelection in 1992, Roemer believed. That would leave the field open for a Republican in 1996. The party had no one to succeed Bush. Roemer dismissed the vice president, Dan Quayle, as an intellectual lightweight unsuited to lead the nation. Roemer's private scenario was that *he* could come out of nowhere, win some primaries, and cop the 1996 Republican nomination. With this vague White House fantasy on his mind, Roemer made a serious tactical error. He crossed Billy Nungesser.

Nungesser was a creepy character who wore red suits to match his slicked-back red hair. He ran a catering business in New Orleans. He was also chairman of the Louisiana Republican Party.

Roemer's mistake was going over Nungesser's slicked-back head and discussing the party switch with White House chief of staff John Sununu. Nungesser felt that this disrespected the majesty of his private empire. He thereafter made a point of not cutting Roemer any slack. Nungesser's state party insisted that Governor Roemer was *not* automatically going to be the Republican nominee for governor. Nungesser decreed that all candidates, Roemer included, would have to sign an affidavit promising to drop out of the race should they *not* receive the party nomination.

Roemer had no intention of signing any such document. The Republicans held their state caucus anyway. In what amounts to an act of spite, they nominated Congressman Clyde Holloway as the Republican candidate for governor. A staunch conservative, Holloway was popular with fundamentalists. Hardly anyone believed he had a chance of winning the election.

One of the few people talking up Holloway's chances was Edwin Edwards. "If Clyde runs, Roemer won't make the runoff," Edwards predicted. "Clyde's a real Republican." Edwards was hardly a disinterested observer. He was running yet again, for the fourth term that Roemer had denied him.

Holloway would be easier to beat than Roemer. Edwards therefore passed on to Holloway a tidbit that his opposition research had turned up. Three years previously, Roemer had told the Baton Rouge *Advocate* that he had voted for Democratic presidential candidate Michael Dukakis. "Dan Quayle helped me make up my mind," Roemer was quoted as saying.

The dig at Quayle wouldn't sit well with Roemer's adopted party. As a Democrat, Edwards couldn't use it, but Holloway could. Anything that helped Holloway would take votes away from Roemer. That, in turn, would help Edwards's chances.

Despite Edwards's tossing him a few bones, and despite the dubious blessing of Billy Nungesser, Clyde Holloway limped along. He never broke decisively into the double digits in the polls. The candidate to watch was David Duke.

Duke had also reinvented himself as a Republican. Like Roemer, he was running without the party's support. Duke's challenge was what he described as his "past." For that, he had the greatest all-around cover story in American politics. He announced that he had found Jesus.

Duke's power base was angry, white, and poor. Many if not most of these people identified on some level with Duke's bad-boy image. But for swing voters not entirely comfortable with a Klansman Nazi governor, Duke provided an out. He said that the swastikas and cross burnings were youthful indiscretions, before he found true religion. Anyone who doubted that did not understand the redemptive power of his walk with the Lord.

Duke had been preparing the ground for some time. Prior to the mid-1980s, he would sound off to journalists on his favored topics of the Holocaust hoax, the genetic inferiority of the nonwhite races, and the person-from-history-I'd-most-like-to-have-dinner-with, Adolf Hitler. That stopped. It was replaced with calls for abolishing welfare and affirmative action.

"I was too intolerant," Duke told Larry King on his show. "I thought the problem was with blacks instead of the welfare system." When challenged to recant his old positions, Duke did, more or less. At a Kiwanis Club forum, he was asked:

Q. Do you believe blacks are genetically inferior to whites?
A. Not inferior but different. I think blacks have different talents.
Q. Do you believe there is a conspiracy by Jews?

A. No, I don't believe there is a conspiracy by Jews.

Q. Do you believe the Holocaust occurred?

A. Yes, there was a Holocaust in which Jews and Christians perished.

Duke's most convincing point was that only he could know what he felt inside. The journalists who doubted his conversion were speculating. The most they could establish was that Duke's "past" was not all that remote. A taped interview from the mid-1980s surfaced in which Duke said that Jews "probably deserve to go into the ash bin of history." A 1989 photo showed Duke shaking hands with the vice chairman of the American Nazi Party.

One of Duke's biggest gaffes came when a TV moderator asked him what church he attended. His answer was the Evangelical Bible Church. Reporters were unable to locate any local church by that name.

Duke had another problem, one endemic in Louisiana politics. "After a rally, the women would flock around him," said Jim McPherson, who had worked on Duke's Senate campaign. "He just took his pick." Duke's tastes ran to Aryan and young. The young part was an issue even in Louisiana. When Duke was in the Louisiana legislature, an irate father showed up to warn him to stay away from his seventeen-year-old daughter, or else.

Aide Linda Melton quit the Duke gubernatorial campaign in disgust. Duke missed an important meeting because he was "out till three or four o'clock in the morning in a real sleazy, sleazy, I mean we're talking redneck sleazy, after-hours club in West Monroe with some really trashy-looking girl."

A CNN reporter interviewing Edwin Edwards suggested that Duke had surpassed him as a womanizer. "Duke is not a womanizer," Edwards corrected. "He is a little-girlizer." The reporter had a point, though. This time around, the sixty-four-year-old Edwards was exploring monogamy with his twenty-six-year-old girlfriend, Candy Picou.

Duke's Shreveport coordinator, a former Klan organizer named David Touchstone, fretted about the age of Duke's dates. He proposed twenty-five as the cutoff point. Campaign worker Billy Hankins agreed. "I told him, 'David, I think maybe 20 is too young.' Duke didn't want to hear that. He was sitting on the floor and he was rubbing his eyes. You could see he was tired, and he was frustrated by this whole thing. He said, 'Look, isn't it enough that I'm trying to save the white race, can't I see who I want to see?'"

The staff was able to persuade Duke by reporting a rumor that a pipe fitter's union was planning to have an underage girl get to Duke and plant ecstasy on him. Said Hankins, "That settled us down some."

In an early survey taken by Robert Teeter, pollster for President Bush, Buddy Roemer was ahead with 33 percent of the vote. Edwards had 27 percent, and Duke had 12 percent. Holloway and other minor candidates were far behind.

Roemer's lead was slim for an incumbent governor running against a man with outsize integrity issues. Blame the jungle primary. The Republican vote was split between Roemer, Duke, and Holloway. Edwards was the only strong Democrat.

In anticipation of the runoff, pollster Verne Kennedy asked voters whom they would vote for between Roemer and Edwards. In early August, Edwards was leading Roemer 51.7 percent to 48.3 percent. A month later, Roemer took the lead, 46.0 percent to 42.7 percent.

Those last two figures add up to well under 100 percent. A surprising thing about the race was the large number of undecided voters, as much as 24 percent in one late-summer poll. Why were people undecided? Roemer was an incumbent, Edwards had been governor for three terms, and Duke, as the prize exhibit of the media's latest freak show, had probably gotten more press than either of them. What more information did people need?

Edwards took first place in the primary, winning 33.8 percent of the vote. Duke came in a strong second (31.7 percent). That meant that Governor Roemer, with only 26.5 percent, was out of the running.

The campaign then entered its truly pathological phase. Louisianans had to decide whether to vote for Edwards or Duke. For some, this was like deciding whether to die slowly in a bear trap or gnaw off a leg.

Edwards called in the hottest political consultant in America, James Carville. Carville was a fellow Cajun, and he swore like a Cajun. Like most star consultants, he owed his fame to his batting average. Over the previous five years, Carville had elected Democratic governors in Pennsylvania, Kentucky, and Georgia. There were other tight races this season, and Carville was in demand. He did not have much time to devote to Edwards or Louisiana. The good news was that he was confident that Edwards would win. It was a matter of getting the biggest margin of victory possible, of demonstrating that Louisiana repudiated Duke's divisiveness.

Speaking of that, the most alarming fact was this: *most whites favored Duke*. It was only by adding in the black vote that Edwards achieved a majority. Edwards was instructed to avoid being seen with large crowds of black people. The rationale was that the swing voters would be mildly racist whites. It was important that they *not* turn on their TVs and see Edwards surrounded by cheering blacks.

Edwards was soon raking in money and endorsements from people who hated his guts. They hated Duke's guts more. "David Duke thinks he hates Jews now," one Jewish fund-raiser for Edwards was quoted as saying. "Wait til we're through with him." Ex-governor Treen—butt of the *60 Minutes* joke—endorsed Edwards. So did the New Orleans *Times-Picayune*, which had long pilloried Edwards's wretched ethics. The press even wrested an endorsement out of President George H. W. Bush. Remember, Edwards was a Democrat *and* a crook. But if he, Bush, lived in Louisiana, he would vote for Edwards.

The most agonized statement came from Buddy Roemer, appropriately enough on Halloween. "I have sat at my desk and cried at the anger, and shock and shame," Roemer began. "I cannot, will not, must not vote for David Duke. It would be suicide for Louisiana. And since my choices are only two, Edwards gets my vote. He does not get my endorsement."

("I'll tell you what happened," Edwards explained. The day after the primary, Roemer "said he was still talking with people about what to do. Which is silly because he knew there was nothing else he could do. We set a meeting. He calls back. He's not finished talking to people. Okay. Fine. Finally, I go to meet with him. He has a legal pad of notes. He's going through all these machinations and details like he's writing the fucking U.N. charter. He says he's not ready. I say, '[O]kay, that's fine, do what you want to do.' Then he calls me at night and says, 'Let me read this to you.' I say, 'Buddy, I don't give a shit.' He says, 'No, I want to get it right.' So he reads the whole fucking thing. And then he says he may want to change a few phrases.")

As David Duke became a national celebrity, the questions got tougher. On *Meet the Press*, Tim Russert asked, "Mr. Duke, can you name the top three manufacturing employers in Louisiana?"

Duke couldn't. After an uncomfortable silence, he said, "We have a number of employers in our state. I couldn't give you the names right off."

The next question was how many people in Louisiana lived below the poverty line. Duke didn't know that, either. "I don't carry around an almanac with me."

In a televised debate for Louisiana Public Television, Edwards held up a map that had appeared in the newsletter of Duke's National Association for the Advancement of White People. It showed a future America, after the NAAWP had moved the ethnic groups around to where it thought they belonged. One surprise was that the Cajuns were to be relocated to Vermont. "As spokesman for the Cajuns, we aren't going to go," Edwards said. "It's cold up there."

The Duke story kept getting weirder and weirder. Bob Hawks, a former Duke campaign manager, told the press that Duke never prayed or talked about religion except when he was campaigning. Klansman Karl Hand said he had seen Duke's pornography collection, and it contained pictures of black men making it with white women. The most eye-opening tale was of Duke's apparently tangential involvement in a 1981 American Nazi plot to take over the Caribbean island nation of Dominica and establish a cocaine factory there.

The bizarre tone of the election was captured in two bumper stickers: VOTE FOR THE CROOK—IT'S IMPORTANT and VOTE FOR THE LIZARD, NOT THE WIZARD. The bumper stickers made the case for Edwards better than anything Carville could do. There was nothing to say in favor of Edwards and no point in pretending there was. But Duke was worse.

A few non–Duke supporters disagreed. "There were many smart, well-intentioned people who saw Duke as the lesser of two evils," wrote blogger Elliot Scott, "not because he was necessarily less evil, but because he was *so* evil that he was actually safe. Edwin Edwards is a crook, a very well-connected, very capable crook. Duke is just crazy (and, yes, also a crook)."

Louisiana energy executive L. L. "Bud" Feikert told *Newsweek*: "I'm going to hold my nose, steady my hand—and it will be shaking—and pull that lever for Edwin Edwards."

Just over 61 percent of the voters did about that on November 16. Edwards won his fourth term. Despite this, 55 percent of whites voted for Duke. Buddy Roemer offered this postmortem: Edwards, who "for twenty years created a hunger for integrity, was saved in the end by having a man run against him who had less integrity."

In his final term as governor, Edwin Edwards delivered about what the voters must have expected. He reinstituted the system of patronage that had been briefly interrupted by Roemer. One of his first acts was to appoint a new head to the Orleans District levee board, the commission responsible for maintaining the levees that protect New Orleans from floods. The new appointee, Robert Harvey, was an attorney whose qualifications included writing a five-thousand-dollar check to the Edwards campaign.

Under Roemer, the levee board had forced the Army Corps of Engineers to agree to build higher levees. Under the new administration, inspections were lax. Edwards had other priorities, such as bringing casino gambling to New Orleans. A new gambling bill passed the legislature. Robert Harvey lured Bally's into opening a riverboat casino at a dock owned by the levee board. In due course the FBI was investigating Harvey for padding the levee board payroll.

Over the next decade, the board was preoccupied with corruption probes and petty feuds with the Army Corps of Engineers. When Hurricane Katrina hit in 2005, the levees failed catastrophically. More than 1,500 people died, and New Orleans was nearly wiped off the map.

By then, Edwards was in federal prison. In 2000 he was convicted of taking bribes from riverboat casino operations and sentenced to ten years. He had married Candy Picou, and when he was sentenced, he suggested she get a divorce rather than wait for him. Picou refused, vowing to bear Edwards's child. "We have some frozen sperm from my reverse vasectomy," Edwards told the press, "and I suppose after I leave here, she'll probably resort to trying to use that."

As he entered prison, Edwards made the last promise of his public career: "I will be a model prisoner as I was a model citizen."

In 1992, David Duke ran for president as a Republican. His momentum vanished as mysteriously as it had appeared. He opened a bar in Metairie with his former campaign manager and studied to become an insurance agent.

In 2002, Duke pleaded guilty to tax and mail fraud. He had mailed thousands of white supremacists and Nazi sympathizers, telling them that he was about to lose his home and life savings. Hundreds of thousands of dollars poured in. In reality, he had already sold his home at a profit and had a number of investment accounts. Duke's financial problem, if he had one, was that he had frittered away money in gambling casinos.

In one sense only, the American system worked. Now that they are convicted felons, neither Edwin Edwards nor David Duke can ever run for U.S. public office again.

Politics may be more colorful in Louisiana, but what happened in the 1991 governor's race is not unusual. When three Republicans run against one Democrat, the Democrat has an advantage that has nothing to do with character, ideology, or qualifications. Republican voters can't vote for all three Republicans. They have to pick one. This can mean that each Republican gets fewer votes than he might have gotten. This phenomenon is called vote splitting. It occurs with party primaries followed by a general election; and when there are no primaries at all, just a single election. In our two-party system, the most familiar form of vote splitting is the spoiler effect. When there is a tight race between the two major candidates, a third-party "spoiler" candidate can take enough votes from one of the front-runners to hand the election to his rival. This happened in the 2000 presidential race, when Green candidate Ralph Nader tipped the balance from Al Gore to George W. Bush in Florida, and thus determined the election. Vote splitting is an invisible hand misguiding the whole electoral process. The consequences are weakened mandates, loss of faith in the democratic process, squandered dollars, and sometimes squandered lives.

This book asks a simple question: Is it possible to devise a fair way of voting, one immune to vote splitting? Until recently, any well-informed person would have told you the answer was a most definite no. They would have cited the work of Nobel-laureate economist Kenneth Arrow and his famous impossibility theorem. In 1948 Arrow devised a logical proof saying (*very* roughly) that no voting system is perfect. Arrow was not talking about hanging chads, confusing ballot designs, hacked electronic machines, or any type of outright fraud. Such problems, though serious, can be fixed. He was talking about a problem that *can't* be fixed. He showed that vote splitting and worse paradoxes can corrupt almost any reasonable way of voting.

This led to decades of lowered expectations, if not outright despair, over voting. Building a significantly better voting system seemed to be impossible. In recent years, scholars have begun to revise this pessimistic view. There are better ways to vote, including some that fall outside the scope of the impossibility theorem entirely. One of the most promising is known as range voting. In December 2000—the month the Supreme Court was deciding whether Bush or Gore would be president—Temple University mathematician Warren D. Smith published an extensive computer simulation study comparing the merits of voting methods. He showed that range voting achieves the greatest overall voter satisfaction, by a large margin, of any widely proposed system. No less important, it stands up better than any other system to attempts to manipulate the vote.

You are already familiar with range voting. It is used in many Internet "polls" and consumer surveys. We use range voting for rating movies, restaurants, athletes, eBay vendors—"everywhere," adds the economist Claude Hillinger, "except where it would matter most, in political elections." That generations of voting theorists had overlooked a practical idea ingrained in popular culture is one of the odder tales in recent scientific and political thought.

The need for a better way of voting has never been more acute. Vote splitting is increasingly part of campaign strategizing. In 2004 Republican donors briefly made headlines by funding a nationwide effort to help Ralph Nader make state ballots. The hope was that Nader would again take crucial votes from the Democratic candidate (John Kerry), perhaps winning a state or two for George W. Bush. The most instructive way to look at this tactic is not as a Republican or a Democrat but as a political consultant. That means keeping a close eye on where the money came from and what it bought. John Kerry spent $310 million on his 2004 campaign. George W. Bush spent $345 million, and Ralph

Nader spent a mere $4.5 million. Yet Nader had tipped the 2000 election and threatened to do so in 2004. This presented an arbitrage opportunity. A relative pittance diverted from Bush's war chest to Nader was judged to be an inexpensive insurance policy. Though it turned out to be unnecessary—Bush won reelection without need of the Nader effect—politics is a game of calculated gambles.

Since 2004, the gaming of the spoiler effect has burgeoned and become thoroughly bipartisan. In the 2006 elections, no fewer than five key races had Democratic money funding spoilers to hurt Republicans, or vice versa. The funds not only aided ballot drives but also paid for TV, radio, and print ads the spoilers could not otherwise have afforded.

Political consultants are hardworking, committed people who get a bum rap about a lot of what they do. But in this case, it's tough to paint what they're doing as anything but villainous. Like terrorists co-opting a government list of soft targets, today's political consultants are exploiting the mathematical vulnerabilities of voting itself. Instead of persuading people to vote *for* their candidates, they are persuading them to vote *against* them—and sometimes winning because of that. Were these new campaign techniques a genetically engineered tomato, they might command more attention than they have. They have gone largely unnoticed by the public, the media, and nearly everyone except the campaign strategists and their clients.

The story of vote splitting is one of political hardball. It is equally a tale of attempts to improve the world through logic (and how rarely *that* works out). In both cases, the story properly begins with Kenneth Arrow's lauded, feared, and long-misunderstood impossibility theorem.

THE
PROBLEM

ONE

Game Theory

Kurt Gödel, the most brilliant logician of the twentieth century, had no interest in politics. He showed no apparent alarm when Hitler became chancellor of Germany. (Gödel closed a 1936 letter with a cordial "Heil Hitler.") He was equally unconcerned when Hitler annexed Austria in 1938. Then, in August 1939, war began. Things quickly got worse in Gödel's Vienna. In November, Gödel was attacked by a gang of Nazi youths. He was not Jewish, but people thought he looked Jewish, or scholarly, or cosmopolitan. Gödel was in the company of his less scholarly girlfriend, Adele Porkert, who worked in a disreputable nightclub. She fought off the Nazis with her umbrella.

Gödel was soon drafted. As he had no intention of fighting, he and Porkert, now married, fled the country. Gödel had a visa and an open invitation to work at the Institute for Advanced Study in Princeton, New Jersey. As things worked out, he and Porkert would spend the rest of their lives in Princeton.

The years rolled by. In 1947 Gödel decided it was time to apply for American citizenship. He needed two American citizens as witnesses. Two of his best friends volunteered. They were Albert Einstein and Oskar Morgenstern (an economist). Like all immigrants, Gödel was supposed to study up on the American system of government. He threw himself into the task. Apparently for the first time in his life, he became interested in the political process.

The day before the exam, he informed Morgenstern that he had uncovered a logical contradiction in the U.S. Constitution. Morgenstern thought this was amusing—until he realized how serious Gödel was about it.

Gödel was famous for discovering a logical contradiction in mathematics. Ever since Euclid, mathematicians had aspired to put logic and math into tidy packages. A set of unquestioned axioms would be given. From those axioms it would be possible to prove all true mathematical statements and to disprove all falsehoods. It would also (presumably) be possible to prove the system's consistency. If it is possible to show that "2 + 2 = 4" is true (as it should be), then it must be impossible to prove that the same statement is false.

This goal seemed reasonable to almost everyone. Then, in 1931, Gödel shattered the millennia-old dream. He demonstrated that no valid logical system can prove itself to be free from contradiction. The gist of Gödel's proof might be rendered like this: Anyone who says he *always* tells the truth is lying. Gödel showed that this statement holds not only for used-car salespeople and politicians but also for the most abstract constructions of logic.

It was this work that brought Gödel renown and led to his esteemed position at the Institute. Morgenstern confided to Einstein that he was worried that Gödel would launch into a rant about the "contradiction" he had discovered in the Constitution during his citizenship exam. The examiner might deny Gödel citizenship just for that. Einstein agreed that they had to make sure this didn't happen.

The citizenship exam was scheduled for December 5, 1947, in

Trenton. Since Adele did not permit Gödel to drive anymore—he had once fallen into such a deep meditation that he forgot he was, at that moment, driving a car—Morgenstern volunteered to drive him. When he picked up Einstein, the physicist got in and turned to Gödel. "Well, are you ready for your next-to-last test?"

"What do you mean 'next to last'?" Gödel inquired.

"Very simple," Einstein answered. "The last will be when you step into your grave."

Einstein could have a morbid sense of humor. But, according to plan, he kept Gödel occupied during the drive. When they got to Trenton, Einstein recognized the judge, Philip Forman, as the one who had administered his own oath of citizenship. Forman pulled Einstein and friends out of line and took them into his chambers. The judge and Einstein chatted while Gödel sat silently. Forman remarked how wise Gödel was to leave Germany and its "evil dictator." "Do you think a dictatorship like that in Germany could ever arise in the United States?" Forman asked.

"I know how that can happen!" Gödel said, and he began his explanation. To Morgenstern's and Einstein's relief, Forman cut him off, telling him he didn't need to go into all that.

Gödel passed the exam. He returned to Trenton on April 2 to take the oath of citizenship. At the ceremony, Judge Forman gave a patriotic speech about American values. It was probably a talk he had given many times. Gödel found himself moved by it (as he recounted in a letter to his mother). He went home feeling that American citizenship was something special and fine. Gödel could switch unpredictably from cold logic to maudlin sentiment, and it was hard for others to tell what would set him off. He adored the Disney film *Bambi*. He saw *Snow White* at least three times.

The **"flaw" that** Gödel found in the U.S. Constitution was in Article V, the one that provides for amendments. It begins:

Article V.

The Congress, whenever two thirds of both Houses shall deem it necessary, shall propose Amendments to this Constitution, or, on the Application of the Legislatures of two thirds of the several States, shall call a Convention for proposing Amendments, which, in either Case, shall be valid to all Intents and Purposes, as Part of this Constitution, when ratified by the Legislatures of three fourths of the several States, or by Conventions in three fourths thereof, as the one or the other Mode of Ratification may be proposed by the Congress . . .

Gödel looked at the Constitution as if it were a set of axioms. Just as the ideal mathematical system should be able to derive any true statement from its axioms, the ideal governmental system should permit any good and equitable constitution to be derived from the original one, by orderly process of amendment. Still, we presumably do not want a Constitution that can amend itself into Nazi Germany, Orwell's *1984*, or some other kind of dystopia.

This is where Article V fails, Gödel felt. By permitting *everything*, it guarantees *nothing*. In principle, the Bill of Rights could be rescinded by a future amendment—just as Prohibition (the Eighteenth Amendment) was repealed by the Twenty-first Amendment. It may be supposed that a two-thirds majority of both houses would never countenance a major erosion of individual liberties. Article V could amend itself. In theory, two-thirds of Congress could vote in a new amendment saying that only a simple majority is required to amend the Constitution. The smaller the threshold, the more likely it is that a strongly motivated faction might manage to pass an amendment that many find unconscionable.

In the 1940s many Americans felt superiority over the totalitarianism existing in Germany, Italy, and the Soviet Union. Wartime rhetoric implied that America had a patent on democracy. Gödel found this "it can't happen here" attitude unconvincing.

In 1932 Adolf Hitler ran in a democratic election for president of Germany. He got 30.1 percent of the vote. That put him a distant second behind Field Marshall Paul von Hindenburg. Under the German system, the first election was followed by a runoff between the top three candidates. Hitler did only modestly better in the runoff, capturing 36.8 percent of the vote. Hindenburg won with 53.0 percent.

"We're beaten; terrible outlook," wrote Hitler's political consultant—Joseph Goebbels. Goebbels could not have guessed how quickly Hitler's fortunes would turn. On January 30, 1933, President Hindenburg appointed Hitler chancellor. Neither of his first two appointees had worked out, and Hindenburg may have felt he was running out of viable candidates.

Less than a month later, communist terrorists burned the Reichstag building. They may have had operational support from the Nazis. The nation's factions put aside their differences to pull together in the crisis. The Reichstag considered a bill to suspend the constitution and give Hitler temporary dictatorial powers. It was not necessarily a crazy idea. The argument was that an enlightened dictator could deal with the crisis better and more quickly than a slow-moving legislative body. The motion passed 441 to 84. It was the first majority Hitler ever got, and the last he would ever need.

It was of course Hitler who was ultimately responsible for Gödel, Einstein, and Morgenstern's trip to the citizenship hearing. None would have been in America otherwise.

After Einstein's death, in 1955, Gödel found himself socially isolated. Morgenstern was perhaps the only real friend he had left in the world. Gödel succumbed to a set of neuroses that made him the talk of Princeton. He feared germs, and wandered the streets in a ski mask to avoid contagion. He spent his last years working on a mathematical proof of the existence of God. He came to believe in ghosts, demons,

"Goebbels, Goebbels, give me back my millions," Hitler says to his tearful propaganda minister in John Heartfield's 1935 photomontage. Goebbels's staff had been accused of embezzling millions, and Hitler's unpopular policies cost him millions of supporters. Hitler epitomizes a troubling paradox: a politician adored by a plurality may be detested by a majority. (*George Eastman House*)

telepathy, life after death, and time travel—the latter based on his own solutions to Einstein's field equations.

Spending time in the company of Gödel made Oskar Morgenstern look almost normal in comparison. Morgenstern too spent his life never quite fitting into any social context. Like Gödel, he had been part of the glittering circle of intellectual luminaries in prewar Vienna. Morgenstern's diaries, now at Duke University, bristle with anti-Semitism. He did not fit in with the Nazis, either. He fled to America, spending much of the remainder of his life in the company of brilliant Jews. At Princeton, he reinvented himself as a man of the world, a connoisseur of wine, women, music, and art. He told people he was an illegitimate descendant of Kaiser Friedrich III. To much of the Princeton University community, however, he was a vain, petty, humorless status-seeker. His stiff Old-World manner inspired his students to tag him *Herr Professor*. Morgenstern once introduced the four younger people working with him—two of them had Ph.D.s, and two were working toward their doctorates—to a European visitor as Dr. Whitin, Dr. Shubik, *"und zwei Studenten* [and two students]." He couldn't bother to give two names. Thereafter, *"zwei Studenten"* became an office punch line.

Whatever his social deficiencies, Morgenstern played a vital role in the community of science. He was a cross-pollinator. When he came across a new and important finding, he would put his own work aside and promote the new idea like a stage mother, nagging people into paying attention. The idea's originator would often be too busy or too unworldly to do so.

Had the muse of genius allotted Morgenstern a steadier flow of great ideas, he might have lacked the time to play this role. A man who cared more about being liked could not have deployed sharp elbows as effectively as he did.

The most impressive of Morgenstern's projects was game theory, the creation mainly of Hungarian-born mathematician John von Neumann. Despite the name, game theory is not primarily about games such as chess or Monopoly or Halo. It is more an exact science of strategy. It explores how rational adversaries make decisions, knowing that their opponents are trying to second-guess or double-cross them. In 1928 von Neumann published the paper inaugurating this field. Like everything else von Neumann did, it was considered brilliant. Then von Neumann moved on to other things.

Morgenstern believed that game theory had important applications to economics. When he came to America, he choose Princeton University over other schools because he wanted to be near von Neumann, one of the true geniuses who worked at the nearby Institute for Advanced Study. There was something almost stalker-like in this move, for Morgenstern had never met von Neumann.

In February 1939, von Neumann attended a lecture Morgenstern gave on business cycles. After the talk Morgenstern cornered von Neumann and told him he was thinking of writing a paper on game theory's applications to economics. Von Neumann said he'd be glad to read it for comments.

Morgenstern showed several drafts to von Neumann. The mathematician tactfully said they needed a little more polish. Von Neumann suggested a collaboration.

With two authors, the "article" grew. When it had become too long to publish in a journal, the two approached Princeton University Press about putting out a slim volume of about a hundred pages. The press agreed. When the authors delivered the typescript at the start of 1943, it came to twelve hundred pages.

The book appeared in 1944 under the title *Theory of Games and Economic Behavior*. Von Neumann generously proposed that the names of the two authors be listed alphabetically. Morgenstern insisted that von Neumann's name go first.

"The skepticism concerning Morgenstern's contribution to the theory of games was widespread," conceded Martin Shubik, one of the most sympathetic of Morgenstern's students. At Princeton, it was generally understood that, for all of his schmoozing with von Neumann, Gödel, and Einstein, Morgenstern was emphatically *not* on their level.

He would sometimes sit in on mathematical seminars and ask questions that appeared to confirm this assessment.

Shubik tells of an excruciating lecture in which Morgenstern spent *three hours* trying and failing to reproduce a result from "his" game theory book. "We would have all been happier," Shubik said, "if Oskar had not attempted to go through formal proofs."

John von Neumann had his talking point down pat.

Q. Johnny, what did Morgenstern *really* contribute? Come on. You can tell.

A. "Without Oskar, I would have never written the *Theory of Games and Economic Behavior.*"

No politician could have handled the question better.

I met Kenneth Arrow on a sunny afternoon at the Stanford Faculty Club. At age eighty-four, he was vigorous and unpretentious enough to arrive for lunch by bicycle. With his helmet checked and lunch in front of us, I began my list of prepared questions. One was about Oskar Morgenstern. At my mention of the name, Arrow winced. "I never knew how well he understood game theory," he said quietly. It had been more than fifty years since Arrow had met Morgenstern. That Morgenstern's memory still had that astringent power says something about the man.

Arrow came to meet Morgenstern through a complex chain of events. Kenneth Joseph Arrow was born in New York City on August 23, 1921, the son of Harry and Lillian Arrow. Both parents were Jewish immigrants raised on the Lower East Side. Harry, a banker, was prosperous during the first decade of Kenneth's life, but when the Depression hit, Harry's bank failed, and the family spent the next decade poor.

When the family had money, they spent a lot of it on books, sets of the world's best literature and encyclopedias. Kenneth was such an avid reader that his mother found it difficult to punish him. When she sent him to his room for having been involved in some mischief, he would simply select an encyclopedia volume and settle down happily with it. Lillian learned that she had to discipline her son by forcing him to go outside and play.

Lillian and Harry, both staunch supporters of Franklin Delano Roosevelt, would discuss politics at the dinner table. The newly impoverished Arrows had to send their son to City College of New York, a school that offered a free education to New Yorkers. The school's faculty had strong Marxist leanings. At City College, Kenneth became fascinated with logic and statistics.

"There was a very famous logician called Alfred Tarski," Arrow explained. "He came to New York for a conference in late August 1939 and was caught here by the outbreak of war." Arrow and his classmates struggled to understand Tarski's idiosyncratic English. One of the words Tarski taught them was as obscure as his pronunciation: *intransitivity*. This idea would become the heart of Arrow's impossibility theorem.

The best way to explain intransitivity is to start with its opposite, *transitivity*. If Bill Gates is richer than Donald Trump, and Donald Trump is richer than you, then it follows that Bill Gates is richer than you. Any relationship that permits such a conclusion is said to be transitive. Many other types of comparisons qualify—"heavier than," "taller than," "is the sister of." Many mathematical relationships are transitive, too. "Greater than," "less than," and "is equal to" are examples. When quantity A equals B, and B equals C, then A has to equal C as well.

An intransitive relationship is anything that does not follow this neat pattern. There are plenty of examples, and we never give most of them a second thought. Raymond is the son of John, and Keith is the son of Raymond. It obviously does *not* follow that Keith is the son of John. Lucas loves Margo and Margo loves Chris. It does not follow that Lucas loves Chris. These are intransitive relationships.

As much as Arrow enjoyed his excursions into arcane logic, "I never thought of this as a way to make a living. This was the Great Depression. The only thing I could dream of doing in mathematics was teaching in high school. I would have been very happy with that; the only problem was, there were no jobs."

The bleak employment picture sent Arrow to graduate work at Columbia University. There he decided that his primary interest was statistics. Harold Hotelling, a statistician in the economics department, was able to offer Arrow a fellowship on the condition that he switch his major to economics.

Hotelling's interests were diverse. In 1929 he proposed a famous riddle of economics, one that is equally important to political theory. There are two "places of business" located "along a line . . . which may be Main Street in a town or a transcontinental railroad," Hotelling wrote. Or, as it's often explained today, the places of business are two ice-cream stands on a crowded summer beach. Where should each stand be located in order to get the most business?

The beach is, say, a thousand yards long, running left to right. The only difference between one stand and the other is location. Beachgoers will naturally favor whichever stand is closest.

One possible arrangement is to have the stands at the 250-yard and 750-yard positions (measured from the far left end of the beach). Then the stand at the 250-yard point will be closest to everyone on the left half of the beach (from 0 to 500 yards). That stand can expect half the ice-cream sales, assuming the customers are evenly scattered over the beach's length. The other stand would get the other half of the business.

This is *not* the answer to Hotelling's puzzle. Here's why. Say you put your stand at 250 yards, and the other vendor is at 750 yards. What's to prevent your competitor from moving in your territory? He could relocate his stand to the 300-yard point. In so doing, he would retain his lock on the whole right half of the beach. (His customers would have to walk farther, but what choice do they have?) At the new location, he would be the closest stand for anyone from the 275-yard point all the way to the 1,000-yard limit. This would give him the lion's share of the business.

You wouldn't have to put up with that. You could leapfrog over him and steal most of his territory. He could counter-retaliate . . . Is there any way of arriving at a sensible truce, where both vendors are satisfied that they could do no better by moving?

Hotelling's answer was yes. The optimal solution is for both vendors to be side by side in the exact middle of the beach. One vendor is just to the left of the precise midpoint and thereby commands the entire left half of the beach. The other vendor is a few inches right of the midpoint and wins the right half.

You may find this answer surprising. Hotelling was *not* saying that this solution was best for the customers. The customers at the far ends of the beach will have a long hike. Hotelling was simply saying this is the way a laissez-faire economy works. Provided no government regulation mandates distance between the stands, they will have incentive to move to the middle.

Many economists believe that Hotelling's model—the "tendency of the outermost entrepreneurs to approach the cluster"—explains some of the minor mysteries of the real world. Why are so many Starbucks located just across the street from *other* upscale coffee shops? Why do all SUVs look alike? Why do TV stations run the news at the same time? Why are the two most popular soft drinks both fizzy brown syrups that taste the same? And why do airlines schedule popular flights to leave within minutes of each other? The answer could be that vendors are competing for the same finite stretch of market "territory." Moving too far from the center would cede too much of the business to the competition. "Buyers are confronted everywhere with an excessive sameness," Hotelling wrote. "Methodist and Presbyterian churches are too much alike; cider is too homogeneous."

Hotelling was well aware that the same principle applies in politics. America's two major parties compete for voters who fall along a left-to-right ideological spectrum. A voter normally favors the candidate whose ideology is closest to her own. Hence candidates of both parties have reason to gravitate toward the middle, to court the swing voters. "Each candidate 'pussyfoots,'" wrote Hotelling, "replies ambiguously to questions, refuses to take a definite stand in any controversy for fear of losing votes."

This model goes only so far. America's two parties *aren't* identical and aren't precisely in the middle. One likely reason is that citizens have the option of not voting and donors have the option of not contributing. If you want ice cream, you've got to hike to the nearest stand. But if the two candidates for office are identical, there is little reason to care who wins.

Arrow absorbed economics quickly. He completed all the required doctoral courses by 1942 and came to the slightly terrifying realization that he had no idea what to do for his dissertation. He thus began a long career as "professional student" (*ein Student*, Oskar Morgenstern might have said).

For a while he drifted from job to job. Then the war intervened, and he worked in weather prediction for the army. This convinced him that the physical sciences were not necessarily more accurate than the social sciences. He thought about chucking an academic career and becoming an actuary for an insurance company. He had heard there was good money in that.

Then Hotelling recommended him for an appointment at the Cowles Commission, the famous economic institute in Chicago. At Cowles, Arrow met many of the great economists of his time. Despite his lack of a Ph.D., he took on his first academic appointment (at the University of Chicago) and a more lasting appointment as husband to Selma Schweitzer. Schweitzer was herself a fellow at Cowles. They married on August 31, 1947. Meanwhile, Arrow continued his search for a dissertation topic.

"John Hicks gave a lecture at Columbia in 1946," Arrow recalled. "He had wanted a definition: What do you mean by saying individual A is better off than individual B?" This deceptively simple question was a vexing problem for economists. Who's better off, a fifty-dollar-an-hour oil field worker compelled to live on a rig in the North Sea, or a worker living a more normal life in Houston, at half the salary? How do you compare the overall welfare of people in a rat-race technological society with those in a more family-oriented third-world culture?

Hicks's tentative definition was that, in order for A to be better off than B, it is necessary that both A and B agree that A is better off. In effect, Hicks was proposing that the two people *vote* on who is better off. Only a unanimous vote would be considered decisive.

Arrow's hand shot up. "What bothered me is that if you have a definition of 'better off,' you'd like to be able to say that if A is better off than B and B is better off than C, then A is better off than C. It does not follow! I could think of examples right away!" Arrow was talking about intransitivity. Hicks had no idea what he was talking about.

"A year later, I'm working on my thesis," Arrow continued. "I'm a great admirer of Hicks's book *Value and Capital* [1939]. But I could see, being the empirical character I am, some problems. I thought my thesis would be fixing them up."

One problem was how corporate stockholders vote on a new director. Provided there are three or more candidates, Arrow realized, it is possible for the results of voting to be intransitive. He devised a simple example, now called the "paradox of voting" or the "Arrow paradox."

Imagine the election is between three candidates whom I'll call Scissors, Paper, and Stone. The voters fall into three factions, each comprising a third of the total vote. One faction likes Scissors the best, Paper second best, and Stone the least. The second faction likes Paper best, Stone second, and Scissors last. The third faction likes Stone best, Scissors second, and Paper last.

Game Theory

	First choice	Second choice	Third choice
Faction A	Scissors	Paper	Stone
Faction B	Paper	Stone	Scissors
Faction C	Stone	Scissors	Paper

This creates a bizarre paradox. *Every* candidate can win a two-way vote. Every candidate can also *lose* a two-way vote.

Take a vote between Scissors and Paper. Factions A and C will prefer Scissors to Paper. Therefore Scissors will beat Paper by a two-thirds majority.

In a similar vote between Paper and Stone, Paper will win, and also by a two-thirds majority.

Now, if Scissors beats Paper and Paper beats Stone, it stands to reason that Scissors will beat Stone. *It doesn't.* In a vote between Scissors and Stone, Stone would win by a two-thirds majority. The outcome is just like the schoolyard game of the same name. Scissors beats Paper, Paper beats Stone, *and* Stone beats Scissors.

This notion strikes almost everyone as illogical, like an M. C. Escher picture of an endless waterfall or staircase. It is a blow to learn that voting, the very bedrock of free societies, is subject to this wild illogic.

The paradox of voting bedeviled Arrow's doctoral work. "Instead of seeing this as an intellectual opportunity, I thought, 'This is a nuisance,'" Arrow said. He naturally thought it presented an insurmountable roadblock to any reasonable model of corporate behavior (he was still focused on stockholder voting). Arrow also had a nagging sense of déjà vu. "I thought I had heard it somewhere before," he said of the paradox. "From that day to this I have not been able to establish whether I had really heard it or not." This belief that the idea might not be original discouraged him from pursuing it. (Indeed, the paradox had been described by the Marquis de Condorcet in the eighteenth century but had been long forgotten.)

"There was a third episode. I got to think, what happens if parties are arrayed left to right?" Arrow applied the paradox to Hotelling's model of politics. He realized that when people's political views fall on a linear, liberal-to-conservative spectrum, the paradox of voting cannot occur.

Let the three candidates be Ralph Nader, Al Gore, and George W. Bush. There are six possible ways of ranking the three candidates, though not all of them make political sense. Whatever your politics, everyone agrees that Nader is on the far left, Gore is a little left of center, and Bush is somewhere to the right of center.

In order to have the paradox, you'd need about a third of the voters to prefer Nader to Gore and Gore to Bush. Okay. Then you'd need another large faction to prefer Gore to Bush and Bush to Nader. That's possible. Finally, you'd need a third faction to prefer Bush to Nader and Nader to Gore. That doesn't compute. It's hard to imagine that Bush supporters would sincerely prefer Nader over Gore.

Arrow sketched a proof that linear ideology prevents a scissor-paper-stone-type voting paradox. *This* insight struck him as unquestionably original and worthy of publication.

"I remember showing this to someone at lunch," Arrow remembered. "Then I picked up a copy of the *Journal of Political Economy* and there was Duncan Black with exactly that idea!"

Duncan Black was Arrow's only rival in founding a modern science of voting. Black taught at the University of Glasgow, far from the academic networks that counted, and lived in a house perched perilously on a cliff. No one at Glasgow quite knew what to make of Black's interest in voting. ("It had been brought to my attention," Black wrote, "that my main effort during the preceding years had produced no tangible result.")

The article that upstaged Arrow had its origin in the war, when Black was watching for air raids from the Green Drawing Room of

Warwick Castle. "Acting apparently at random, I wrote down a single diagram and saw in a shock of recognition the property of the median optimum."

This was Black's *median voter theorem*. The "median voter" is the voter in the exact middle. Half the voters are more conservative than the median voter, and half are more liberal.

In order for there to be a median voter, it's necessary that everyone's political views be assignable to a point on a neat left-to-right line. That may or may not be a good approximation to reality. But when there is a median voter, votes between pairs of candidates will be transitive, and Arrow's disturbing paradox can't occur. Black's theorem demonstrated that the median voter is the ultimate focus group. Whichever of two candidates the median voter prefers will win a two-way vote.

This seconds the conventional wisdom of politics. Pollster Richard Scammon and strategist Ben Wattenberg once semi-seriously remarked that the ultimate bellwether is a "forty-seven-year-old wife of a machinist living in Dayton, Ohio." The presidential candidate who captures *her* vote will win the election. There is nothing too mysterious about this. The median voter, like everyone else, favors the candidate whose views are closest to her own. This means that the candidate who captures the center will win a two-way race.

Six years into his peripatetic career as grad student, Arrow accepted an unusual job. He agreed to go to California to think about nuclear doomsday.

The RAND Corporation was the greatest monument to von Neumann's—and Morgenstern's—game theory. RAND began as the air force's Project RAND (for *R*esearch *AN*d *D*evelopment), a scientific consultancy initially contracted to Douglas Aircraft. Conceived as a peacetime Manhattan Project, RAND was recruiting many of the nation's best minds to ponder the challenges of the nuclear age.

Arrow heard about RAND from his wife's former employer, Abe Girschick. "This Air Force thing at that point was a wild, far-out place, open to all kinds of ideas," Arrow said. "The idea was that because of the new nature of warfare, particularly the bomb, all the old views were wrong . . . It was an invitation to take a very wild point of view."

RAND took pride in hiring a diverse group of specialists and encouraging everyone to talk to one another. Over the years, RAND's scholars and consultants have ranged from John Nash to Condoleezza Rice. In its first decade, however, the guiding spirit of the place was unquestionably John von Neumann.

"Everyone sat up in great awe" when von Neumann spoke, Arrow said. Politically, von Neumann was conservative and a hawk. He believed that game theory provided useful models for nuclear deterrence and arms races. RAND's people pondered questions such as would the Soviet Union launch a first strike against the United States if it meant losing twenty million people in the counterattack? Would building a hydrogen bomb enhance or diminish U.S. security?

Arrow's title was research statistician and mathematician. He was asked to analyze the deployment of America's nuclear submarines. The submarines were constantly in motion so that the Soviets would never know where they all were at any given time and would thus be unable to destroy all the subs in a surprise first strike. Knowing that some American submarines would be able to launch a counterattack against the Soviet Union—and knowing that the Americans knew the Soviets knew this—were cornerstones of the policy of deterrence.

Arrow now questions how much of this work ended up being useful to American defense. "People were *trying* to be helpful," he said. "But really, we were making up our military problems by talking to each other." Many of RAND's most influential contributions far transcended the defense issues that inspired them. The impossibility theorem is one of the best examples of that.

"It was in this context that Helmer, one day at coffee—they had terrible coffee—said the United States after all is an *abstraction*. There are lots of people in the United States. They have different interests, different political values. So even assuming you had a value structure for every individual, in what sense do you have a value structure for the United States?"

Olaf Helmer was a philosopher. RAND was broad-minded enough to suppose that philosophers might have useful input in defense strategizing. Helmer's point was that game theory assumes the participation of "players" with precisely defined motivations. How could President Harry Truman or General Secretary Joseph Stalin speak and act for their nations?

Truman at least had been democratically elected. But how could he represent the people who had voted against him, or the people who had voted for him only because they thought Thomas Dewey was even worse? There were American hawks who couldn't build H-bombs fast enough. There were American pacifists clamoring for immediate unilateral disarmament. For almost anything that some American believes, there is another American who believes the exact opposite. The same was true of the Soviet Union, even if its people could not dissent openly.

Arrow's off-the-cuff response to Helmer was "Oh! That is nothing, Abram Bergson has written on that type of thing." Bergson, then at Columbia, was an expert on the Soviet economy. This was a tricky matter, for the Soviet gross national product could not be measured by market valuation, as with capitalist economies. Bergson devised the concept of a "social welfare function," a numerical measure of a society's well-being. He had not fully addressed how societies make choices, however. Helmer suggested that Arrow write something on the subject.

"I just started playing around," Arrow said modestly. "It took me about two days to decide I was on the wrong track because I was looking for some solution. It didn't occur to me that there was no solution."

Arrow's result, the impossibility theorem, shows that indeed there is no solution for some of the problems of voting. The theorem was published first as a RAND research report in the fall of 1948. Almost

Walt Kelly's 1948 cartoon depicts the metaphor that inspired Kenneth Arrow: cold war as chess game between Harry Truman and Joseph Stalin. When democrat and dictator represent millions, who moves? (© *Okefenokee Glee & Perloo, Inc. Used by permission; Collection of the Harry S. Truman Library*)

immediately it was a sensation. It became Arrow's long-delayed dissertation topic and was republished as a 1951 book, *Social Choice and Individual Values*.

The theorem was so original that its first reactions included puzzlement and incomprehension. Columbia University economist Al Hart was charged with reviewing Arrow's dissertation. Theodore Anderson remembers Hart coming into his office and saying, "Ted, would you look at this? Don't tell me if it is correct, tell me if it is important."

TWO

The Big Bang

The small, insanely competitive women's figure skating world is still seething over an incident at the 1995 World Championship. At one point in the competition, the top three skaters were Chen Lu of China (first place), Nicole Bobek of the United States (second), and Surya Bonaly of France (third). All three had completed their performances, the judges had scored them, and the media had reported their preliminary rankings. Then fourteen-year-old American Michelle Kwan took the ice. When Kwan's performance was factored in, she came in fourth place. The odd thing is, Kwan caused Bobek's and Bonaly's standings to flip. Bobek dropped to third place and went home with a bronze medal. Bonaly rose to second place and took home the silver.

In other words, before Kwan skated, Bobek was judged a better skater than Bonaly. Afterward, Bonaly was a better skater than Bobek, according to the same judges. No judge had changed his or her mind about the two skaters; their votes for them had already been cast.

You may think there must have been something funny about the formula used to combine the judges' rankings. Trust me—there wasn't. If I explained the whole voting system, you would nod your head and say, *That sounds fair.*

During the men's competition of the 1997 European Championship, nearly the same thing happened. This time the top three skaters were Alexei Urmanov, Viacheslav Zagorodniuk, and Philippe Candeloro, in that order. The final contestant, Andrejs Vlascenko, came in last *of six.* Adding in the votes for Vlascenko caused Candeloro to move up to second place. Candeloro went home with a silver medal because the judges hadn't liked the way Vlascenko skated. Meanwhile, Zagorodniuk dropped to third place, forfeiting a silver medal because Vlascenko came in last.

This "Great Flip-Flop" touched off a firestorm in the skating world. Immediately afterward, International Skating Union (ISU) chairperson Ottavio Cinquanta admitted that something was wrong with the judging system. He vowed to fix it. Skating columnist Sandra Loosemoore disagreed. She felt the old system was okay and that the ISU should be more concerned with educating the public about these possible flip-flops. Loosemoore suggested including a printed copy of the scoring method in skating program booklets, incorporating announcements about it on the public address system, and providing a "technical liaison" to explain scoring to the media. She proposed that flip-flops be viewed as "something that adds significantly to the suspense of the event!"

The ISU nonetheless rolled out a new judging system in 1998. Under the system, Cinquanta promised, "If you are in front of me, you will remain in front of me!"

He was wrong. Cinquanta apparently had never heard of the impossibility theorem. If he had, he would have known that he was trying to do exactly what Kenneth Arrow had proved impossible. Loosemoore quickly provided an example of a case where the ISU's new system would fail miserably, and she cited a statistical analysis claiming that the new system was actually *worse* than the old one.

There are many situations where everyone can't have his or her own way. A group must arrive at a choice that is binding on all of its individual members. What is the best way to do this? Political philosophers had been asking that question for ages. Arrow's novel approach was to recast it as a question in pure logic. He observed that social choices generally follow a set of rules—a constitution, a parliamentary procedure, or a cultural tradition. These rules are legalistically precise to minimize the possibility of dispute.

In Arrow's terminology, any system for devising a social choice is called a *constitution*. You can compare Arrow's constitutions to voting machine software. The constitutions take the voters' ballot markings as input. They tally the votes according to a precise, step-by-step algorithm. Then they output the winners.

A constitution does not have to be fair or democratic or even reasonable. It could be like a hacker's rigged voting software, slanting the election in favor of a desired candidate. Of course, the important question is how to devise a constitution that *is* fair and logical. This is what Arrow tried to do—until he discovered it couldn't be done.

Americans are so used to "one person, one vote" that they often imagine this is the only sensible way to vote. It's not. (In fact, we'll see that it's about the *least* sensible way to vote!) "One person, one vote" is known as a plurality vote because the winner is the candidate who receives the largest number of votes. Many other voting methods, such as instant-runoff voting, use ranked ballots. Instead of just marking your favorite candidate with an X, you mark that candidate 1, and then mark your second-place choice 2, your third-place choice 3, and so on. This ranked, or preferential, ballot is used throughout the world, though rarely in the United States.

Arrow's proof assumes a ranked ballot. In so doing, it includes the familiar plurality vote as a special case: a plurality vote constitution simply says to ignore all but the first-place choices. Arrow's analysis therefore covers virtually every voting system used in elections throughout the free world, plus systems not even imagined today.

One important feature of voting is *not* included in Arrow's analysis, though. This is strategic voting. Sometimes people intentionally vote for someone other than their true favorite. An example is a supporter of a third-party candidate who votes for the more acceptable of the two major-party candidates. Such a voter is pretending to prefer the major-party candidate because she doesn't want to "throw away" her vote on a favorite who has no chance of winning.

Arrow assumes complete honesty on the part of the voters. You might imagine that, instead of ballots, a polygraph test verifies each voter's sincere preferences about the candidates. Could you use this flawless knowledge about voter preferences to devise a perfect voting system? This is essentially what Arrow asked. The answer is no.

In order for Arrow to make a compelling case, it was necessary to set some specific conditions. He began with the claim that any reasonable way of voting (constitution) must meet a set of commonsense conditions. In Arrow's original proof there are five conditions. I will give a simplified (but equivalent) version with just four.

One condition is *transitivity*. "If a man says he likes Republicans better than Democrats and Democrats better than Communists, then we think he is strange indeed if he also says he likes Communists better than Republicans," as political scientist William H. Riker once put it. Arrow stipulates that every voter must have transitive preferences. Someone who prefers a Republican to a Democrat and the Democrat to a Communist *has* to prefer the Republican to the Communist.

We already know that there are cases where two-way votes of transitive voters can produce an intransitive outcome. Arrow therefore demands transitivity of the election's outcome, too. A useful voting system has to be decisive and identify one unambiguous winner. Arrow further requires that the outcome be a full ranking of all the candidates. We want to know not only who won but also who came in second, third, and so on.

A second condition is that the voting system must respect *unanimity*. In the unlikely event that *every single voter* prefers candidate Adams to Buchanan, then Adams should beat Buchanan in the final tally. Any other result is ridiculous.

You may wonder why we need this condition when unanimity is unheard of in a real election with thousands or millions of voters. Wouldn't it make more sense to demand that when a substantial *majority* of the voters prefer Adams to Buchanan, Adams is preferred in the outcome?

Notice that any voting system that always respects the desires of a "substantial majority" will also respect unanimous desires. Unanimity is actually the *least* demanding condition we can ask for. This keeps Arrow's result as far-reaching as possible.

A third condition is a no-brainer: *nondictatorship*. Suppose that whenever there's a big decision to be made, every citizen goes to the polls and marks a ballot. It's all a pretense. Only one vote counts, and that's Joe Stalin's. This is a dictatorship (even if everyone does go through the motions of voting). The nondictatorship condition says, reasonably enough, that there must not be a dictator-voter who always gets his way, no matter how everyone else votes.

Arrow had to include the nondictatorship condition because a dictatorship—hardly a fair voting system—can easily obey his other conditions. Assuming that Joe Stalin knows his mind, the above system is transitive. Also, our dictatorship never violates the unanimous will of the people. When *everyone* (including Joe Stalin) votes for increasing the vodka ration, more vodka it is. Of course, when everyone *except* Joe Stalin votes for vodka, it's another story.

Arrow had one more condition. He gave it a wordy label: *independence of irrelevant alternatives.* It is best introduced with a few examples. One of the most memorable is due to the Columbia University philosopher Sidney Morgenbesser (1921–2004), a specimen of a particularly rare brand of genius, better remembered for his wit than for anything he published. According to the story, Morgenbesser was in a New York diner ordering dessert. The waitress told him he had two choices, apple pie and blueberry pie. "Apple," Morgenbesser said.

A few minutes later the waitress came back and told him, oh yes, they also have cherry pie.

"In that case," said Morgenbesser, "I'll have the blueberry."

Cherry pie is what Arrow calls an "irrelevant alternative." It is irrelevant because, given the chance to order cherry pie, Morgenbesser rejected it. But something you don't want anyway shouldn't cause you to change what you *do* want. When the two options were apple and blueberry, Morgenbesser preferred apple. Fine. Then cherry was added to the menu. It would have made perfect sense for Morgenbesser to switch his order to cherry. It would have made sense for him to stick with apple. Switching to blueberry was crazy!

The Great Flip-Flop is an example of a vote failing to meet independence of irrelevant alternatives. The gold- and silver-medal winners should not flip because of a skater who came in sixth. So Arrow pro-

posed, as a commonsense condition, that whether candidate A beats B should *not* depend on any "irrelevant" third-party C. To give one final example, the obvious one, whether Al Gore beats George W. Bush should not depend on whether Ralph Nader is in the race. As both the figure-skating and the political examples show, people can get pretty upset when this condition is violated.

You may not feel that this and the other conditions say everything there is to say about fair elections. That's okay. Arrow's conditions, like Euclid's axioms, were purposely kept minimal. The important thing is that all are absolutely necessary preconditions of any reasonable democratic system. Arrow derived a conclusion whose shock waves are still being felt. He proved that it is impossible to design a voting system meeting these commonsense conditions. It is like squaring the circle or designing a perpetual-motion machine. *It can't be done.* Consequently, *any* voting system of the broad class described by Arrow has serious problems.

Arrow called this result an impossibility theorem. But "when I used that term at the Cowles Commission, the director, Tjalling Koopmans, felt that it was too pessimistic." On Koopman's advice, Arrow switched to the more upbeat name "general possibility theorem" in his dissertation. Afterward, he and almost everyone else reverted to the more accurate—and dismal—name.

The audacious nihilism of Arrow's proof was quickly compared to Gödel's. "The search of the great minds of recorded history for the perfect democracy, it turns out, is the search for a chimera, for logical self-contradiction," wrote MIT economist Paul Samuelson in 1952. "New scholars all over the world—in mathematics, politics, philosophy, and economics—are trying to salvage what can be salvaged from Arrow's devastating discovery that is to mathematical politics what Kurt Gödel's 1931 impossibility-of-proving-consistency theorem is to mathematical logic."

No century before the twentieth could have been shocked by the revelation that the social contract is founded on as flimsy a foundation as mathematics itself. It was partly for this work that Arrow won the 1972 Nobel Prize in Economics (shared with John R. Hicks) "for their pioneering contributions to general economic equilibrium theory and welfare theory." The Nobel committee's press release identified the impossibility theorem as "perhaps the most important of Arrow's contributions to welfare theory." Arrow himself rates the theorem as his most important achievement, and it has been cited more than any of the other papers he has published in a long, diverse career as an economist.

Like Michelangelo's Sistine Chapel, the impossibility theorem was so breathtakingly original that it made everyone else's work in voting theory look old-fashioned. A couple of academic careers were probably stunted as a result. Abram Bergson, whose work had been the jumping-off point for Arrow's, sat on the panel quizzing Arrow for his doctorate. "Obviously, he was a little miffed," Arrow recalls, "but very fair." Some conjecture that Arrow ultimately cost Bergson a Nobel Prize.

A sadder case was the perpetually underappreciated Duncan Black. Black claimed that he discovered the paradox of voting in 1942. Not until November 1949, however, did he and R. A. Newing submit a paper to *Econometrica* describing the paradox. It took eighteen months for the journal to accept it. The editor insisted that Black cite Arrow's paper (which went far beyond Black's). Feeling cheated of priority, Black withdrew the paper and had it printed privately as a booklet titled *Committee Decisions with Complementary Valuation*. Few ever saw it. Twenty copies remained in Black's house at his death. Black himself must have written the jacket copy: "Whatever the merits or demerits of the book, it can safely be said that there is no other which has attempted to deal with this subject."

Black was not entirely out of the loop. In December 1948 the RAND Corporation's Joseph Goldsen wrote Black that "a group of

American mathematicians and political scientists" were interested in his work and would appreciate receiving offprints. Black had never heard of the RAND Corporation. He checked it out with the British Consul in San Francisco. An official informed him that "the activities of the Rand Corporation are highly classified" and the "United States Air Force would much prefer that, if you decided to respond to Mr. Goldsen's enquiry, it should be communicated to the Corporation through themselves." Black must have decided he wanted nothing to do with the RAND Corporation and its highly classified activities. He never replied to Goldsen.

For the past half century scholars and journalists have struggled to understand what the impossibility theorem means. It is possible to find in the literature counterparts to Elisabeth Kübler-Ross's stages of denial, anger, bargaining, depression, and acceptance. Kübler-Ross was characterizing reactions to impending death—and as some saw it, Arrow's work was a death knell for any idealistic notion of democracy. It has struck many as a portentous comment on the human condition. We can't connect, we can't find consensus, we can't get along.

"During the 1930s and 1940s there was a pervasive sense of dismay and defeat among the intellectuals of the West over what they took to be the inevitability of the triumph, both external and internal, of fascist or communist alternatives to democratic capitalism," historian S. M. Amadae wrote in *Rationalizing Capitalist Democracy* (2003). Authoritarian states were moving toward centrally planned economies. This was the wave of the future, and it worked (or so Lincoln Steffens said). In the United States there was a new eagerness to justify previously unquestioned Western values. Could the uncertain workings of democracy and individual choice compete with scientifically planned economies?

The RAND Corporation was a focus of America's collectivist panic.

Its creation was an attempt to beat the Soviet planners at their own game(s), to show that reasoned, scientific policy decisions could be compatible with American democracy. This meant, in other words, that RAND's elite would devise ways to make sound decisions on behalf of the American masses. Amadae has termed this doctrine "rational choice" and wrote that "it is no exaggeration to say that virtually all the roads to rational choice theory lead from RAND." Amadae interprets Arrow's theorem as "part of the campaign to reassert the tenets of governmental rule legitimized by popular consent, but not susceptible to fascist or authoritarian perversions."

Mathematics is no respecter of ideology. What Arrow ended up proving did not exactly help the case for democracy. Perhaps his theorem resonated all the more deeply for this reason. It articulated a central anxiety of the age, that democracy and individualism might in some deep way be inadequate against the collectivist, authoritarian alternative.

Social Choice and Individual Values was published during the peak of Joseph McCarthy's communist witch hunt. In a climate already suspicious of intellectuals who criticized the American system, Arrow's work was easily miscast. "I gave a talk on this at the December 1948 meeting of the Econometrics Society," Arrow said. "There was a fellow there, a Canadian economist named David McCord Wright. He said that he hadn't seen the value of *freedom* mentioned anywhere in this. As he was going out, he said to a mathematician who was interested in economics, a fellow named Kenneth May: 'Oh! Arrow and Klein are communists!'" Lawrence Klein was the meeting's chairman. Arrow was more amused than offended because Wright must not have known May. "May was a real leftie," Arrow says. "He probably *was* a communist."

Among those who attended to what Arrow was saying, the effect was more to reconcile people to the status quo than to make them want to tear it down. One reaction to Arrow's theorem was that it echoed the oft-quoted wisdom of Winston Churchill in a 1947 House of Commons speech: "Many forms of Government have been tried, and will be tried in this world of sin and woe. No one pretends that democracy is perfect or all-wise. Indeed, it has been said that democracy is the worst form of government except all those other forms that have been tried from time to time."

That was the optimistic view. To look at it another way, Arrow's theorem says that election outcomes can be decided by quirks of procedure as much as the voters' authentic wishes. That better recalls a remark, probably apocryphal, attributed to Joseph Stalin: "Those who cast the votes decide nothing. Those who count the votes decide everything."

Upon the 1972 announcement of Arrow's Nobel Prize, Paul Samuelson supplied the now-standard journalist's gloss: "What Kenneth Arrow proved once and for all is that there cannot possibly be . . . an ideal voting scheme."

To some extent, Arrow's theorem refutes the notion of a "will of the people." We all believe in a public will, envisioning it in our own political image—that is to say, as decisive and self-consistent. This belief makes it easy to be optimistic about democracy. Voting is then a way of channeling the public will. The many different ways of designing ballots and tallying votes can be thought of as competing road maps of the same region. Though different in superficial ways, all show the same territory. Because of that, it shouldn't matter which map (voting system) we use. All are going to get us where we need to go.

We all know that the map is not the territory. What if there were no territory—only maps? Arrow's theorem says that there are situations where the "will of the people" is ill-defined, where rational people are collectively irrational. A decisive voting system will come up with a winner, but that winner may differ from the winner decided under another voting system that *also* sounds fair and reasonable. There may be no unique democratic outcome.

———

Is there any way around this? Arrow's result applies only when there are three or more candidates. A simple majority vote between two candidates is as fair as anyone could desire.

Much voting *is* between two alternatives. There are yea-or-nay votes for parliamentary motions and yes-or-nos for ballot referenda. In elections for office, America's two-party system often provides a de facto binary choice.

The role of the two-party system in avoiding electoral paradox was recognized long before Arrow. In an 1885 book, *Congressional Government*, future president Woodrow Wilson argued that the two-party system must present voters with clear-cut, either-or choices. Wilson was an Anglophile taking as his model Victorian England. Writing at a certain remove from the rough-and-tumble of British politics, he believed that the tightly disciplined British parties offered voters a clear philosophical choice lacking in America. Why can't the Democrats and Republicans be more like the Tory and Labour parties? Wilson wanted to know.

One thing Wilson did *not* know was that he would one day become president only because the two-party system *failed*. In 1912 ex-president Teddy Roosevelt's independent candidacy split the Republican vote, leading to Wilson's victory. Had there been a single Republican running, Wilson almost certainly would have lost.

Upon closer inspection, two-way choices are the exception in politics. There are always more than two people wanting to run for an important office. Most of them bow out when they fail to gain their party's nomination. Every bill or referendum put to the vote is one out of the infinity of bills or referenda that potentially could have been proposed. When we rank-and-file voters have a two-way choice, it's because someone more powerful has decided what that two-way choice is going to be.

Harvard economist Amartya Sen aptly called Arrow's theorem "the big bang." From out of nothingness, it created the ever-expanding universe of social choice theory. Scholars quickly set about finding ways to interpret and build upon Arrow's work. I will have more to say later about the ever-morphing perceptions of the impossibility theorem. For the moment, let me add this caveat: *The devil is in the details.* I have defined Arrow's conditions informally. His result is not a philosophical thesis but a demonstration in pure logic, contingent on the precise formulation given in his paper. Arrow himself made a slight error in his original publication, discovered by Julian Blau in 1957 and corrected in the second edition of *Social Choice and Individual Values.* This underscores the far greater hazard of reducing Arrow's theorem to a maxim such as "no voting system is perfect."

Oskar Morgenstern was dying. An aggressive spinal cancer racked his body and sapped his spirit. As his own health ebbed, Morgenstern was attempting to look after Kurt Gödel, who was also dying—and was almost out of his mind. The logician had lately become convinced that he was being poisoned. He hinted that one doctor was prescribing a poisonous drug. He asked another doctor whether he was an impostor impersonating the "real" doctor.

Morgenstern asked one of Gödel's physicians for an opinion. Was Gödel a danger to himself or others? The doctor thought he was okay, if only he'd eat. Gödel ate so little that his weight had diminished to sixty pounds.

In fact, Gödel would survive Morgenstern.

Sometime in 1976, Morgenstern received a paper from an acquaintance, a mathematically trained magazine editor named George A. W. Boehm. People were always sending Morgenstern papers, hoping he would vet them or convey them to an even more distinguished authority. Boehm's paper described a novel voting system. It purported to prevent the spoiler effect—to encourage honest voting—and perhaps even to keep the Hitlers of the world from power over majorities who disliked them.

The amazing thing about the system was how *simple* it was. A single mimeographed sheet described it in full.

Morgenstern filed away Boehm's ingenious scheme. He was too sick a man to do much with it.

THREE

A Short History of
Vote Splitting

The most popular take on the impossibility theorem has been stoicism: *voting isn't perfect—get past it.*

That imperfection is most visible in spoilers and vote splitting. As University of California at Irvine mathematician Donald Saari put it, the 2000 presidential election was "a beautiful example of Arrow's theorem at work."

How common is it for a presidential election to go to the "wrong" candidate because of a spoiler? The answer is complicated by the electoral college as well as by the imponderables common to any game of historical make-believe. Pundits have routinely assumed that a majority of Ralph Nader voters in 2000 "would have" voted for Al Gore. They're supposing that, had Nader's plane crashed a few days before the election, most of his supporters would have gone to the polls and voted for Gore. Ignored is the near-certainty that many Nader voters would not have voted at all had their candidate not been in the race.

The major parties go to an awful lot of trouble to get their supporters into the voting booth. Without a candidate and a get-out-the-vote effort, many people don't vote.

Rather than asking, "What if such-and-such a spoiler never ran?" it is more instructive to imagine a version of history in which the candidates and voters and campaigns were the same, the only difference being the system for counting the popular vote. Suppose that every third-party voter had been required to specify a "second choice" among the two front-running candidates. All the third-party-candidate votes would have been transferred to their supporters' second choices and wouldn't have gone wasted. (This is almost, but not quite, how the system known as instant-runoff voting works.) The adjusted popular votes would then determine the electoral votes, as they do now.

There was no popular vote in the first few presidential elections. The 1828 race was the first held under the modern rules: a two-party system, with popular and electoral college voting similar to today's. The first spoiler-determined election under these rules was that of 1844.

Both of the major parties were running slave-owners for president in 1844. The Democrats settled on James Polk, a Tennessee attorney and congressman largely unknown to the public. Polk sided with his party in approving a platform that championed the annexation of Texas as a slave state. The Whig Party nominated Henry Clay. It was his fourth run for president. Clay was both a slave-owner and an abolitionist. He opposed the annexation of Texas and advocated resettlement of freed slaves in Africa. Well known and widely respected, Clay probably would have won, had it not been for James Birney.

Birney was an abolitionist attorney and publisher running on the Liberty Party ticket. Of the candidates, he alone called for an immediate end to slavery. Clay ended up getting 48.1 percent of the popular vote to Polk's 49.5 percent. Birney got 2.3 percent, more than Polk's popular-vote margin of victory. That's significant because the vast majority of Birney's supporters presumably would have favored Clay over Polk.

Polk got 170 electoral votes to Clay's 105. Birney got no electoral votes at all. There were only a couple of states where the Birney vote might have made a difference. One was New York. Clay would have needed about 67 percent of the Birney vote to win New York. He almost surely would have gotten it, had Birney supporters been able to name a second choice. That would have shifted New York's 36 electoral votes from the Polk column into Clay's. Clay then would have won the election 141 to 134. He conceivably could have won Michigan, too, but this would have required practically all of Birney's supporters to favor Clay.

Despite owing his victory to an abolitionist, Polk refused to take the abolition movement seriously. In his diary, he complained that "the agitation of the slavery question is mischievous and wicked, and proceeds from no patriotic motive by its authors. It is a mere political question on which demagogues and ambitious politicians hope to promote their own prospects for political promotion. And this they seem willing to do even at disturbing the harmony if not dissolving the Union itself."

Finding himself in failing health, President Polk chose not to run for a second term. It was probably the right decision. He came down with cholera the night after he laid the cornerstone of the Washington Monument. Within four months of leaving office, Polk's slaves were placing their master in the cold, cold ground.

In 1848 both major parties courted Zachary Taylor, a hero from the battle of Buena Vista in the Mexican War. As a political creature, Taylor was uniquely malleable. He had never held office. He had never even voted.

FOOTRACE, PENSYLVANIA AVENUE.
Stakes $25.000.

Henry Clay (far right) has the lead on James Polk (tumbling figure at center) in H. Buchholzer's cartoon of the 1844 election. Polk ultimately beat Clay owing to spoiler James Birney (not shown). The twenty-five-thousand-dollar stake was the president's annual salary.

Taylor agreed to run as a Whig. This left the Democrats scrambling for an alternative. Ex-president Martin Van Buren, then sixty-five, announced that he wanted to run again. (He had wanted to run in 1844, too.) His party wouldn't have him. The Democrats nominated Lewis Cass of Michigan. Van Buren felt insulted and ran on the Free Soil ticket, taking a more antislavery stance than Cass did. Democrats were split between loyalty to their party's former president and the party's current candidate. This gave Taylor a victory he had done little to merit. Van Buren's 291,661 popular votes were more than double the margin by which Taylor beat Cass.

Taylor won 163 electoral votes to Cass's 127. Van Buren got no electoral votes. Had 90 percent of the Van Buren vote favored fellow Democrat Cass over Taylor, Cass could have picked up Massachusetts and Connecticut. This would have had him tied with Taylor 145 to 145 electoral votes. The election then would have been settled in the House of Representatives. Had about 94 percent of Van Buren's supporters favored Cass, Cass could have gained New York and Vermont as well. Lewis Cass then would have won 187 to 103 and become the twelfth president.

The 1860 Democratic convention was a disaster. Meeting in Charleston, the Democrats immediately began bickering over the federal government's right to restrict slavery. Unable to decide on a candidate, the party called a time-out. They reconvened weeks later in the more neutral venue of Baltimore. Another deadlock followed, and the southerners bolted. With only northerners left, Stephen Douglas won the nomination. Douglas was the architect of the Kansas-Nebraska bill permitting the admission of new slave states. The southern Democrats

THE PRESIDENTIAL FISHING PARTY OF 1848.

Zachary Taylor (right) catches all the electoral vote "fish," leaving none for Martin Van Buren (far left), the Liberty Party's John Hale (center left), or Democrat Lewis Cass (center). An 1848 Currier and Ives print.

This 1860 Currier and Ives lithograph is one of the more surreal illustrations of vote splitting. Published after the politically suicidal split of the Democratic Party, it shows "Honest Abe" ready to slurp down helpless Democrats Stephen Douglas and John Breckinridge.

regrouped in Richmond and nominated the strongly pro-slavery John Breckinridge.

The split greatly advanced the fortunes of the Republican nominee, Abraham Lincoln. Though a lukewarm abolitionist during the campaign, Lincoln was the only candidate who did not have good things to say about the institution of slavery. He ceded some of his potential support to the new Constitutional Union Party and its candidate, John Bell. Bell's platform could be described as "anyone but Lincoln." He appealed to people who sensed that a Lincoln victory would break up the union, and who couldn't see themselves voting for a Democrat. Bell drew most of his support in border states, where the threat of war was keenly felt.

All four of the candidates won some electoral votes and double-digit popular vote percentages. Despite that, it was not an especially close race. Lincoln was way ahead.

	Popular Vote (%)	Electoral Votes
Lincoln	39.8	180
Breckinridge	18.1	72
Bell	12.6	39
Douglas	29.5	12

Historians have long questioned the legitimacy of Lincoln's victory. For that matter, so did the seven Confederate states that seceded between Election Day 1860 and Lincoln's inauguration. They were protesting what they saw as a flawed voting system.

A candidate who won the North, and *only* the North, would have enough electoral votes to win. The Lincoln campaign had made a strategic decision to write off the South entirely. Back then, parties printed and distributed their own ballots. The Lincoln campaign did not bother to print ballots for the Deep South. Douglas alone ran a nationwide campaign, and (unusual for the time) the candidate himself traveled widely. In the absence of reliable polls, he thought he had a shot at winning the South. This misjudgment may have cost him the election.

The motivations of Bell and Breckinridge have fascinated historians. Both knew there weren't enough electoral votes in the South for them to win. Bell seems to have wanted to use the spoiler effect to preserve the union. His objective apparently was to prevent Lincoln from getting a needed majority of electoral votes. This would throw the election to the House of Representatives, where Bell might have been a power broker in electing someone more moderate than Lincoln.

By one speculative theory, Breckinridge intended to use the spoiler effect to break up the union. He hoped to take enough votes from Douglas so that Lincoln would win. This would provide a pretext for

1860 again. John Bell (right) vainly glues the map back together as Lincoln and Douglas claw apart the West and Breckinridge clutches Dixie to his heart. Published by Rickey, Mallory and Co., Cincinnati.

the South to secede, securing a final solution to the abolitionist problem. A more believable analysis, advanced in William Davis's 1974 biography of the politician, is that Breckinridge (who accepted the nomination reluctantly, on the urging of Jefferson Davis) concurred with Jefferson Davis's belief that Bell would be a spoiler, taking votes mainly from Douglas and causing the detested Lincoln to win. Breckinridge entered the election in order to strike a deal with Douglas and Bell. They would *all* pull out in favor of a suitable compromise candidate to be determined. The plan ran aground when Douglas, and perhaps Bell, refused to go along—so goes the theory.

Had it not been for the vote splitting, Douglas certainly would have beaten Lincoln in the popular vote (a vote of unenslaved males only). Virtually all of Breckinridge's and Bell's supporters would have sided with Douglas rather than Lincoln. Douglas still would have lost the electoral vote, though. He was the second most popular candidate in many states—a significant distinction in this election—but second place counts for nothing in the electoral vote. Douglas won just two states, New Jersey and Missouri. Four of New Jersey's electors cast their votes for Lincoln, so Douglas got only 12 electoral votes.

Adjusting for the Breckinridge/Bell spoiler effect, Douglas might have gained all the southern states and picked up California and Oregon from Lincoln. This would have given him about 130 electoral votes. (I am throwing in South Carolina's 8 electoral votes even though the state still didn't hold a popular vote.) Lincoln would nonetheless have had 173 electoral votes and the victory.

The best explanation for why Lincoln won is the electoral college.

Between the Civil War and the Great Depression, the Democrats won only three presidential elections. At least two, and possibly all three, were due to spoilers.

James G. Blaine was a two-time secretary of state who had served in both houses of Congress. He is today remembered for championing what was then a Republican core value, the separation of church and state. Blaine might instead have been remembered as the twenty-second president, had it not been for another wedge issue, the prohibition of alcohol.

The temperance movement thrived in the years of Reconstruction. Its supporters tended to be Republican women. They couldn't vote; they could write and give speeches. Judith Ellen Foster's pamphlet "The Republican Party and Temperance" cast the 1884 race, Grover Cleveland v. James Blaine, as a referendum on moral values, temperance above all. Foster termed the Democratic Party the "open ally of the saloon." "We want the Democratic Party to bite the dust," wrote another crusader, Frances Willard of the Woman's Christian Temperance Union, "and will do the utmost to work its final overthrow."

Despite this zeal for crushing Democrats, the male Republican leadership kept the temperance movement at arm's length. The latter was pressing for an anti-alcohol plank in the Republican platform. That would have been political suicide. Too many voters drank.

There was a growing Prohibition Party, founded in 1869 and lately showing muscle in state races. In 1884, it nominated John St. John, a former Kansas governor who had helped make the state dry. As a presidential candidate, St. John did surprisingly well. He drew most of his support from Republican ranks. After it became clear that the race between Blaine and Democrat Grover Cleveland was a tight one, the Republican Party asked St. John to drop out. He refused.

There was such a thing as opposition research even back then. The Republicans learned that St. John had had an early marriage he didn't talk about. In other words, he was divorced. This was considered a dreadful scandal. The Republicans launched a vitriolic attack on St. John's character.

St. John was so incensed that he focused his campaign on New York, a state where he had a chance of tipping a raft of electoral votes to Grover Cleveland. More remarkably, the Democrats quietly funded St. John's New York campaign. They got their money's worth. Cleveland won *only* because of St. John's spoiler candidacy.

Cleveland achieved a slim plurality of the popular vote (48.5 percent) and 219 electoral votes to Blaine's 182. St. John was unquestionably a spoiler. In New York he pulled 24,999 votes, while Cleveland's margin of victory over Blaine was only 1,047. Flipping New York's 36 electoral votes to Blaine would have put Blaine in the White House.

(There was also Greenback candidate Benjamin Butler, who got more votes nationally than St. John did. The Greenback Party started with many Republican supporters [in the 1870s] and ended up merging into the Democratic Party [in the 1890s]. Some have argued that Butler hurt Cleveland more than Blaine. Yet even if *all* of Butler's votes had come out of Cleveland's total, which no one believes, Blaine would have won New York and the election—had it not been for St. John. De-

AT HIS OLD TRICKS AGAIN OUT WEST.
James G. Blaine. "I will now, in confidence, tell in 50,000,000 people."

Republican "magician" James Blaine attempts to turn beer into water in an 1884 Thomas Nast cartoon. Looking on skeptically is Prohibition Party candidate John St. John, the spoiler who made Blaine's presidential ambitions disappear.

pending on your estimates, Blaine could have picked up Connecticut and New Jersey as well.)

In 1892 Grover Cleveland, who had been ousted after one term, ran against the Republican incumbent Benjamin Harrison. Cleveland regained office with only 46.0 percent of the popular vote. There were two strong third-party candidates. Populist James Weaver is often considered a spoiler. He commanded 8.51 percent of the popular vote and 22 electoral votes. Prohibition candidate John Bidwell received 2.24 percent of the popular vote and no electoral votes.

Bidwell's support would have come largely out of the Republican vote. The sympathies of Weaver's voters are less clear. Weaver had been an abolitionist and Republican. After the Civil War, the Republicans increasingly became the party of big business. This left some of its supporters, Weaver among them, feeling abandoned. In 1878 he joined the Greenback Party. This called for silver coinage and an eight-hour workday. Weaver served in Congress with the backing of the Greenback and Democratic parties.

The Democratic Party gradually swallowed up most of the Greenback Party. Weaver again resisted. He helped organize the Populist Party circa 1891. This promoted direct election of senators, government ownership of railroads and telephone and telegraph lines, and a graduated income tax (a double novelty because there was no federal income tax at the time). Though the forty-hour workweek and federal income tax were considered radically leftist, the party also had a nativist, reactionary streak. The Populists endorsed Democratic candidates in local Western races and Republicans in the South.

In 1892 Weaver probably hurt the Republicans most by siphoning off the African American vote. Blacks had voted Republican in past elections. Weaver was the first presidential candidate to court the black vote as seriously as he did. In some southern states, he captured practically all of the "Republican" vote—meaning blacks who were willing to walk past the hooded Klansmen at southern polling stations to vote against the Democratic machine. Weaver polled 36.6 percent in Alabama, versus just 3.95 percent for Republican Benjamin Harrison.

Harrison would have needed something like 84 percent of the Weaver vote in swing states to win. He then might have gained the four states Weaver won (Colorado, Idaho, Kansas, and Nevada); wrested Illinois, Indiana, West Virginia, and Wisconsin from Cleveland; and picked up the 10 electoral votes cast for Weaver or Cleveland in the split-vote states of California, North Dakota, and Oregon. Harrison then would have squeaked past Cleveland 227 to 221. But probably the Weaver vote was *not* decisive because none of the swing states were in the South.

Tycoons J. P. Morgan and Henry Clay Frick raised two million dollars for Teddy Roosevelt's 1904 reelection campaign. It was a bad investment. The fiercely independent Roosevelt's trust-busting continued unabated. At the end of his second term, Roosevelt announced his intention to retire, and the big capitalists were glad to see him go. His vice president, William Howard Taft, became the Republican candidate in 1908. Taft vowed to continue Roosevelt's policies, ensuring the outgoing president's endorsement. Roosevelt began his retirement with a safari in Africa, where J. P. Morgan hoped that "a lion would do its duty."

Taft succeeded Roosevelt as president. Once in office, he sided with Wall Street interests. That and an assortment of personal slights, real and imagined, led Roosevelt to feel betrayed. He ran against Taft in the 1912 Republican primaries, calling the sitting president a "fathead" and "dumber than a guinea pig." Taft's partisans dominated the 1912 Republican convention in Chicago. When Roosevelt failed to win the nomination, he and his supporters stormed out and held their own convention a few blocks away. They founded a Progressive Party, with Roosevelt as its candidate.

The 1912 race has become a textbook case of vote splitting. Roosevelt may have been more universally admired than any American president since George Washington. He had the satisfaction of beating Taft by 27.4 percent to 23.2 percent of the popular vote. That adds up to a slim majority for the combined "Republican" vote. Yet Democrat Woodrow Wilson had a plurality, with 41.8 percent. Wilson won the electoral vote contest easily, getting 435 votes to Roosevelt's 88 and Taft's 8. In the usual analysis, Roosevelt would have beaten Wilson, had the Republicans nominated him instead of Taft. Taft could have beaten Wilson, too, had he run without Roosevelt's challenge.

The situation is less pat than it is often presented. The Socialist Party's Eugene V. Debs got an impressive 6.0 percent of the 1912 popular vote. In his campaign speeches, Debs attacked the Democratic Party nearly as much as the robber barons. "Where but to the Socialist Party can these progressive people turn?" he asked. "Every true Democrat should thank Wall Street for driving them out of a party that is democratic in name only and into one that is democratic in fact." Debs clearly took votes from Wilson, while Taft and Roosevelt took votes from each other. Furthermore, a Prohibition Party candidate, Eugene Chafin, got 1.4 percent, most of which probably came from the Republicans.

If Debs's votes were reassigned to Wilson, and Chafin's to the Republicans, Roosevelt would have needed to pick up 94 percent or more of Taft's votes to win. Or vice versa: Taft could have won by picking up 94 percent of the Roosevelt vote. The former scenario is more plausible. Had they been forced to choose between Wilson and Roosevelt, Taft's capitalist base would have preferred a moderate Republican to a liberal Democrat. Were Roosevelt's supporters required to name a second choice, some probably would have favored Wilson over Taft.

Let's focus on Wilson v. Roosevelt, then. With 94 percent or more of the Taft vote counting toward Roosevelt, Roosevelt would have picked up Maine, New Hampshire, Massachusetts, Rhode Island, Connecticut, New York, New Jersey, Illinois, Iowa, Kansas, Nebraska, North Dakota, Montana, Wyoming, New Mexico, Idaho, and Oregon. Roosevelt would have *lost* California. This is one of the six states that Roosevelt did, in reality, win. He won it (over Wilson) by a mere

174 votes. The main reason Roosevelt did so well in California was that Taft didn't make the ballot. Roosevelt was listed as a Republican *and* a Progressive, leaving Taft to pick up a handful of write-in votes. But California was a strong state for Debs. The Socialist got 79,201 votes. Wilson would easily have won California had it not been for Debs.

California split its electoral vote. Eleven votes went for Roosevelt and just two for Wilson. Let's assume that had Wilson won the state's popular vote, he would have received all 13 electoral votes. Roosevelt then would have picked up 191 electoral votes and lost 11. He would have been elected president 268 to 266. Had California's electors still cast a few votes for Roosevelt (which seems likely), his margin would have been a few votes larger.

FLOOR-MANAGER TAFT: "HOLD ON, COLONEL—YOU CAN'T DO THE GRIZZLY BEAR WITH THAT DEAR OLD LADY!"

The bust of Lincoln scowls at the scandalous behavior of William Taft and Teddy Roosevelt in a 1912 Edward Kemble cartoon. The "Grizzly Bear" was a dirty-dancing craze of the early 1900s.

Ross Perot was a Dallas IBM salesman who chafed at the computer company's bureaucracy. With a thousand-dollar loan from his wife's savings, Perot founded Electronic Data Systems. When EDS went public in 1968, the company's value increased by a factor of ten, and so did Perot's net worth. Perot sold his stake to General Motors for $700 million in 1984.

Perot ran EDS as a tight ship. The dress code was enforced by checking skirt lengths with a tape measure. But EDS took care of its own. In 1979 Perot organized a daring mission in which EDS employees and a Green Beret rescued two EDS staffers from an Iranian prison. Suddenly Perot was a swashbuckling corporate folk hero. He had served no elective office when he announced on CNN's *Larry King Live* that he was willing to run for president in 1992.

In June, the high point of Perot's popularity, some polls ranked him ahead of both George H. W. Bush and Bill Clinton. Perot spent about sixty-five million dollars of his own money on the campaign. This gave him the luxury of quitting the race in midsummer, pouting eleven weeks, and then plunging back in at the start of October. As to why he'd quit, he claimed that Republican dirty tricks experts were attempting to wreck his daughter's wedding by circulating a faked nude photo of her. It was this sort of talk that led critics to charge that Perot was unstable and the notion of him as president downright scary.

"In the final analysis, Perot cost me the election," George H. W. Bush wrote. Though Perot got not a single electoral vote, he polled 19.7 million popular votes. That is nearly four times the margin by which the incumbent Bush lost to Bill Clinton. Senator Bob Dole pointed out, accurately enough, that 57 percent of the electorate had voted *against* Clinton. Democrats countered that 62 percent had voted *for* a change. Clinton confided to consultant Dick Morris that the Republicans in Congress "never saw my presidency as legitimate. They see me as accidental, illegitimate, a mistake in a three-way race."

Perot was hard to pigeonhole ideologically. Some saw in his pro–abortion rights stance a "moderate," others a "libertarian." Perhaps more than anything, he played off a broken campaign promise. "Read my lips: no new taxes," went the most memorable line of Bush's acceptance speech at the 1988 Republican convention. Then, in 1990, Bush did raise taxes, for complex political reasons. Most of the hardcore Perot supporters wanted to limit taxes and also wanted to believe that politics was simple, not complex. They felt Bush had betrayed them.

Had at least 67 percent of Perot votes gone to Bush in key states, and the rest to Clinton, Bush would have won. The Republican would have picked up Maine, New Hampshire, Connecticut, New Jersey, Ohio, Wisconsin, Iowa, Kentucky, Georgia, Colorado, Montana, and Nevada, for an additional 106 electoral votes. That would have given Bush 274 votes to Clinton's 264.

Despite the widespread conviction that Perot hurt Bush more than Clinton, scant poll data supports this. A survey by Gerald M. Pomper asked Perot voters to name their second choice. Pomper reported that 38 percent of Perot voters favored Bush as second choice, 38 percent favored Clinton, and the others said they would not have voted at all, had they not been able to vote for Perot, or they would have voted for still another third-party candidate. If this is anywhere close to being accurate, the Perot vote was not decisive.

Polls can be misleading, of course, and those asking for "second choices" of people voting for potential spoilers may be particularly troublesome. The media was branding Perot an egotist for not stepping down and letting the two-party system take its course. Pomper's subjects could have anticipated that the poll's results would be trumpeted as evidence of Perot-as-spoiler. Some may have tried to protect their candidate by insisting that they would sooner have voted for Clinton than Bush.

It is also important to recognize that many Perot supporters *did* vote for Bush. The ones who didn't were more likely to have some particular reason to dislike Bush. Perot himself fell into this category.

Perot believed, as did many Americans, that large numbers of U.S. POWs were still being held in Vietnam. The sad fact now appears to be that most of the "missing" were shot down while flying secret missions over Cambodia and Laos. The United States did not want to admit to illegal missions and had therefore listed soldiers as missing when they would have otherwise been presumed dead. Perot became an advocate for getting to the bottom of the POW/MIA question. The Reagan administration tried to quiet him, first by letting him see classified documents, and then by having Vice President Bush give him a tactfully stern talking-to. Perot took *that* the wrong way. He concluded that George Herbert Walker Bush was his enemy.

So were the Vietnamese. And the Black Panthers. Perot accused the Vietnamese of hiring Black Panthers to assassinate him. Perot also came to believe that his own campaign consultant, Ed Rollins, had signed a lifetime contract with the CIA when it was run by Perot's old nemesis, George H. W. Bush. In Perot's mind, Rollins was actually a mole for the Bush campaign.

Perot could have pulled out of the race. He could have thrown his support behind Bush, with or without exacting political promises. He didn't do that because of his grudge against Bush. "In politics, nothing ever happens by accident," said Franklin Delano Roosevelt. "If it happened, you can bet it was planned that way." Being a spoiler is not just about the math of voting. It is about *spite*. And there is no better illustration of that than the 2000 election.

Harry Levine is a sociologist at Queens College. An ardent liberal, he long admired Ralph Nader and had used one of Nader's books in his classes. But Levine was alarmed at the prospect of Nader becoming a spoiler in the 2000 election. Unlike most Nader supporters, Levine saw a way out.

Toward the end of World War II, the United States contemplated an alternative to the bombing of Hiroshima and Nagasaki. It was to take Japanese observers to a remote part of the Pacific for a demonstration of the atomic bomb. Once they grasped what they were dealing with, and that the same thing could be used on Japan, they would surrender. No bombs need have been dropped on the cities.

Levine thought that Nader could do much the same thing. Nader could withdraw from battleground states such as Florida to avoid taking crucial votes from Al Gore. He could put all his energy into the "safe" states where he couldn't possibly affect the electoral outcome. Nader would get a big turnout in those states, bigger than he could by spreading his resources all over the map. He could then point to the

The Bush family has seen the spoiler effect from both sides, implies Mike Lane's 2004 cartoon. (*Reprinted with permission of PoliticalCartoons.com*)

states where he withdrew and claim that Gore won *only* because he had pulled out. Assuming that Gore won, this would give Nader clout with the new administration. He could then use that to advance his environmental and progressive causes.

What could be simpler? All Levine had to do was get the message to someone close to Nader. He got his chance when Nader made a campaign swing through New York. In Levine's words, this turned out to be a voyage into "Nader's own Lewis Carroll alternate reality—to the other side of the looking glass."

It was Nader who started the Carrollian allusions. In a Madison Square Garden rally that Levine attended with his teenage son, Nader likened Al Gore and George W. Bush to Tweedledee and Tweedledum. Gore's and Bush's politics were so close that it made no difference which won.

The next day, Levine attended a smaller political meeting, in Greenwich Village. Leaning against the wall was filmmaker Michael Moore. Moore was then best known for *Roger and Me*, a film that Nader had backed. Levine introduced himself to Moore and mentioned being upset about the Tweedledee and Tweedledum line. Bush and Cheney were real right-wingers, he said. Al Gore and Joe Lieberman were far from perfect, but anyone who cared about what Ralph Nader stood for had to find them preferable.

Moore nodded without saying much. Levine went on. There should be a website telling progressives in which states it was safe to vote for Nader. Moore said there was going to be a site like that. They also planned to encourage vote swapping. People in safe states could agree to vote for Nader instead of Gore, in return for people in battleground states voting for Gore instead of Nader. "We're going to do it," Moore said.

"Great," Levine said. "But the web site also needs to tell people the states where it is too close to vote for Nader—so people know to hold their nose and vote for Gore in those states."

As Levine remembers it, "Moore instantly turned and looked hard at me. His face got flushed, red, and he puffed up like one of those fish that expand when threatened. In this red, puffed up and very angry state he started yelling at me, leaning into me, and repeatedly poking his finger into my face.

"'You can't say that!' Moore blustered. 'You can't say that! You can't say that! You can't say that!'"

Going by some polls, the most popular presidential candidate of 2000 was Arizona senator John McCain. At one point, McCain's CNN/ Gallup approval rating was 66 percent. That put him ahead of Al Gore (59 percent) and George W. Bush (57 percent). In another poll, a quarter of the public said they would vote for McCain *even as a third-party candidate*. Hardly anyone was willing to go out on that kind of a limb for Gore or Bush. That the third most popular candidate ended up in the White House is testimony to the skills of Bush's strategist, Karl Rove.

Much of what American political consultants do amounts to exploiting the mathematical quirks of the plurality vote. One of those quirks is that the way people vote generally depends on how they think *other* people will vote. The plurality ballot is not kind to those who "throw away their vote" on someone who can't win. Most voters try to make sure they vote for someone that a lot of other people will be voting for.

One of Karl Rove's major themes during the Republican primaries was that McCain didn't have a chance. "At the end of the day, there will be 30 members of the 55 Republicans in the U.S. Senate for George W. Bush, despite the fact that one of their own is running," Rove declared. "If you are the establishment choice on the Republican side, you are the inevitable nominee. No ifs, ands, or buts." In short, Bush was "inevitable." Republicans who happened to prefer McCain needed to face reality and switch their vote.

The Bush campaign raised far more money than McCain's, allowing Bush to enter every primary. McCain had to concentrate his resources on a few states. One of the states where both candidates ran was New Hampshire. There McCain beat Bush by nineteen points.

The next state was South Carolina. The Bush TV ads turned nastier, claiming that McCain was a creature of corporate PACs, an odd charge in a Republican-versus-Republican fight.

"Y'all haven't even hit his soft spots," South Carolina state senator Mike Fair told Bush.

"We're going to," Bush promised, but we're "not going to do it on TV."

Negative campaigning is highly effective for reasons psychological, political, and mathematical. In the various primaries in 2000, Bush ran against McCain, Steve Forbes, Alan Keyes, Gary Bauer, and Orrin Hatch. Suppose a primary voter likes McCain best, and Bush almost as much. McCain would most likely win that vote. The fact that the voter likes Bush almost as much, and better than a whole field of other contenders, counts for nothing. That leaves the Bush campaign with two remedies: do either something to make Bush *more* popular or something to make McCain *less* popular.

There is a real asymmetry here. Plausible negatives are easier to fabricate. You can hardly start a *positive* rumor. ("*Psst!* Bush was a war hero, just like McCain, only he's too modest to talk about it.") Voters are much more likely to believe a negative rumor, a dark secret the candidate and the "liberal media" (or "right-wing media") are covering up. Delivered just before Election Day, a rumor can have more credibility than news.

The rumor mill began turning in South Carolina. Bob Jones University law professor Richard Hand sent out an e-mail message claiming that McCain "had chosen to sire children without marriage." Church flyers took a different tack, identifying McCain as "the fag candidate." South Carolina voters also began receiving mysterious phone calls, supposedly from pollsters, offering further insinuations about the Arizona senator. It was implied that McCain's wife, Cindy, was a drug addict; that McCain was one of those crazy Vietnam vets who might go berserk at the slightest provocation; and, again, that McCain had an illegitimate black child. The faint connection to reality was that the McCains had adopted Bridget, a dark-skinned Bangladeshi child, from Mother Teresa's orphanage.

When Professor Hand was told that McCain had *not* fathered an illegitimate child, Hand replied, "Wait a minute, that's a universal negative. Can you prove that there aren't any?"

The press generally assumed that Karl Rove was behind the smear campaign. If correct, Rove did a good job of keeping his fingerprints off it. "We had no idea who made the phone calls, who paid for them, or how many calls were made," said McCain's campaign manager, Richard H. Davis. "We never did find out who perpetrated these smears, but they worked."

Bush and McCain met face to face at a debate. McCain turned to Bush and shook his head.

"John," Bush answered, "it's politics."

"George, everything isn't politics."

During a commercial break, McCain went on about the smear campaign. Bush insisted he knew nothing about it. He said they should put this behind them, and he offered his hand.

"Don't give me that shit," McCain said. "And take your hands off me."

Like most politicians in a two-party system, McCain ultimately withdrew from the race and endorsed his former opponent. But he likely would have beaten Gore more decisively than Bush was able to do.

Ralph Nader had a hard time keeping political consultants. Like a Mafioso, he had decided he could trust only blood. He had anointed a nephew, Tarek Milleron, as his principal campaign advisor. Milleron looked eerily like a younger clone of his uncle. He was about thirty, handsome, and smart. He dressed as if he were applying for a job on General Motors' legal staff. Harry Levine ran into Milleron at another

THE CHOICE

Ann Telnaes's Pulitzer Prize–winning cartoon finds slim pickings for the voter in the middle. The electoral process often eliminates the most popular candidate. (In 2000 that may have been John McCain.) (© 2000 Ann Telnaes. All rights reserved. Reprinted with permission of Ann Telnaes in conjunction with the Cartoonist Group)

Nader event and made one more pitch. He repeated the story about the atomic bomb and Japan. Nader need only *demonstrate* his spoiler effect, not use it as a weapon of mass destruction.

Milleron's body language sent the wrong signals. He told Levine that a Bush victory might be a good thing for progressives. It is a well-known fact, he said, that it is easier to raise money for environmental causes when people feel threatened.

Levine countered that a Gore administration would still be better for environmental causes overall than a Bush administration. They should help Nader's voters to avoid being spoilers.

"We are not going to do that," Milleron snapped.

"Why not?"

"Because we want to punish the Democrats, we want to hurt them, wound them."

Milleron's remarks would have been no surprise to those who followed Nader's career closely. Not many voters did.

Nader came to public attention in 1965 with the publication of a bestselling book, *Unsafe at Any Speed*. In it, he attacked the automobile industry for putting profits above customer safety. The title was intended literally. Nader told of a boy who had gored himself on a Cadillac tail fin and died. It was a parked car.

Nader was soon testifying regularly before Congress. He became such a popular figure that, in 1968, Democratic presidential hopeful George McGovern asked him to be his running mate. Nader refused.

In 1972 novelist Gore Vidal (a cousin of Al Gore's) was cochairman of a group calling itself the New Party. Vidal thought Nader would be an ideal presidential candidate. Nader again begged off. He said he was afraid he might split the Democratic vote, leading to the reelection of Richard Nixon. In his opinion, that would *not* be a good thing.

Nader could do the political math as well as anyone. He knew the Republicans were less sympathetic to his causes than the Democrats. What happened between 1972 and 2000? The country turned right, and Nader didn't. Reagan, a hugely popular president, preferred to staff his regulatory agencies with executives from the industries being regulated. Washington became a hostile environment for consumer activists.

In 1992 Nader campaigned briefly in the New Hampshire primary, then dropped out of the race. It might have been expected that the return of a Democrat to the White House would restore Nader's influence. It didn't. Bill Clinton refused to have anything to do with Nader. Just before Clinton signed a bill relaxing the fifty-five-mile-an-hour speed limit, Nader practically begged for five minutes of face time. He wanted to make his case that a higher speed limit would cause hundreds of additional fatalities. Clinton never responded.

It was the same story with Al Gore. "The vice president has no time to meet with Mr. Nader," he was told. This was surprising because

Nader had worked with Gore and had rated him one of the ten senators most sympathetic to his views. Nader got on the phone and was put through to the vice president. Gore would not commit to a meeting. The call ended with Gore saying, "Well, I'll see." He never called back.

Nader ran for president on the Green Party ticket in 1996. He told *Mother Jones* magazine that Clinton ought to be known as George Ronald Clinton—a recombinant political monster. Asked by the *Mother Jones* reporter whether his candidacy wouldn't actually help elect Bob Dole, Nader pointed out that in the 1992 New Hampshire primary, 52 percent of his votes came from registered Republicans. That statistic needs some context. In 1992 Nader was promoting the idea that ballots should have a choice marked "none of the above." In the event that "none of the above" got a plurality of votes, no one would win, and another election (or elections?) would be held. Nader told the New Hampshire voters to vote for him *if* what they really wanted to say was "none of the above." Many of the 6,311 voters who voted for Nader were probably registering their distaste for the other candidates. New Hampshire is a conservative state, and it is not surprising that just over half the Nader voters were Republicans.

The New York Times also tried to pin Nader down on the spoiler scenario. "If I really wanted to beat Clinton," Nader said, "I would get out, raise $3 or $4 million, and maybe provide the margin for his defeat. That's not the purpose of this candidacy."

As his 2000 campaign commenced, Nader announced plans to raise five million dollars for his most intense fight yet. A *Rolling Stone* reporter confronted Nader with what he'd said in 1996. "Since you're planning to raise $5 million and run hard this year, does that mean you would not have a problem providing the margin of defeat for Gore?"

"I would not—not at all," Nader answered. "I'd rather have a provocateur than an anesthetizer in the White House. Remember what [Reagan secretary of the interior] James Watt did for the environmental movement? He galvanized it. Gore and his buddy Clinton are anesthetizers."

By all accounts, Nader viewed George W. Bush as something less than human. It was Al Gore who was a moral being accountable for his actions. In Nader's mind, Gore needed to be punished, and the country was better off with Bush because a Bush presidency would be such a catastrophe that it would send the country veering leftward. Many of Nader's associates thought this reasoning was insane. One of them, Gary Sellers, created an uncomfortable moment at a Washington, D.C., fund-raiser in August 2000. "Ralph, this is shaping up to be Ross Perot all over again," Sellers charged. "You'll be the Perot of the left. It will be very destructive."

The room went silent. "Oh, Gary," Nader said, "I wish I could be as clairvoyant as you. Don't you worry. George Bush is so dumb, Gore will beat him by 20 points."

Sellers told biographer Justin Martin that Nader "had a personal animus toward Gore. Gore had moved to the center and that enraged Ralph. Gore also did not return his phone calls. It was clear that Ralph's feelings were hurt. This was the kind of thing you'd expect from an adolescent. It was embarrassing. He was furious and he was going to teach Gore a lesson."

Vote-swapping websites sprang up in the campaign's final weeks. Nader stonily refused to endorse them. "We opposed it," Nader's campaign manager Theresa Amato explained. "Our campaign theme was, vote your conscience, not your fears. Ralph Nader's position was that people should vote for who they want and not engage in elaborate schemes."

A week before the election, California attorney general Bill Jones, a Republican, sent a cease-and-desist letter to the creators of one such site, VoteSwap2000.com. It said that vote trading was a felony punishable by three years in prison. For aiding thousands of such crimes, site creators Jim Cody and Ted Johnson were looking at multiple consecutive life sentences.

Jones cited California Election Code sections 18521 and 18522, which ban buying and selling votes. Applying this to Internet vote trading to avoid a spoiler effect was, to say the least, creative. To avoid trouble, Cody and Johnson shut down the site. Five other state officials elsewhere, all Republican, filed similar complaints.

Liberal forces came down equally hard on Nader himself. *The New York Times* editorialized on "Mr. Nader's Misguided Crusade." The paper had little problem with Nader's positions, only with his "engaging in a self-indulgent exercise that will distract voters from the clear-cut choice presented by the major-party candidates." As *Nation* columnist Christopher Hitchens remarked, the *Times*'s editorial position was the exact opposite of Voltaire's: "I respect what you have to say, but I will fight to the death to prevent you from saying it."

In August, Robert F. Kennedy, Jr., wrote an op-ed piece for the *Times* claiming that Nader had said that he would vote for Bush, were he compelled to choose between Bush and Gore. This was an urban legend zipping around the Internet. Nader wrote the *Times* to deny it (sort of). "I have never said I would vote for George W. Bush, whom I have strongly criticized across the country, if forced to chose between him and Al Gore. Indeed, I have never stated for whom I have ever voted or expect to vote for since the 1960s, though it can be assumed that I will vote for Green Party candidates this year."

"I will not speak his name," James Carville said of Nader. "I'm going to shun him, and any good Democrat, any good progressive ought to do the same thing." Within the Gore campaign, the Green Party candidate was known as "That Bastard" or "the Grim Reaper."

By one hopeful theory, Nader was playing a game of chicken. He was trying to pressure Gore to move to the left. Then he would drop out of the race. By midsummer Nader still hadn't blinked. Gore made overtures to Nader via intermediaries. Myron Cherry, a Gore aide who had worked with Nader in the 1970s, called Nader and laid out the options. If Nader withdrew from the race, Gore would listen to what he had to say. He would give Nader real power in the administration, such as helping decide the head of the Environmental Protection Agency.

Nader "responded like I'd joined the devil," Cherry said. "He would not talk to me and indicated we had nothing to offer him. It was like we were pariahs."

It was not just the Democrats who had to worry about a spoiler. Two right-wing candidates were competing for Bush's conservative base. Pat Buchanan was running on what was left of Ross Perot's Reform Party, and Harry Browne was running as a Libertarian.

In recent years, the Libertarians have been as much a thorn in the side of the Republicans as the Greens have been to the Democrats. This fact gets overlooked perhaps because there has not been a Libertarian spoiler in a presidential election (yet). In congressional races, however, the Libertarians have accomplished a lot—for the Democratic Party. The most powerful Democrat in the Senate would not be there had it not been for a Libertarian spoiler. In 1998, Nevada's Harry Reid, now the Senate majority leader, squeaked by Republican John Ensign by a mere 428 votes. A Libertarian named Michael Cloud drew 8,044 votes in the same race. Similar scenarios elected Democratic senators in Georgia (Max Cleland in 1996) and Washington (Maria Cantwell in 2000). Libertarian spoilers also tipped two 2000 House races to Democrats (Jane Harmon of California and Rush Holt of New Jersey).

Much of the Libertarian rhetoric is a looking-glass version of Nader's. In a 1997 issue of *The Libertarian Enterprise*, L. Neil Smith proposed that the Libertarian Party zero in on Republican incumbents who had won by a margin of 5 percent or less. The Libertarians should put all their resources into running strong candidates against the vulnerable Republicans, "the object being to *deny* them their five percent and put Democrats in office in their place."

It wasn't that Smith wanted tax-and-spend Democrats to run the country. Rather, he expected the Republicans to come crawling to the Libertarians and adopt their liberal views on social issues. Exactly how that would sit with the religious right was left unsaid.

Fortunately for George W. Bush, Harry Browne and Pat Buchanan together polled less than a third of the votes that Ralph Nader did. In the final days of the race, Buchanan stopped campaigning in battleground states. He chose not to risk being responsible for a Gore victory. At least some of Nader's team proposed a similar tactic.

Nader's longtime goal had been to win 5 percent of the popular vote. That would qualify the Green Party for federal funding in 2004. Nearly all Greens also wanted Gore to beat Bush, barely. These two goals depended on Gore's having a greater-than-5-percent lead on Bush. That was looking less and less possible. Nader's advisors suggested that he spend the last days in New York, California, and possibly Texas. California and New York are the two most populous states; their liberal populations were receptive to Nader's message; and since they were firmly in Gore's camp, progressives in these states could vote for Nader with a clear conscience. Texas was just as certainly Bush's, and Nader had enough support in Austin to make that a logical stop.

Nader brushed aside these ideas. His final itinerary included the contested states of Florida (November 4), New Hampshire (part of November 6), and Pennsylvania (Election Day, November 7). He "went into the swing states thinking that's where the press was, that's where he would get publicity," explained Nader's media consultant Bill Hillsman. "But I warned him, 'Only if you want more stories about being a spoiler.'"

The spoiler label didn't bother some Nader voters. On the night of the election, blogger Matt Welch heard one Nader supporter boasting, "I wouldn't vote for Al Gore if he was running against Adolf Hitler."

Bill and Hillary Clinton watched the 2000 election returns in New York City in the company of publisher Harold Evans. As states blinked red or blue on the TV screen, the president supplied statistics on how badly Nader had penalized Gore in each state. A little after 8:00 p.m., the networks retracted their premature projection that Florida would go to Gore.

"I want to kill him," Evans seethed, meaning Nader. Hillary, who had just been elected senator, replied, "That's not a bad idea."

She was not the only Democrat turned homicidal. Perhaps the most shocking line came from from Michael Dukakis: "I'll strangle the guy with my bare hands." The longtime foe of capital punishment was talking about Ralph Nader, of course.

For weeks, Nader campaign workers had existed in a bubble of denial. They hoped that Gore would win, Bush would lose, and Nader would somehow make a respectable showing. Cheering erupted at the Nader headquarters whenever the networks declared that Gore had won a contested state. After the networks retracted the Florida projection, NBC's Tom Brokaw asked Nader some pointed questions about his role in the election. "Screw the corporate media," one Nader staffer said, off camera.

In the wee hours of the day after the election, Nader went home to watch further returns on his black-and-white TV set.

The morning after the election, Matt Welch recorded this exchange between Nader and Pat Buchanan at the National Press Club. Nader arrived with a big grin on his face. He had won only 2.73 percent of the popular vote. No matter; he had made a difference after all.

"Fearless leader!" Buchanan called. "Hey, fearless leader!" Nader finally understood what was going on, and the two shook hands warmly.

"Congratulations, you ran a terrific campaign," Buchanan said.

"Well, Pat, you know how hard it is to challenge this entrenched two-party system!"

For nearly everyone, a message of the 2000 election was how inexact a science vote counting is. Republicans and Democrats bickered over mismarked and absentee ballots in Florida and other battleground states. Ultimately, the Supreme Court ruled on procedural details of the Florida count. Bush won by five electoral votes (and lost in the popular vote).

Ralph Nader's 2,883,105 votes were concentrated in liberal states on the coasts that Gore already had locked up. There are only two states where Nader was a plausible spoiler, Florida and New Hampshire. In every other state that went for Bush, the Nader vote was smaller than the Bush-Gore difference.

The official Florida count credited Bush with 2,912,790 votes and Gore with 2,912,253. Bush won the state by just 537 votes. The disputed hanging chads, dimples, butterfly ballots, and absentee ballots might have changed these figures either way by hundreds, conceivably thousands. Nader got 97,488 votes, Buchanan received 17,484, and Browne got 16,415.

That leaves little doubt that Gore would have won under a spoiler-proof voting system. Had the Nader voters favored Gore over Bush by even a 51 percent margin (with similar figures for Buchanan and Browne voters favoring Bush), that would have been enough to tip the vote to Gore. Or, had 100 percent of the Buchanan and Browne votes gone to Bush, and just 68 percent of the Nader vote to Gore, Gore would have won.

A nationwide *ABC News* poll taken just after the election asked Nader voters whom they would have voted for between the two front-runners. Forty-seven percent said Gore, 21 percent said Bush, and the rest said they would not have voted at all. This poll was taken as Nader voters were being reviled for spoiling the election, and they must have known that any Nader voter who admitted favoring Gore over Bush would look foolish to most of America. Even so, and excluding the abstainers (as we're doing throughout this analysis), the ABC numbers

FOUR

The Most Evil Man in America

In the past few election cycles, the spoiler effect has taken on unprecedented strategic importance. It is best to begin by saying something of the profession responsible for that. Political consultants are an
American invention. At least until recently, other nations with long
democratic traditions did not have professional campaign runners. It is
sometimes claimed that consulting goes back to the early years of the
republic. Thomas Jefferson's advisor, John Beckley, is cited as an early
example of a "political consultant."

A much stronger claimant to that title would be Marcus Alonzo
Hanna (1837–1904). Hanna's first career was as one of the great in-
dustrialists. He sagely built an empire in the burgeoning iron and coal
businesses, sparing no effort in suppressing the midwestern labor
movement. It was only after Hanna turned fifty that his interests
shifted to politics. Though he served as senator from 1897 until his
death, he is best remembered for managing the career of William
McKinley. With Hanna's help, McKinley won two terms as Ohio gov-

imply that 69 percent of Nader voters favored Gore, and 31 percent favored Bush. That implies that Gore would have won Florida.

A similar calculation shows that Gore could have won New Hampshire provided that over 72 percent of Nader voters there favored Gore over Bush. The most likely electoral outcome for the 2000 election, had it not been for the Nader (-Buchanan-Browne) spoiler effect, is that Gore would have picked up Florida and conceivably New Hampshire, winning by at least 291 electoral votes to Bush's 246.

Let me recap. Five presidential elections were probably decided by spoilers (1844, 1848, 1884, 1912, 2000). At least two others (1892, 1992) are questionable cases. In still another race (1860), four-way vote splitting and the electoral college created such ambiguity that it was a factor in precipitating civil war.

In 1844, an abolitionist spoiler put a slave-owner in the White House.

In 1848, a former Democratic president sabotaged the Democratic Party's chances.

In 1884, a Prohibition Party candidate helped elect a supposed "ally of the saloon."

In 1912, a former Republican president prevented the reelection of a Republican president.

In 2000, a consumer and environmental advocate elected the favored candidate of corporate America.

There have been 45 presidential elections since 1828. In at least five, the race went to the second most popular candidate because of a spoiler. That's over an 11 percent rate of catastrophic failure. Were the plurality vote a car or an airliner, it would be recognized for what it is—a defective consumer product, unsafe at any speed.

ernor and two as president. As the Republican presidential candidate, McKinley refused to travel because of the frail health of his wife. His opponent, Democrat William Jennings Bryan, was a renowned orator, traveling the country by train. Hanna rose to the challenge by designing a campaign that relied on advertising to an unprecedented degree. He raised $3.5 million (roughly $80 million in today's dollars, and about twelve times what the Bryan campaign spent). Hanna sent mail to everyone who had voted in 1896, some of it ethnically targeted; he produced the first political publications in Yiddish.

Hanna's efforts changed the American political equation forever. For the first time, dollars could be converted directly into votes (legally, even). After McKinley's landslide victory, no serious presidential candidate would ever again run without professional guidance.

Today's consultants are defined by electronic media, scientific polling, game-theoretic strategizing, and (not the least) a down-and-dirty ethos. These elements scarcely coexisted before the 1960s. The political decade started with the four debates of John F. Kennedy and Richard Nixon. People who heard the first debate on radio judged it to be a draw. Those who watched on television knew that Kennedy had won. To the TV audience Nixon, recovering from a knee injury, looked pale, uncomfortable, and unpresidential. He had lost weight, his shirt didn't fit, and he had refused makeup to cover his five-o'clock shadow.

Consultants' sales pitch soon became "Don't let what happened to Nixon happen to you." The profession's ranks swelled through the 1960s. It was in that tumultuous decade that Joseph Napolitan coined the term *political consultant*. Napolitan worked for JFK, Lyndon Johnson, and nine foreign heads of state. His 1972 book, *The Election Game and How to Win It*, described its subject in much the terms that RAND's strategists were using for nuclear showdowns. By then, game theory was in vogue with political strategists, and Arrow's theorem was a trendy buzzword. "Campaigns are like arms races," said former Federal Elections Commission chair Trevor Potter. "You didn't know you needed another battleship until the other country had one."

Today there are something like seven thousand political consultants in America. This number is said to have tripled in the 1990s. Consultants have successfully expanded the franchise to downticket races that had never used professionals before. America's top practitioners are in demand all over the free world. This is one of the few industries in which outsourcing means hiring an American.

The term *political consultant* has long been a grab bag for a heterogeneous set of practitioners—campaign managers and strategists, producers of TV and radio ads, pollsters, fund-raisers, mailing list managers, and a variety of lesser advice-givers dealing with everything from hair to diction. Consulting is a highly competitive field, with college degree programs, a trade journal (*Campaigns and Elections*), and professional organizations. The lure of money and power is so potent that buzz-worthy politicians are flooded with résumés and promises to work for next to nothing. Everyone hopes for a string of successes that will launch a career. The field has approximately the burnout rate of film school graduates. The lucky few juggle half a dozen campaigns by private jet, while the majority end up pondering what else to do with their lives. About the only certainty is that the nature of campaigns shifted seismically in the last third of the twentieth century. And if there is one consultant most responsible for what campaigns have come to be, it is Lee Atwater.

Harvey Leroy Atwater was born in Atlanta on February 27, 1951. His high-school coach told Lee's mother that he would never be a football player: "He's not mean enough." That was an assessment others would find it necessary to revise. The view of former representative Pat Schroeder, a Colorado Democrat, is typical: "Lee Atwater is probably the most evil man in America."

As a consultant, it was Atwater who combined the science and the sleaze. "If I've done an innovative thing," he once told *The Atlanta Con-*

stitution, "it's consciously having this working formula, which has proved invincible in every campaign." He explained that he used polls in order to zero in on the specific issues on which voters disagreed with an opposition candidate. These issues became the themes of the campaign.

There was a little more to it than that. Atwater fought dirty. "While I didn't invent 'negative politics,'" he wrote, "I am among its most ardent practitioners."

Like consultants, negative campaigning is nothing new. In the 1828 presidential race, Andrew Jackson's opponents accused him of *cannibalism*. The same charge was brought against John Fremont in 1856. This may help put today's attack ads in perspective.

The Whigs claimed that Democrat Martin Van Buren wore the finest ladies' corsets under his suit. He ate off golden utensils and spent a fortune on diamonds, rubies, French vases, and imported beauty creams, all charged to U.S. taxpayers. The 1844 race was enlivened by the interesting claim that Henry Clay had broken every one of the ten commandments. In 1876 Democrat Samuel Tilden declared his intention to run a clean campaign against Rutherford B. Hayes. The Republicans declared that Tilden had syphilis and was an unprincipled drunkard scheming to bring back slavery. Tilden's people then claimed that Hayes had gone insane and shot his mother.

The parade of calumny continues well into the twentieth century. In 1948 Lyndon Johnson, running for the Senate against Coke Stevenson, instructed a campaign worker: "Go out there and tell 'em Coke was caught having sex with a farm animal."

The worker was aghast. "But you know that's not true!"

"Of course it's not true. That's not the point. Tell it anyway, and make him deny it."

Then something happened to politics in the middle of the twentieth century. The smears receded. For a few decades, campaigns were more civil than they had been, or would be. The biggest factor was television.

Prior to TV, citizens sat on front stoops and discussed politics. Campaigners frequented bandstands, bars, general stores, and fraternal clubs. They well knew that a nasty rumor about an opponent could tip an election. Then mass media, air-conditioning, and the move to the suburbs created a new political universe. People spent less time in public places and more time isolated in cars, cubicles, and tract homes. Hollywood provided a new set of celebrities, better looking and more uninhibited than the ones in Washington. Politics began commanding a narrower slice of the nation's attention.

The first generation of modern political consultants was in the business of selling candidates on TV. This was an era when sitcom husbands and wives slept in separate beds, when broadcast law mandated "equal time" for opposing viewpoints, and when the network news shied away from anything not suited to family audiences. John F. Kennedy let his lovers frolic in the White House pool, confident that no one would dare report his womanizing. These attitudes circumscribed what was possible in a paid TV ad.

In the 1980s, the Reagan administration relaxed equal-time requirements for broadcasters, greatly expanding the range of political commentary. It was this move that ultimately made possible Rush Limbaugh, Fox News, and Air America Radio. Cultural changes weighed in, too. Relaxed attitudes toward sex and profanity, the profusion of cable TV channels, and the rumor-intensive Internet eventually took campaigning back to where it had always been: the gutter.

In 1978 Atwater was consulting on Carroll Campbell's race for a South Carolina congressional seat. Campbell's main opponent was a Democrat, former Greenville mayor Max Heller. In July, Campbell hired pollster Arthur Finkelstein to survey likely voters.

Today Finkelstein is famous as the man who made *liberal* a dirty word in campaign ads. (He was also one of the first gays to be married in Massachusetts.) One of Finkelstein's poll questions for Campbell reportedly ran like this:

> Choose from the following characteristics that best describe Campbell and Heller: (a) honest, (b) a Christian man, (c) concerned for the people, (d) a hard worker, (e) experience in government, (f) Jewish.

This was an edgy question for the time. Max Heller was Jewish. Arthur Finkelstein was Jewish. While everyone knew that religion and ethnicity affected political decisions, these were topics rarely broached so baldly in a campaign's private poll. Finkelstein's poll found that South Carolina's voters were willing to vote for a Jew. But they drew the line at voting for someone who did not believe in Jesus Christ as savior.

It might seem that being Jewish implies, to high probability, disbelief in Jesus-as-savior. Poll data often display this kind of casual illogic. In Atwater's version of this story, he passed along the poll results to the "Twelve-dollar Man," Don Sprouse. A minor candidate for the congressional seat, Sprouse had earned that nickname by running a tow service that advertised a flat twelve-dollar fee. Politically, he was a joke. His campaign consisted of his driving around the state in a motor home and talking to whoever would listen.

"Now, don't use it," Atwater supposedly said, "because we're going to do it right before the election."

Sprouse called a news conference the next day. He blasted Heller for not believing that the savior had come. A Jew had no business representing the Christian people of South Carolina's fourth district, he charged.

Assuming the poll data were anywhere near correct, Sprouse's tirade must have hurt Heller. Campbell won the congressional seat.

This incident became a blueprint for many of Atwater's later tactics. Religious intolerance had been converted into votes. The candidates, the press, and other consultants wanted to pretend that the voters were "better" than they were. Atwater was willing to exploit the voters' dark side.

He was also willing to exploit the strategic value of a minor candidate. Sprouse said things Campbell wouldn't have dared say. No one could blame Campbell for what Sprouse said, but Campbell could benefit. Sprouse's attack presumably caused some Heller supporters to switch their votes to Campbell, and others to switch their votes to Sprouse. Even the latter switch was good for Campbell because Heller was the candidate he had to beat.

Political consultants always have to worry about money. The coverage of Sprouse's attack on Heller was free publicity. When the candidates made more edifying speeches, the media couldn't care less.

Atwater's most notorious invention is "push-polling." This came about in another South Carolina race, two years later. Atwater was managing Ronald Reagan's 1980 presidential campaign in the South and concurrently working as a pollster for South Carolina congressman Floyd Spence. Spence's opponent was attorney Tom Turnipseed, a Democrat with an unusually checkered history. Turnipseed had been a conservative working for George Wallace's 1968 presidential run until Wallace fired him for drinking. Turnipseed joined a twelve-step recovery program, remaking his life and his politics. In 1977 he entered the gubernatorial primaries as a liberal Democrat. During this campaign he disclosed that he had suffered depression as a teenager and had undergone electroshock treatments.

In the 1980 race, Turnipseed learned that Atwater's people were phoning white suburbanites and presenting themselves as independent pollsters. Their "polls" contained confusing questions designed to leave the false impression that Turnipseed belonged to the NAACP, a big negative with white voters in South Carolina.

This was perhaps the first push poll. The point of such a poll is to change voters' opinions rather than to sample them. A push poll will pose questions such as "How would you feel if you learned that Tom Turnipseed was a member of the NAACP?"

Turnipseed complained about the phony polls. "I'm not going to respond to that guy," Atwater said of the charges. "What do you expect from someone who was hooked up to jumper cables?"

The "jumper cables" remark became emblematic of the new, nasty politics and its foremost practitioner, Lee Atwater. Even Atwater's mother, Toddy, was taken aback when she saw Turnipseed on television. According to Atwater biographer John Brady, she tearfully confronted her son by phone. "Lee, this man said the most terrible things about you on TV, that you were a dirty tricks artist."

"Mother," Atwater replied, "I'm gonna be in politics all my life, and people are gonna say things like that."

On April 27, 1985, Vice President George H. W. Bush assembled his extended family to brief them on his plans for running for president in 1988. He had chosen Atwater to run his campaign. It was an unusual choice. Despite his being the Republican Party's wunderkind, it was unclear how well Atwater's dirty-south politicking would play on a national stage. Atwater seemed an especially odd match for Bush. The vice president's aristocratic upbringing prized fair play. He said he did not want a negative campaign, and neither did his wife.

Bush had Atwater give a presentation to the assembled family. Two of Bush's sons played the skeptics. The one known as "Junior" or "W" was concerned that Atwater would still be working for the consultancy firm of Black, Manafort, Stone, whose Charles Black represented Jack Kemp, another Republican candidate.

"If there's a hand grenade rolling around George Bush, we want you diving on it first," Jeb Bush told Atwater.

"Well, if you're so worried about loyalties," Atwater said, "then why don't one of you come here in the office and watch me, and the first time I'm disloyal, see to it that I get run off?"

"W" got that job. His time spent with Atwater was an education in the new campaigning. Atwater assembled an "oppo" team ("opposition research") headed by James Pinkerton. It was a political Manhattan Project devoted to finding dirt on Bush's opponent, Massachusetts governor Michael Dukakis. The team had more than a hundred researchers working around the clock in eight-hour shifts, with a budget of $1.2 million. Six researchers went to Massachusetts in a motor home in order to pore over twenty-five years of back issues of the local newspapers for anything that Michael or Kitty Dukakis might ever have said or done that could be embarrassing. "The only group I was very interested in having report to me directly was opposition research," Atwater said.

Word of this massive operation got back to Dukakis by way of South Carolina Democrat Pug Ravenel. "They're going to try to tear you a new one," Ravenel warned.

"I've been in negative campaigns before," Dukakis answered.

"Whoever ran that campaign was no Atwater," Ravenel said. "Atwater is the Babe Ruth of negative politics."

Dukakis insisted on taking the high road. "I felt that keeping it positive was (a) the way we wanted to do it, and (b) the way that we *should* do it—not just in an ethical sense, but because that was what people were looking for."

To test the oppo team's findings, Atwater set up a focus group in Paramus, New Jersey. Fifteen Democrats who had voted for Reagan in 1984 and were now leaning toward Dukakis were assembled in front of a one-way mirror. On the other side sat Atwater, pollster Robert Teeter, and media consultant Roger Ailes (later CEO of Fox News).

The moderator asked the voters how they would feel if they learned that Dukakis: had vetoed legislation requiring reciting of the Pledge of Allegiance in schools . . . was opposed to capital punishment . . . had let convicted murderers leave prison on weekend passes? The reaction to the murderers' weekend passes was galvanic. Erstwhile liberals instantly turned against Dukakis.

The prison furlough program had not been Dukakis's idea. It had been inaugurated under his Republican predecessor, Francis W. Sargent. But Dukakis supported the program, and in 1976 he vetoed a bill that would have barred first-degree murderers from the furloughs.

Atwater's team was not the first to take note of this. Al Gore had used the furlough program against Dukakis in the Democratic primaries, citing two cases where furloughed Massachusetts criminals had committed murder while out.

Atwater's team found a case that Gore hadn't mentioned. William Horton, Jr., had been serving a life sentence for a 1974 stabbing murder when he was released on furlough on June 6, 1986. He ran away, and ten months later, in Maryland, he terrorized a young couple. He knifed the man twenty-two times and raped his fiancée twice. Horton was black, and the victims were white.

Atwater felt he had hit the jackpot. Anticipating resistance from the Bushes, he took videotapes of the focus group to the Bush compound in Kennebunkport so that the candidate could judge the effect for himself. Bush was sold. It was time to go negative.

The Bush campaign was at pains not to mention Horton's race as such. Atwater referred to Horton as "Willie," apparently believing that the invented nickname sounded more black. The media took the cue. A reporter called "Willie" Horton in jail and asked him whom he supported for president. "Obviously, I am for Dukakis," he said.

"Did you hear about Willie's endorsement?" Atwater asked reporters. "I assume the reason he endorsed him is that he thinks he'll have a better chance of getting out of jail if Dukakis is elected. I don't know if Dukakis would let him out, but I think there'd be a better chance."

The two so-called "Willie Horton" TV ads became the template for negative ads thereafter. In midsummer a political action committee briefly aired an ad that showed a mug shot of Horton. The PAC was not officially connected to the Bush campaign, which permitted Atwater and Bush to disown responsibility for it. The ad was quickly withdrawn in a storm of controversy—that is, free publicity, in which the media again found cause to report that "Willie" Horton was a black man who had raped a white woman. It was followed by an official Bush campaign ad attacking the furlough program. The official ad didn't mention Horton, nor did it need to.

In a televised debate with Bush, moderator Bernard Shaw asked Dukakis, "Governor, if Kitty Dukakis were raped and murdered, would you favor an irrevocable death penalty for the killer?"

"No, I don't," Dukakis began, "and I think you know that I've opposed the death penalty during all of my life." Dukakis had been expecting a question on capital punishment, just not one so personalized. Unrattled, he delivered his canned response. Dukakis's poll numbers dropped five points after the debate. Conservative pundits attributed the drop to that question. Red-blooded Americans liked candidates to show more outrage to hypothetical questions.

The Dukakis campaign decided not to cry racism over the Horton ads, consultant Susan Estrich said. "'We can't afford to alienate white voters,' I was told by many in my party and my campaign; whites might be put off if we 'whine' about racism."

One difference between the Bush and Dukakis campaigns was the tenure of their consultants. Atwater and Ailes remained firmly in charge of Bush's campaign. Dukakis hired and fired a whole stable of consultants. In fact, he hired Estrich twice and fired her once. (He hired her the second time after deciding he couldn't fire his campaign's highest-ranking woman.) The number of people giving Dukakis advice kept increasing.

Dukakis called Mario Cuomo, a mentor, to ask him what to do about Atwater's attacks. Cuomo's advice was "Hey, don't pay any attention to that stuff. Just let it go."

For most of the campaign, Dukakis followed that counsel. "After the campaign was over, I realized it was the worst advice he had ever given me."

The Most Evil Man in America

People resent negative advertising—if you ask them whether they resent negative advertising. "But they sure do remember it," James Carville adds. In late October the Dukakis campaign ran an ad showing Dukakis watching one of Bush's attack ads and switching off the TV in disgust. "I'm fed up with it," the candidate said. "Haven't seen anything like it in twenty-five years of public life. George Bush's negative TV ads: distorting my record, full of lies, and he knows it."

The ad failed to budge the sagging polls numbers. Finally, the Dukakis people jumped the shark with their own attack ad. It presented Angel Medrano, a heroin dealer who killed a pregnant mother while on a federal prison furlough. The pregnant mother bit reeked of a too-calculated attempt to top the untoppable. Medrano was identified as one of "his [Bush's] furloughed heroin dealers," an unconvincing attempt to hold the vice president responsible for anything that happened in the federal prison system.

Bush won the election with 53.4 percent of the popular vote. He beat Dukakis by nearly eight points. To the political consultant profession, the 1988 race became an essential case study. It was a controlled experiment. Bush had decided to go negative and Dukakis hadn't (until the end). The results spoke for themselves.

The 1988 election also left a queasy sensation. Atwater had opened a Pandora's box. Henceforth, would anything be off-limits? The Washington rumor mill said that Bush had a long-running affair with an aide named Jennifer Fitzgerald. In earlier campaigns, this would have been a nonissue. But with standards in free fall, it was hard to tell how the Democrats might respond.

Atwater's own prodigious womanizing was legendary. A steady stream of lithesome Republican women visited the consultant in his office. Atwater was in the habit of telling his female friends that the Secret Service had to sweep the room for bugs every few hours—so they would have to be quick.

It's alleged that Atwater struck a deal with the Dukakis campaign. If they didn't mention the Fitzgerald rumor, the Republicans wouldn't bring up a similar infidelity rumor about Kitty Dukakis. The media was not party to any such deal. In Kennebunkport, CNN's Mary Tillotson asked Bush if he was having an "adulterous" affair. Bush blew up and refused to answer. He delegated his son, George W., to tell everyone, "The answer to the 'A' question is a big 'N-O.'"

After the election, Bush Sr. named Atwater head of the Republican National Committee. One of the items on Atwater's agenda was recruiting African Americans to the Republican Party. On that issue, David Duke was shaping up to be a major embarrassment. Duke was then running for the Louisiana State Legislature and was already talking up a run for governor in 1991. Atwater found a rule saying that the executive committee of the RNC could pass emergency resolutions. He passed one condemning Duke and excommunicating him from the Republican Party. Atwater also taped an anti-Duke commercial for black radio stations. These efforts boomeranged. The fact that the national Republicans and black radio stations hated Duke only energized Duke's supporters. As Duke defiantly told the press, "I'm just as Republican as Lee Atwater."

At the age of thirty-nine, Atwater was cracking one of his best Michael Dukakis jokes when he had a violent seizure. His doctors discovered a golfball-size tumor in his brain. It was untreatable.

"I can't imagine me getting back in a fighting mood," he told friend and journalist Lee Bandy. "I don't see how I'm ever going to be mean."

This was truer than any reasonable observer would have guessed. Atwater turned to spirituality. He tried out different approaches, religious and secular, to coping with death. One advisor told him to draw up a list of regrets. This was to include all the people he had wronged in his life. Atwater made it a point to contact all these people and apologize.

That included Tom Turnipseed, Michael Dukakis, and dozens of others who had been victims of his attack ads. Atwater apologized to a woman he had dated in college, whom he had tried to trick into having sex with all of his fraternity brothers. During a Christmas retreat at a vacation home, he painstakingly confessed every extramarital affair he could remember to his wife—and to a couple of friends who had dropped by to wish them Merry Christmas.

Atwater went public with his apologies in a *Life* magazine profile that ran the month before his 1991 death. Most surprisingly, he renounced his trademark character assassination and dirty tricks in favor of . . . peace and love. "My illness helped me to see what was missing in society is what was missing from me: a little heart, a lot of brotherhood."

Atwater's deathbed repudiation of negative campaigning was to have no discernable effect on his profession. Even those consultants who were philosophically opposed to his tactics had already found that they had to adopt them or perish. Darrell West of Brown University reported that 35 percent of ads were negative in 1976, about when Atwater was starting to make a name for himself. This proportion rose to 83 percent in 1988. You don't need statistics to know that it is now asymptotically approaching 100 percent. *The New York Times* found that the 2006 elections were conducted in "the most toxic midterm campaign environment in memory." Of at least thirty new House and Senate race ads rolled out the last week of September 2006, only three were positive. Strategists from both parties said they expected the percentage of negative ads aired by Election Day to be over 90 percent.

Atwater gave the appearance of being unconflictedly amoral in his professional life. He had convictions, of course. His personal politics were corporate-libertarian. He was pro-choice and dismissed the religious right as the "extra-chromosome crowd." He held it was okay to exploit fake polls, bigotry, innuendo, or anything else to elect the candidates he believed were best for America. His professional legacy was to bring political consultants into near-congruence with the cold warriors of the RAND Corporation and the Kremlin. Running a campaign became a game in which it was necessary and expected to seize every strategic advantage possible. The essence of political consulting is thinking about the previously unthinkable.

Atwater liked to compare his strategizing to the "nine-dot puzzle." You are given a simple grid of nine dots. The challenge is to draw four straight lines that run through all nine dots without lifting pen from paper.

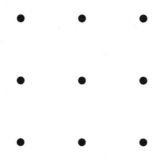

The solution is to look beyond the implicit grid, to ignore the "rules" that aren't rules at all. After the 2000 election, Atwater's successors did just that.

FIVE

Run, Ralph, Run!

Karl Christian Rove was born on December 25, 1950. That makes him two months older than Lee Atwater, a fact that surprises people today. Many think of Atwater as Rove's mentor and imagine him to be a generation older.

"We're not alike," Rove once said of himself and Atwater. Atwater was the frat boy, athletic, loud, charming to women. From youth, Rove was chubby, bespectacled, and studious, his hair going thin. Atwater's first post-college job was managing Rove's unusually bitter campaign for national chairman of the College Republicans. Rove won, but thereafter it was Atwater's career that eclipsed Rove's. By age thirty, Atwater was a celebrity working for Ronald Reagan and living the Washington high life. Meanwhile, Rove plugged away in Austin, Texas, working in political direct mail. This was the plain sister of political consulting, a side of the business that many were ready to write off. By the 1990s, the buzz was all about the Internet. In the brave new digi-

tal world, Bill Clinton pollster Dick Morris predicted, direct-mail consultants "would be the first to go."

He was wrong. Direct mail is the one part of politics that keeps a
scorecard. Most of politics is faith-based. Candidates buy TV ads and
phone banks because they *believe* it will help. A direct mailer trolling
for campaign cash knows exactly who responds to what pitch and with
how much.

Rove took that analytic approach with him as he ascended to the
apex of his profession. It was largely his doing that the 2000 presidential race became the first nationwide, reasonably scientific test of the
effectiveness of campaign techniques. The Republican Party performed
experiments with the statistical sophistication of, at least, a psychology
post-grad. These experiments went by the name of "metrics." Republicans set aside parts of voter lists as controls and did not subject the
people on them to the usual phone or mail pitches. Then, in follow-up
interviews, they compared the controls with people who had been
contacted, to see if there was a statistically meaningful difference in
whether and how they voted.

One widely publicized finding was that only 6 percent of the electorate were true swing voters, capable of being persuaded into voting
for either major party. Rove condensed this information into a mantra:
"There is no middle." More emphasis was placed on making sure that
diehard conservatives voted.

There is little doubt that the battery of analysts also paid close attention to the Nader spoiler effect. The Green left had elected Bush as
surely as the religious right had. And beginning with the 2002 midterm
elections, Republicans started aiding potential spoilers who might hurt
Democrats.

This trick, too, has a long history. I have already mentioned that the
Democrats financed spoiler John St. John's New York campaign in
1884. The Republicans were accused of a similar tactic in the 1908
presidential race between William Taft and Democrat William Jennings
Bryan. Socialist Eugene Debs, a potential spoiler, traveled the nation in

Karl Rove counts the votes in a 2004 Internet cartoon. In the public imagination, political consultants have often replaced politicians as the prime villains of public life.

a "Red Special" train giving whistle-stop speeches. Samuel Gompers, head of the American Federation of Labor, charged that Republican donors had secretly paid for Debs's train in order to fragment the Bryan vote and elect Taft. Gompers and his union had endorsed Bryan.

The Socialist Party attempted to refute Gompers by publishing a list of the names and addresses of the fifteen thousand donors who had helped pay for the train. As the train cost thirty-five thousand dollars, the average donation was a little more than two dollars. I am not aware of anyone having gone to the trouble of checking the political affiliations of the fifteen-thousand-name list. The Debs vote tipped a few extra states into Taft's column but was not decisive. Taft won overwhelmingly.

Modern attempts to game the spoiler effect date from July 2002. John Dendahl, chairman of the New Mexico Republican Party, quietly offered "more than $100,000" to the Green Party *if* they would run candidates in New Mexico's first and second Congressional districts. The Greens were relatively strong in New Mexico, and they had already been spoilers in local races. The difference was that the Republicans were now willing to pay cash for services that had previously been free.

Unlike the Republicans, the Greens are not a top-down hierarchy. They vote on everything. At the Greens' state convention, Dendahl's top-secret offer was put to a formal vote and rejected. Some of the delegates went straight to the press. Their story now was that the Republicans had offered them $250,000 to play spoiler, and (in classic Green-speak) they said, "We disavow and condemn any attempts to manipulate or use New Mexico voters as pawns in the game of politics as usual."

This forced Dendahl to backpedal. "I wouldn't have walked across the street to recruit a Green candidate," he told CNN's Kate Snow. "But I'm not the be-all and end-all of political knowledge. And when somebody in Washington says to me, 'We want to give a bundle of money to the Greens,' I'll deliver the message." Dendahl refused to disclose the identity of the mystery benefactor. The inevitable assumption was that, whoever wrote the check, Karl Rove was the mastermind behind the offer.

The New Mexico offer reminded Texas journalists James Moore and Wayne Slater of an earlier incident in Texas: Karl Rove's "six-pack." In 1991 Rove was managing Rick Perry's bid to unseat Democrat Jim Hightower for Texas agriculture commissioner. From out of nowhere, a "six-pack" of obscure candidates challenged Hightower in the Democratic primary. "They pretty much admitted they are Republicans," Hightower complained. "They've certainly never been active in the Democratic party." The Texas Farm Bureau, traditionally a Republican group, paid the six-pack's filing fees. "There's no evidence that Rove was directly connected," wrote Moore and Slater in *Bush's Brain*, "but it is inconceivable that the Texas Farm Bureau acted on behalf of Rove's client without his approval in 1990, and equally unlikely that the Republican party acted without his knowledge more than a decade later in New Mexico."

It is also inconceivable that Republican strategists didn't closely follow the Green Party's plans for the 2004 presidential election. They were to be disappointed. The Greens nominated David Cobb, and Cobb was no Ralph Nader. The media scarcely paid any attention. Better news for the Bush reelection campaign was that Nader *was* running again, this time as an independent.

Nader's 2004 run struggled with problems that hadn't existed four years earlier. The first was 2000 itself. It is one thing to be told that Nader might be a spoiler; it is another thing to see it play out on CNN. Not everyone who voted for Nader in 2000 was ready to do it again. There were technical hurdles, too. Lacking even a minor party's organizational help, Nader would have a hard time getting his name on state ballots.

The average citizen imagines that the people collecting ballot signatures in the mall parking lot are civic-minded volunteers. In most cases, they're not. They're eleven-dollar-an-hour temps, often flown in from out of state. Much of the old ward-heeling has gone corporate.

The Nader people knew they needed professional help to collect ballot signatures. For example, Nader needed 14,694 signatures to make the ballot in Arizona. The best way to show what a long shot that was is to jump ahead in time to November. Nader was destined to get only 2,773 votes in the entire state.

The companies that collect ballot signatures are partisan. No Democratic firm would take Nader's business, not after 2000. In spring 2004 the Nader campaign approached Arno Political Consultants, a well-known outfit based in a suburb of Sacramento. Arno was as Republican as Republican gets. It also did work for the private sector, including many of the firms that Nader had vilified over the years: Wal-Mart, Occidental Petroleum, Phillip Morris.

"I thought it would be bad for us to go in with anyone like Nader," Michael Arno explained. "And even though I don't know Bush personally, I have a relationship with some of the people close to him."

Arno referred the Nader people to Jenny Breslin of Florida-based JSM Inc., an equally strange bedfellow. JSM people were already contracted to raise signatures for a conservative ballot initiative, Protect Arizona Now, that would deny public services to illegal immigrants. JSM agreed to collect signatures for Nader in Arizona. The Nader campaign paid two dollars per signature.

It appears that the JSM people were sent out with both the Protect Arizona Now and Nader petitions on their clipboards, and they encouraged people to sign both without worrying overmuch about whether that made any sense. It *didn't* make any sense. In the June issue of *The American Conservative*, Nader's former opponent Pat Buchanan asked him point blank whether illegal immigrants should be eligible for welfare. Nader answered that undocumented aliens "should be given all the fair-labor standards and all the rights and benefits of American workers, and if this country doesn't like that, maybe they will do something about the immigration laws."

The people who signed both petitions either didn't know what they were doing—or else they knew *exactly* what they were doing. They might have reasoned that Nader could again be crucial to a Bush victory.

Meanwhile, Nader got some unexpected free help. It came from Sproul and Associates. Sproul, a major contractor of the Republican National Committee, specialized in collecting signatures and had a reputation for pushing the ethical envelope. It might have had less of a reputation had it paid its employees more promptly. In 2004, Eric Russell walked into a Las Vegas FBI office with a bundle of Democratic voter registration forms. Russell said he had retrieved the forms from Sproul's trash. Apparently, in the rush of the Nevada voter registration drive, Sproul people sometimes let Democrats fill out the forms. Then they threw them away. Daren Gray, one of the Democrats whose form was trashed, was "pretty mad," according to a Las Vegas TV report. Russell said he blew the whistle because Sproul hadn't paid him all his wages.

Derek Lee, of a company called Lee Petitions, told blogger Max Blumenthal that two of Sproul's canvassers were paid to collect signatures to get Ralph Nader on the Arizona ballot. Blumenthal contacted the two canvassers (Aaron James and Diane Burns) by phone. Both were "clearly nonplussed; when asked if they were hired by Sproul to get signatures for Nader, both hung up."

The Nader signatures wouldn't do anyone any good unless the Sproul people got them to Nader. That delicate handoff was managed at a budget motel in Scottsdale. The motel room was the headquarters of JSM's Jenny Breslin. Meghan Rose, a former consultant for the Republican National Committee, reportedly delivered the Sproul-gathered signatures to Breslin's people, who then mixed them in with the other Nader petitions. Max Blumenthal reported,

> Confronted with the accusation that she served as the baglady for Sproul's Nader ballot scheme, Rose would not issue an outright denial.
>
> "I do not work for Nathan Sproul," she stated repeatedly. "I don't even know how you got my name."
>
> Asked again to confirm or deny the accusation, Rose became testy. "I didn't do anything. I've shaken Nathan Sproul's hand once," she said.
>
> Reached by cellphone, Jenny [Breslin] refused to speak directly to the accusation that Rose delivered Sproul's Nader petitions to her, referring the question to Sproul, who could not be reached.

Sproul did speak to *The Arizona Republic*: "I'm not being paid by anybody to do petitions [for Nader], and I've not paid anybody to do petitions."

Sproul's denial would have been easier to believe had this been an isolated incident. It soon became clear that there was a nationwide Re-

Reality was stranger than Drew Sheneman's 2004 cartoon. Republican donors paid for Nader ballot drives in Arizona, Michigan, New Mexico, and Oregon. (© *Tribune Media Services, Inc. All rights reserved. Reprinted with permission*)

publican effort to get Nader on the ballot. It was accompanied by a reverse effort by Democrats to keep Nader off the ballot.

Oregon's ballot requirements are a relative cinch. A candidate need only assemble a thousand registered voters in a nominating convention and have them sign a petition. Nader had soared past this requirement in 2000. But his April 2004 convention failed to attract the needed thousand.

Nader vowed to try again on June 26. Polls were showing a tight race in Oregon, and neither major party was leaving much to chance. A Democratic e-mail urged Democrats to attend Nader's convention, where they were supposed to crowd out authentic Nader supporters and *refuse* to sign the petition.

One of the new features of the 2004 political landscape was a law limiting the amount of money that large donors could give to political parties. One consequence of this was the diversion of massive amounts of cash to independent PACs and "527" advocacy groups. The 527s were able to play hardball on behalf of the parties. In Oregon, the Republicans aided Nader through two conservative-though-technically-not-Republican groups, the Oregon Family Council and the Citizens for a Sound Economy (CSE). The first was an antiabortion group; the second was a pro-corporate organization that stood for almost everything that Nader was most against. CNN asked Nader why CSE would be helping his campaign. Nader replied that the group was "opposed to Congressional pay raises." It was a *brilliant* answer. As consultant Jeff Cohen noted, this was "perhaps the one issue out of a thousand that Nader and CSE have in common."

Both conservative groups mobilized supporters to show up at Nader's convention and sign the petition. The CSE phone script explained this otherwise inexplicable request as a chance to "pull some very crucial votes from John Kerry." It was all for naught. Nader again failed to make a thousand signers. In late July it was reported that the campaign had not submitted the signatures that were collected, "apparently embarrassed at how many will be shown to be registered Republicans."

A Nader spokesperson put an Ayn Rand spin on accepting Republican help: "It's a free country. People do things in their own interest."

In Michigan, Nader petitions were available at the state's Republican Victory Centers. The Michigan party's executive director, Greg McNeilly, boasted of having bagged a thousand Nader signatures himself and said that "it is my fervent hope" that Nader would take votes away from Kerry. The Michigan GOP effort collected forty-five thousand signatures for Nader, more than Nader needed (thirty thousand signatures) and nearly nine times what his anemic campaign was able to do. Republican campaign worker Nick De Leeuw filed the collected Nader signatures with the Michigan Board of Canvassers, and when the Michigan Board of Appeals deadlocked on whether to put Nader on the ballot, a Republican attorney filed suit.

"We won't take any signatures from them [the Republicans]," vowed

Nader spokesman Kevin Zeese. After all, Nader was advocating the impeachment of President George W. Bush. Hours later, however, Zeese revisited the issue. Nader *might* accept the Republican signatures, he said, provided the campaign failed to get the nomination of the Reform Party. "We have to get on the ballot somehow."

On July 9, Nader's vice-presidential candidate, Peter Camejo, issued another emphatic, soon-to-be-retracted denial. "We don't want that money," Camejo insisted, referring to a *San Francisco Chronicle* report that said that one in ten of Nader's big-money donors had also donated to Republican candidates. A few days later Camejo was saying, "It is conceivable that pro-Bush, pro-Republicans believe we have a right to be on the ballot. We will not establish lie detector tests for people who give us money." And "Republicans are human beings too."

Candidates are advised to collect twice the required number of signatures. Many signatures are inevitably disqualified, even without the extraordinary circumstances of the 2004 race. The twenty-thousand-odd signatures Nader got in Arizona was cutting it close. The Democrats challenged Nader's signatures, and he was left with about 550 short of the needed amount. He also failed to make the ballot in Oregon. He succeeded, however (with Republican help), in Michigan and New Mexico.

There was another potential spoiler in the 2004 race, one Karl Rove knew all too well.

Roy Moore was a West Point graduate, a Vietnam vet, and slightly out of his mind—or such was the implication of more than one of the nicknames he went by. In Vietnam, Moore had been called "Captain America," a name not as admiring as it sounds. A strict disciplinarian, Moore was so unpopular that he slept with sandbags around his bunk to protect himself from fragmentation grenades. At the University of Alabama law school, a professor tagged him "Fruit Salad" because he was always coming up with crazy ideas. One of his crazier ideas was to become a professional karate fighter. He tried this in the early 1980s, after he resigned an assistant D.A. post and before he moved to Australia to become an outback cowboy.

In the 1990s Moore ended up back in Alabama and back in the judiciary. In 1995 he put up a hand-carved wooden plaque of the ten commandments in his courtroom and began opening court with prayer. The ACLU sued his pants off. He thereby earned his most lasting nickname, the "Ten Commandments Judge."

Moore shed no tears over his predictable loss in the ACLU suit. In 1997, when a federal judge ordered him to remove the plaque, he replied, "If the feds want this plaque down, tell them to send U.S. marshals to tear it down."

Rallies were held in Moore's behalf. Many Alabama politicians agreed wholeheartedly with him, and others felt they had better look like they agreed wholeheartedly with him. Alabama governor Fob James vowed to "call out the State Police and to mobilize the National Guard, if necessary, to prevent anyone from attempting to remove the plaque." The plaque stayed.

In 2000, Moore ran for chief justice of the Alabama Supreme Court. His opponent, Harold See, was being advised by the tireless Karl Rove. See's campaign must have looked like such a slam dunk that Rove could have phoned it in. Rove had a killer pitch he'd used many times in southern judicial campaigns. He painted his opponents as wealthy, tasseled-loafer-wearing opportunists making millions out of ridiculously high damage awards.

The loafer didn't fit Moore. He was already a folk hero for his plaque. He beat See and celebrated the victory by commissioning a two-ton granite version of the plaque and placing it in the rotunda of the Alabama Judicial Building.

As 2004 approached, Moore began testing the waters for a presidential run on the Constitution Party ticket. The Constitution Party's 320,000 members made it the third largest American party, bigger than the Greens. A Moore candidacy threatened to split Rove's coalition

right along the perforation between the social and economic conservatives. (Ohio Constitution Party vice chair Patrick Johnston was the author of the essay "Why Christians Should Not Vote for George Bush.")

"The possibility that Roy Moore could challenge President Bush in
November may not be costing Karl Rove any sleep—yet," wrote *Salon's*
Fred Clarkson. "But the chance that the popular conservative judge
could do to Bush what Ralph Nader did to Al Gore in 2000—split his
ideological base, and cost him the presidency—has analysts crunching
numbers and weighing Moore's chances."

In another election, Moore might have been an easy target for a
smear. But Rove's game plan for 2004 was to turn out the voters who
most admired Moore. Branding Moore a nutcase, even if the message
couldn't be traced back to Bush, could disenchant social conservatives
and discourage them from voting at all.

One of Moore's pet ideas was a "Constitutional Restoration Act,"
which he co-drafted in 1996. In March 2004, two Alabama Republicans introduced the bill in Congress. The text said that "the Supreme
Court shall not have jurisdiction to review" any matter involving "ac-
knowledgment of God as the sovereign source of law, liberty, or government." One of the sponsors, Senator Richard Selby, bravely predicted
they had enough votes for passage.

The bill fell into the black hole that exists at the center of every
congressional committee. Bush, meanwhile, campaigned on his support of a constitutional amendment banning gay marriages. Washington observers saw this as a nod toward people like Roy Moore (who
complained that "there's nothing to keep three men and a horse from
getting married"). Moore didn't take the bait. He fretted that Bush's
bill had too many loopholes. "Some judge would probably let a man
marry his sister or daughter" under Bush's amendment, he complained.

It is difficult to gauge a third-party non-candidate's support from
polls. The voters who most admired Moore would not necessarily be
voting for him. "I personally like Judge Roy Moore," said Roberta
Combs, president of the Christian Coalition. "I admire the stand he

took for the Ten Commandments. But I definitely don't think he should run. I think he could hurt the president."

Others were already redrawing the electoral vote map. "After you have divided up the secure Bush states and identified places where 1 or 2 percent of the vote might make a difference," consultant Tanya Melich said, "there is really only one—and that's Florida." *The Nation* columnist Micah Sifry conjectured that Moore might steal Bush's hold on Colorado and Oregon, too, to the benefit of John Kerry.

"It's time for Democrats to stop shaking their fists at Ralph Nader," wrote Timothy Noah, "and to start flattering and cajoling Moore. They need this man to run for president." Noah proposed that Bill Clinton favor Moore with one of his late-night phone calls, Barbra Streisand offer to sing at his church, and Kerry consultant Bob Shrum cut all of Moore's TV spots for free.

The *Montgomery Advertiser* found it hard to believe that Moore would turn spoiler and help elect Kerry. "But, if Alabamians have learned anything from Moore's past, it's that logic doesn't play much of a role in the decision-making of the Ten Commandments judge."

Logically or not, Moore decided not to run for president. The Constitution Party nominated Michael Peroutka, an attorney who resigned his post at the Department of Health and Human Services after deciding that none of the agency's programs was constitutionally permissible. In November, Peroutka eked out a minuscule 0.12 percent of the vote.

Bush did not need Nader to win reelection. His popular vote margin over Kerry was nearly seven times the Nader vote. Libertarian Michael Badnarik did nearly as well as Nader did, and Badnarik presumably hurt Bush's total more than Kerry's.

Despite that, the Republican drive to collect signatures for Nader already appears to have been a watershed. What was done furtively in 2004 has since been done openly. Aiding spoilers has become the steroids of campaign strategy. With the performance enhancement possible, who's going to worry about long-term consequences?

SIX

Year of the Spoiler

In November 2005, U.S. representative Randy "Duke" Cunningham, who had run as a born-again Christian and "a congressman we can be proud of," pleaded guilty to mail fraud, tax evasion, and accepting $2.4 million in bribes. A special election followed in June 2006 to fill Cunningham's seat representing the prosperous coast north of San Diego. The Fiftieth Congressional District was solidly Republican. The Republican candidate, former congressman Brian Bilbray, ought to have won without breaking a sweat. Yet polls showed a close race between Bilbray and his Democratic opponent, Francine Busby, a woman with almost no political experience. Busby was a member of the Cardiff school board.

The loss of a Republican congressional seat months before the November midterm elections would have been particularly humbling to the party. The GOP raised five million dollars to aid Bilbray's campaign, compared to a still-impressive two million for Busby. This bought packs of consultants, hours of air time, and the kind of dirty politicking that

Americans had come to accept as normal. A Busby ad juxtaposed Bilbray's picture with a trash can. A Bilbray ad insinuated that Busby was soft on child pornography. Whatever.

Though a moderate Republican in general, Bilbray was a foaming-at-the-mouth immigration hawk. The Fiftieth District had relatively few Latinos and a lot of whites who feared an invasion from the south. Bilbray supported building a continuous border fence from the Pacific Ocean to the Gulf of Mexico. In one of his ads he was shown driving a bulldozer, keeping "Tijuana sewage" off California's beaches.

The race's potential spoiler was William Griffith, a crew cut–shorn West Pointer who taught geometry in Carlsbad and had hosted a TV math show. Griffith was a Republican running as an independent on an anti-immigration platform. He maintained that he was *more* anti-immigrant than Bilbray. How that was possible was unclear.

Griffith's support hovered at around 4 percent, or roughly the margin of error in the polls showing Bilbray and Busby as tied. Griffith spent two thousand dollars of his own money on his campaign. That bought some gas money and a website that said that Bilbray was "most assuredly NOT conservative" and that called Busby "a classic tax-and-spend liberal."

Then something odd happened. Voters in the Fiftieth District began getting phone calls telling them to vote for Griffith. No one was more puzzled at that than the candidate himself. "I do not know who's conducting the phone campaign on my behalf," he wrote on his website. "I am grateful for the enthusiasm of those who know what I stand for, and want to promote my candidacy." But, he admitted, "I don't know if they're doing it for me or as a tactic against Bilbray."

The mystery was solved when ads touting Griffith began running on conservative talk radio, saying in part:

> Think lobbyist Brian Bilbray's a conservative when it comes to immigration? Think again . . . Lobbyist Bilbray isn't the candidate to secure our borders. You have a choice. Independent William Griffith is en-

dorsed by the San Diego Minutemen and San Diego Border Alert because he opposes guest worker programs, amnesty, and the hiring of illegal immigrants. Francine Busby supports John McCain's position on
immigration—stronger enforcement at the border, better support for
border agents, and no amnesty. When it comes to immigration, don't
expect lobbyist Brian Bilbray to fix Washington, or fix our borders. I'm
Francine Busby, candidate for Congress, and I approve this message.
Paid for by Francine Busby for Congress.

The Busby/Griffith ads set a new high-water mark for candor.
Busby approved the message, and there was a token pitch for Busby
herself—but, remember, these ads targeted the Rush Limbaugh demo-
graphic, who weren't about to vote for a feminazi educrat. The point of
the ad was to get Bilbray supporters to switch to Griffith, a candidate
who couldn't possibly win. Bilbray complained to reporters that it was
"unheard of" for a candidate to run ads for an opponent.

You would have had to follow the campaign business closely to be
aware of a precedent. Here's one: In November 2005, some Virginia
voters received an "Official Democrat and Progressive Voter Guide."
The guide had scant praise for the Democratic candidate for governor.
Tim Kaine, it said, had "turned his back on the issues you believe in."
The guide also said that "Russ Potts is the only candidate who will
stand up for progressive principles." It ticked off seven issues in which
Potts took a liberal stance and Kaine was more moderate.

Potts was a liberal Republican state senator running as an independent. Potts had not sent the handsomely printed guide. To find out who
did, alert voters had to read the fine print running vertically alongside
the picture of Kaine. Looking like a photo credit, it read, "Paid for and
authorized by Virginians for Jerry Kilgore." Kilgore, the Republican
nominee, had watched his initial lead over Kaine erode to a single percentage point: 45 percent for Kilgore versus 44 percent for Kaine in a
poll taken shortly before Election Day. Hoping to split the Kaine vote
by touting the liberal credentials of Potts, the Kilgore campaign had

sent the fake "official" guide to residents of Washington, D.C., suburbs where Democratic turnout was high.

One of Kilgore's accomplishments as Virginia attorney general had been to help pass the state's "Stand by Your Ad" law, which makes candidates responsible for the content of their political ads.

Blogger Nicholaus Norvell called 2006 "the year of the 'Spoiler.'" Though Joe Lieberman's independent bid for his own Connecticut U.S. Senate seat commanded most of the national attention, three- and four-way races were unfolding all over the nation. So were attempts to game the spoiler effect.

A May 2006 SurveyUSA poll showed that the Honorable Rick Santorum was the least popular member of the entire U.S. Senate. Santorum was the third most powerful Republican senator, an up-and-comer already hinting at a presidential run, and a man fighting for his political life.

As with all the Republican incumbents of 2006, Santorum's ties to President Bush and the Iraq war had gone from being a plus to a minus. If anything, he had been more gung ho on Iraq than Bush himself. In a June 2006 speech, Santorum announced that he'd seen secret documents proving that Saddam Hussein's weapons of mass destruction had finally been located (a newsworthy claim that the president was not making.)

Polls showed Santorum trailing Democratic challenger Bob Casey, Jr., the son of a former governor. Both sides launched blistering negative campaigns. The Santorum effort surreally included a Republican dressed in a duck suit who shadowed Casey at public appearances. He was "Bob the Duck," there to remind voters that the Democrat was ducking the issues. Actually, there was more common ground between Casey and Santorum than might be expected from the tone of the campaign. Like Santorum, Casey was a pro-life Roman Catholic. He was for staying in Iraq and against gun control.

The one candidate representing the stereotypic liberal position on these issues was the Green Party candidate, Carl Romanelli. Romanelli had zero chance of winning and little of making the ballot. For that he would need 67,070 signatures. The Green Party had only 20,000 members in Pennsylvania. In June the Luzerne County Green Party nonetheless raised $66,000 to pay for Romanelli's petition drive. All twenty contributors were identified by the press as Republican or conservative donors, a few of them hiding behind misspelled names or names of household members. Another thirty dollars came from a liberal, namely the candidate himself.

Politically, Santorum and Romanelli were like matter and antimatter. If they shook hands, they'd annihilate. "This is politics," Santorum told the press on a campaign swing through the Pittsburgh suburbs. "It's no surprise when you're an incumbent, it helps to have more people on the ballot." Romanelli was equally blasé about the arrangement. "I have friends in all political parties," he said. "It's just that my Republican friends are more confident about standing with me than my Democratic friends. And as a group, my Republican friends are a little better off."

The friendly Republican money was funneled to JSM, one of the companies that had collected Nader signatures in 2004. JSM turned in 93,000 names. The Democrats lost no time in challenging them.

On a steamy week in August, volunteers from the Democratic and Green parties began poring over the signatures in Harrisburg. Two representatives of the Santorum campaign observed—it was their money. As the fifth day began, the group had gone through 11,000 signatures and had about 82,000 to go. Green volunteer Tom Lingenfelter leaned over the table to hear Democratic Party attorney Shawn Gallagher speak. "He threw his forearm up at me" is Lingenfelter's story. "I put my arm up and his arm hit mine." The Democrats say Lingenfelter started it. Lingenfelter cursed Gallagher, there was some shoving, and a court officer, Bob Snook, stepped between the two to break it up.

Another Green, John Ryan, entered the fray. The fight spilled into the hallway as Snook gouged Ryan's eyes and began choking him. Snook called the police. Six officers responded.

The Green Party has a list of ten key values, of which the fourth is *nonviolence*. Ryan insisted he was defending himself and didn't know Snook was a court officer. "I thought he was just another insane Democrat."

Like most things in politics, this new trend is about money. Through August 2006, Rick Santorum's campaign was said to have raised twenty-one million dollars, compared to eleven million raised by Casey. In a campaign manager's wildest dreams, the extra ten million might buy ten extra percentage points in the November vote. Figure a million dollars per percentage point as an off-the-cuff estimate of what it costs to buy votes in a state like Pennsylvania.

The sixty-six thousand dollars that Santorum's supporters spent on Romanelli's signature drive was pin money. Yet an August poll showed Romanelli getting about 5 percent of the vote in a three-way race. No one expected Romanelli to retain all those votes in November. The JSM signatures might be thrown out. These were the risks the Republican donors were taking. But say that, on the average, the sixty-six-thousand-dollar investment in Romanelli could be expected to decrease the Casey vote by 1 percent. The race was between Santorum and Casey, so decreasing the Casey vote is just as good as increasing the Santorum vote. The upshot is that sixty-six thousand dollars spent on Romanelli's signatures could do about as much for Santorum as a million dollars spent on his own TV ads (which were mostly attacking Casey anyway). Gaming the spoiler effect can be an order of magnitude more cost-effective than conventional campaign techniques. For consultants, this was the real lesson of the Year of the Spoiler.

Five candidates ran in the 2006 Republican primary for Arizona's Eighth Congressional District. The most popular was the most conservative, and he may have been the most unelectable. Polls implied that

Randy Graf, a former pro golfer and founding member of the Minuteman border vigilantes, was likely to win the primary. The polls also predicted that Graf would then go on to lose to the likely Democratic candidate, Gabrielle "Gabby" Giffords.

The National Republican Congressional Committee determined that Graf had to be cut loose. They chipped in at least $122,000 (some reports said more than $200,000) on ads for another Republican candidate, Steve Huffman. It was highly unusual for the national party to meddle in state primaries. "We don't comment on strategy," said the National Republican Congressional Committee's Ed Patru.

Huffman was a moderate. According to the polls, he was the only Republican who stood a chance of beating Giffords. He likely would have beaten Graf, too, had his vote not been split by a second moderate Republican, Mike Hellon. There was pressure on Hellon to drop out, and he ignored it.

The Democratic National Committee saw the Republican ante and raised it. Before the primary, the DNC funneled money to pay for a barrage of attack ads targeting Huffman. That would help the ultraconservative Graf and lead to an easy victory for Gabby Giffords.

The Eighth District includes some of the most porous border with Mexico. "When it came time to secure our borders, Steve Huffman was missing," the Democrats' ads said. "If we can't trust Huffman to show up for work, how can we trust him to protect us?" Huffman held DNC chairman Howard Dean personally responsible for the attack. The other Republican candidates blamed the Republican National Committee's Ken Mehlman for favoring Huffman. Asked for his opinion of the Republican National Committee, GOP candidate Mike Hellon was concise: "They're idiots."

He had a point. The Democrats' money was better spent this time. Their designated Republican loser, Graf, won the primary by six points over Huffman. Graf had no problem with the fact that Democrats helped buy his victory. "Gabby Giffords wanted me," he told supporters. "Gabby Giffords has me."

———

Texas governor Rick Perry, a Karl Rove protégé from way back, was in hot water for reasons only partly of his making. Maybe the least of his worries was the Democratic challenger, Chris Bell. There were also two strong independents, Carole Strayhorn and Kinky Friedman.

Carole Strayhorn was a state comptroller and former Austin mayor who had planned to challenge Perry for the Republican nomination. The chance of succeeding against a Rove hand-pick in Texas was slight. Strayhorn dropped out of the Republican race and retooled for an independent run. Friedman was the most colorful candidate, the thinking man's Jesse Ventura. He was a country rock singer and lyricist ("They Don't Make Jews Like Jesus Anymore"), the author of faux-autobiographical detective novels (*The Love Song of J. Edgar Hoover*), and a bit player in *Texas Chainsaw Massacre 2*. He appealed disproportionately to citizens who did not normally vote. Asked where he got the signatures for his ballot petitions, he answered, "Thank God for bars and dance halls."

Texas is one of the states that makes it insanely difficult to qualify for the ballot. Both Friedman and Strayhorn had to collect 45,540 signatures within a two-month window. Strayhorn made a media event of turning in 101 boxes containing 223,000 signatures. The gesture backfired when the press noticed that Friedman turned in an also-ample 169,000 signatures, and his fit in 11 similar-size boxes. Strayhorn's boxes were mostly full of air.

Texas law says nothing about full boxes. By supplying nearly five times as many signatures as required, Strayhorn should have breezed through the certification process. Nevertheless, the Perry-appointed Texas secretary of state, Roger Williams, took his own sweet time examining the signatures. Strayhorn sued Williams over the delay, and ultimately both she and Friedman made the ballot.

In late January 2006 Wayne Slater of *The Dallas Morning News* analyzed Strayhorn's campaign-contribution report. He determined that "more than half of her largest contributions . . . came from givers with a history of backing Democrats." Contributions included twenty thousand dollars from Ben Barnes, a Democratic former lieutenant governor. Much of the money was from trial attorneys. "This is a never-before-seen hostile takeover attempt by Democrats' most recognized puppeteers, personal injury trial lawyers," sniped Perry's political director, Alfredo Rodriguez.

Strayhorn's father had been the longtime dean of the University of Texas law school. It wasn't just lawyers, though; Strayhorn was raking in money from the gamut of Democratic stalwarts. Strayhorn explained by saying that it was a two-way race. Democrats were helping her because they knew that only a Republican could win in Texas.

Friedman preferred to say it was two-way race between Strayhorn and her ego. The polls did not much support Strayhorn's claim, either. Perry was in the lead, and Democrat Chris Bell was usually second. Most polls had Strayhorn third or even a distant fourth. To her Democratic contributors, tossing money at Strayhorn was like making a hard break shot in pool. It was impossible to predict what was going to happen; anything that broke up the status quo was likely to be good. Certainly aid to Strayhorn hurt Perry, the least palatable candidate of all to most Democrats. To further confuse things, there was a Libertarian candidate, James Werner, who threatened to be a spoiler's spoiler. "I would be pleased if I could cost any of my opponents the election," Werner boasted.

Ben Westlund took the opposite position. Early in his independent run for Oregon governor, Westlund made an explicit vow *not* to be a spoiler. He apparently had some kind of mental block about breaking campaign promises, for in August 2006 Westlund gracefully bowed out of the race. He had been polling about 10 percent in a tight contest between Democratic incumbent Ted Kulongoski and Republican challenger Ron Saxton.

That still left several potential spoilers in the race. The most prominent was the Constitution Party's Mary Starrett. The Constitution Party candidate is often expected to be a troglodyte. Starrett was more of an Ann Coulter hottie, a former morning-TV anchor with perfect hair. "Some people I've talked with say, 'If I vote for you, it might throw the race to Ted Kulongoski,'" Starrett admitted. "And I say, 'So what? What's the difference? There is no difference between Saxton and Ted. It's just Tweedle-dee and Tweedle-dum.'"

The Republicans needed Starrett to disappear. An attorney by the name of Kelly Clark had long been the Republican point man in Oregon. Clark determined that the Constitution Party had failed to comply with an antiquated law requiring parties to publish advance notice of their nominating convention in newspapers of general circulation. Clark filed a complaint with the State Elections Division to strike Starrett from the ballot.

Ron Saxton's campaign denied having anything to do with the complaint. Starrett turned nasty, bringing up Kelly Clark's personal history. In 1992 Clark stalked an ex-girlfriend, broke into her home, and had what the courts termed "sexual contact without consent." He pleaded guilty to third-degree sexual abuse and was disbarred for two months. Starrett also reminded the press that Clark once shared office space with political boss Neil Goldschmidt, an admitted pedophile.

After cooling down, Starrett offered the olive branch to Clark. In her apology, she had occasion to mention Clark's criminal past again, but only in passing, and only twice.

Oregon secretary of state Bill Bradbury ruled that Starrett would stay on the ballot. Bradbury was a Democrat. Starrett boasted that campaign money was rolling in—"Talk about pennies from heaven"— and she had plans for a preelection TV blitz. That requires the kind of money that Constitution Party candidates don't usually have. Was it coming from, uh, Democrats? "We're getting money from some heavy hitters who don't want Ron Saxton in office," Starrett explained.

We are witnessing a bipartisan mainstreaming of the spoiler effect as a tool for political strategizing. It is easy to blame spoilers, and easier to blame everyone's favorite villains, political consultants. Some may feel that there ought to be a law against such a thing. It is harder to contemplate any workable legislative remedy. A law might prevent one political party from giving money to another, but much of politics is already conducted by 527 advocacy groups and other doppelgangers with no official connection to the Democrats and Republicans. It is surely a citizen's constitutional right to contribute to a Green candidate, even if that citizen has also contributed to Republicans, as it is to give money to Libertarians and to Democrats.

When hackers corrupt software, we blame the hackers. We also recognize that the software must be changed to prevent the hacking. A voting system is software. It describes how to compute a winner from the raw data of marked ballots. To be useful software, voting systems must work with people the way they actually are. Voters, candidates, and strategists can be insincere, scheming, spiteful, and even self-destructive. When such people are able to use the system to defeat the overall will of the voters, blame is properly laid on the system itself.

Can anything be done to eliminate the spoiler effect? Is there a better, fairer way of voting?

THE
SOLUTION

SEVEN

Trouble in Kiribati

Few topics engaged eighteenth-century French intellectuals as much as *America*. Benjamin Franklin was the toast of Paris. Lafayette made a sensation by hiring two Native American houseboys. Books, pamphlets, and plays on the semi-mythic New World were brisk sellers. As one such tract eulogized,

> America offers the prospect of a vast land populated by several million men who, thanks to their education, have been made immune to prejudice and inclined to study and reflection. No distinction of rank or pull of ambition can deter these men from the natural desire to perfect their minds, to apply their intelligence to useful research, to aspire to the glory that comes with great works and discoveries. Nothing there keeps part of the human race in an abject state, condemned to stupidity and destitution. There is therefore reason to hope that by producing as many men devoted to the increase of knowledge as in all of Europe,

America will in a few generations double the mass of knowledge and the speed of its accumulation.

These incredibly misguided words flowed from the pen of Marie Jean Antoine Nicolas de Caritat Condorcet, known as the Marquis de Condorcet. Born in Ribemont, France, on September 17, 1743, Condorcet was a gentleman mathematician and more than a little vain about his American connections. He knew Thomas Paine, Benjamin Franklin, and Thomas Jefferson. In 1785, Condorcet was named an honorary citizen of "New Haven dans la Nouvelle Yorck" (as the *Journal de Paris* scrambled the geography). He thereafter published a number of anonymous pamphlets as "un bourgeois de New-Haven" or "un citoyen des Etats-Unis."

"America for Condorcet was a mental experiment," Princeton historian Robert Darnton wrote. "Having never traveled far from Paris, except for one visit to Voltaire's estate near Geneva, he remained free to design the country he wanted in his imagination."

Condorcet's halcyon view of America was of a piece with his belief in the ability of science to promote human happiness. "All errors in government and in society are based on philosophic errors," he asserted, "which in turn are derived from errors in natural science." Condorcet was the quintessential liberal. In his day, that term had nothing to do with big government or a welfare state. (The government of Louis XVI was *trés grande*, all for the welfare of the *moi* who was the state.) Liberals were those who championed the rights of individuals. Condorcet believed not only that common people should have the same rights as kings, but that women should have the same rights as men, blacks should have the same rights as whites, and that slavery and capital punishment should be forever abolished. He discussed these ideas with Thomas Jefferson, though not all of it sank in. Jefferson thought highly enough of the Frenchman's ideas to translate a portion of Condorcet's abolitionist essay, *Reflections on Black Slavery*. James Madison and Condorcet each wrote similar bills of rights for their nations' constitutions.

One point on which Condorcet lacked tolerance was religion. His strict Catholic upbringing succeeded only in instilling in him the most intense distrust of all faiths, Catholicism included. One of his epigrams was that he hoped to see a day in which priests and slaves were to be found only on the stage, as tragic mementos of a less enlightened past.

Condorcet's somewhat tactless manner was softened by a happy marriage. The year he turned forty-three, Condorcet married the twenty-two-year-old Sophie de Grouchy. She was a revolutionary, a near genius, and one of the most beautiful women in Paris. The Condorcets ran a glittering salon and were frequent visitors to others'.

Three years into the marriage, the French Revolution intervened. Condorcet supported the Republican cause. He became secretary of the Assembly and wrote much of a draft of the new French constitution. However, he favored sparing the lives of Louis XVI and Marie Antoinette, as part of his principled stand against capital punishment.

Maximilien Robespierre's more vindictive faction, the Jacobins, came to power and sent Louis and Marie to the guillotine. They also threw out Condorcet's constitution with its bill of rights. When Condorcet objected, he was declared an enemy of the Revolution.

Condorcet went into hiding. During this miserable time, he wrote one of his most absurdly optimistic works. Its title can be rendered in English as *Outline for a History of the Progress of the Human Mind*. Condorcet's last days are recorded in an anecdote. With ragged appearance and a wounded leg, he went into a village tavern and asked for an omelet. "How many eggs in your omelet?" the keeper is supposed to have asked.

"A dozen," Condorcet answered.

"What is your trade?"

"A carpenter."

"Carpenters have not hands like these, and do not ask for a dozen eggs in an omelet."

Condorcet was found out and imprisoned. He died under mysterious circumstances in a provincial prison cell in Bourg-la-Reine on March 29, 1794. Some guess he was poisoned. The irony of this Panglossian optimist's death was not lost on one commentator, who wrote, "Condorcet himself perished a victim of the French Revolution, and it is to be presumed that he must have renounced the faith here expressed in the necessary progress of the human race toward happiness and perfection."

Condorcet had a rival in Jean-Charles de Borda (1733–1799). In a 1775 letter, Condorcet dismissed Borda as

> what they call "a good Academician" because he talks in Academy and likes nothing better than to waste his time drawing up prospectuses, examining machines, etc.; and especially because, realizing he was eclipsed by other mathematicians, he abandoned mathematics for petty experiments . . . Some of his papers display talent, although nothing follows from them and nobody has ever spoken of them or ever will.

Condorcet may have envied Borda, who had seen Condorcet's promised land of America. Borda, a minor hero of the American Revolution, captained the French ships *La Seine* and *La Solitaire* in the Caribbean and off the American coast. The British captured Borda in 1782. They released him after a short term of captivity, and he returned to France.

There he pursued a career as a mathematician and surveyor. A share of his fame rests with his role in devising the metric system. Borda was chairman of the Commission of Weights and Measures, which included many of the great scientists of the age, among them Condorcet, the chemist Antoine Lavoisier, and the mathematician

Pierre Simon Laplace. The illustrious group considered defining the fundamental unit, the meter, as the length of a pendulum that would complete precisely one swing per second. Accurate clocks could be carried to any corner of the globe, and a simple experiment with string and a plumb bob could determine the accurate length.

Borda rejected the idea. He did not like the fact that it made the meter dependent on the second, since the second was not an even-power-of-ten unit (being one sixtieth of a minute). The second was "Babylonian," to use Borda's pejorative. He insisted that the meter instead be set to one ten-millionth of the distance from the North Pole to the equator.

Borda's definition required an accurate measurement of the globe. No one had ever been to the North Pole. It was like talking about running a tape measure to Neptune. Borda concluded that it would suffice to measure one tenth of the distance. Surveyors carrying the white flag of the French king were sent out to measure the meridian from Dunkirk to Barcelona. By then the Revolution was in full swing. Battles ceased as soldiers gaped at the surveyors in amazement.

Once the survey was complete, a former royal jeweler made a platinum bar of the proper length for the French archives. Those wanting to know the precise length of a meter had to make a pilgrimage to Paris. Largely because of that, distant America decided *not* to adopt the metric system. (Jefferson had lobbied to adopt it.) The new nation's only concession was to adopt a "metric" system of money, with each dollar rationally divided into one hundred cents.

Borda wanted to do for voting what he had done for weights and measures: make it scientific. He came to a conclusion that surprised many of his colleagues. Democracy is not always fair.

On June 16, 1770, Borda revealed this fact to the world in a talk at the Royal Academy of Sciences. His speech was not published and has been lost. Fourteen years later, however, he spoke on the subject again.

This time the talk appeared in the academy's journal, the foremost scientific periodical of the time, edited by the Marquis de Condorcet.

"It is an opinion generally held," Borda wrote,

> and I know not whether it has ever been objected to, that in an election by ballot the plurality of voices indicates the will of the electors, that is to say, that the candidate who obtains such plurality is necessarily he whom the electors prefer to his competitors. But I am going to make it plain that this opinion, which is true in the case where the election is conducted between two candidates only, may lead to error in all other cases.

Borda then gave a lucid explanation of what we now call vote splitting. Two candidates competing for nearly the same constituency may split the vote, allowing a less popular third candidate to win. "One may compare them exactly to two athletes who, after having exhausted themselves against each other, are subsequently vanquished by a third who is weaker than any of them."

Vote splitting throws into question any election between three or more candidates. A familiar example—one studied by contemporary social choice theorists—is the voting for the Academy Awards. The 2005 winner for Best Picture, *Crash*, had come and gone in theaters so quickly that many Americans could not recall having heard of it. *Crash* reportedly made less inflation-adjusted money than *any* Best Picture winner ever. Meanwhile, the critical buzz for another nominated film, *Brokeback Mountain*, had been so intense that entertainment editors felt obligated to explain why it had failed to win. "Perhaps the truth really is, Americans don't want cowboys to be gay," theorized *Brokeback* screenwriter Larry McMurtry.

Largely overlooked was the fact that *Brokeback* was competing against another gay movie, *Capote*, a biographical picture about novelist Truman Capote. Assuming that a largish group of Academy voters were uneasy about *Brokeback Mountain*'s theme, *Capote* would have been competing for the same finite pool of gay-friendly voters.

That was not the only complication. The audience for *Capote* must have overlapped significantly with another nominee, *Good Night and Good Luck*, a tale of 1950s TV newsman Edward R. Murrow's confrontation with Senator Joseph McCarthy. Both *Capote* and *Good Night and Good Luck* explored the moral dilemmas of journalists who become part of the story. Both were dead-on works of historical recreation, with actors portraying vintage-TV personalities whose looks, voice, and mannerisms were known to baby-boomer audiences.

The two remaining nominees stood apart. *Munich* was about terrorism at the 1972 Olympics, and *Crash* was a crime drama about race relations in contemporary Los Angeles.

The Academy of Motion Pictures Arts and Sciences uses a system called the single transferable vote for its nominations. (More on that later.) It then reverts to a standard plurality vote for the nominated films. By this rough analysis, *Capote* was probably hurt the most by vote splitting, *Brokeback Mountain* and *Good Night and Good Luck* were hurt less, and *Crash* and *Munich* were hurt the least. As the Academy does not release vote counts, it is impossible to say whether this was the determining factor in *Crash*'s winning. What is certain is that the core audiences for nominated films overlap to different degrees. This penalizes some movies and rewards others for reasons that have nothing to do with the voters' assessments of the films.

In 2002, New York University political scientist Steven Brams and Bloomington, Indiana, software engineer Paul Hager investigated the Academy Award voting from 1952 through 1996. They found that independent critical judgments, such as the American Film Institute list of 100 top movies and the Internet Movie Database's top 250 movies, agreed with one another more than they agreed with the Academy's Best Picture winners. Brams and Hager concluded that there is "no way of knowing whether the Oscar winners reflect the artistic judgment of the Academy voters or the vagaries of a seriously flawed voting method."

It would hardly have been in the optimistic spirit of his age for Jean-Charles de Borda to identify a problem and not provide a rational solution. Lacking Arrow's proof that a perfect voting system is impossible, Borda set out to devise one. His system is now known as the "Borda count" or the "method of marks."

The voter ranks all the candidates, from most to least preferred. This can be done by putting numbers next to the names on the ballot. To tally a Borda vote, you add up the numerical rankings given each candidate on all the ballots. When first-place choices are indicated with a one, a low score is good. The candidate with the lowest score has the greatest overall support, and that candidate wins.

Another, entirely equivalent method is to award points for each ranking. With three candidates, first place could be worth two points, second place, one point, and third (last) place, zero points. When you tally this way, the candidate with the highest total wins.

The Borda count may be better known to sports fans than voters. It is the system used to decide Major League Baseball's most valuable player, football's Heisman trophy, and the player rankings for NCAA sports. The "voters" are sportswriters, and the "candidates" are players. The Borda count also figures in the complex formula that determines eligibility for bowl games. (This uses rankings from the Harris and *USA Today*/ESPN college football polls.)

Whenever there are more than two candidates, Borda's system lets voters express themselves more fully than a plurality vote does. One way to see this is with a David Duke–type candidate whom people either love or hate. Because ardent supporters will rank the candidate first, he may do well in a plurality vote with many candidates. The fact that a majority of people may greatly dislike the candidate is ignored.

In the Borda count, voters' dislike is also factored in. The love-him-or-hate-him candidate will be taken down a few notches. Most would agree that this makes sense.

Yet there was something dreadfully wrong with his system that Borda did not see. The French Academy of Sciences didn't see it, either. That august body adopted the Borda count in their voting on new members, starting in 1784.

The following year, the Marquis de Condorcet published his own theory of elections, as part of a treatise whose title might be translated *Essay on the Application of the Theory of Probability to Plurality Voting*. Condorcet's book is notorious as one of the most confusing, pretentious, attention-span-challenging works in the French language.

> We must state at once that Condorcet's work is excessively difficult; the difficulty does not lie in the mathematical investigations, but in the expressions which are employed to introduce these investigations and to state their results: it is in many cases almost impossible to discover what Condorcet means to say. The obscurity and self-contradiction are without parallel, so far as our experience of mathematical works extends; some examples will be given in the course of our analysis, but no amount of examples can convey an adequate impression of the extent of the evils. We believe that the work has been very little studied, for we have not observed any recognition of the repulsive peculiarities by which it is so undesirably distinguished.

This review, in Isaac Todhunter's *History of the Mathematical Theory of Probability* (1865), must have scared off generations of English readers. Condorcet's book is a rambling study of how the theory of probability (a hot topic of the time) may be applied to human affairs. In a discussion of voting, Condorcet restates Borda's point about vote splitting.

A famous mathematician pointed out the drawbacks of the conventional election method before we did and suggested a system whereby each voter ranks the candidates in order . . . Although the famous mathematician who suggested this method has not published anything on the subject, I felt I should mention him here . . . When this essay was printed, I knew about this method only because various people had mentioned it to me. It has since been published in the *Mémoires de l'Académie*.

Condorcet is playing coy; he was editor of the *Mémoires de l'Académie*. At any rate, he then described his own ideas on voting. Observing that there is no problem when there are only two candidates, he proposed holding two-way votes between every possible pair of candidates. The proper winner would be the one who beat every other candidate in a head-to-head match. Such a winner is now called a "Condorcet candidate" or "Condorcet winner."

In the 1991 Louisiana governor's race, it is likely that Buddy Roemer would have beaten Edwin Edwards in a two-way vote, with David Duke out of the picture. It is almost certain that Roemer would have beaten Duke in a two-way vote. Roemer also would have beaten Clyde Holloway and the other very minor candidates. Assuming these guesses to be correct, Roemer was the Condorcet winner. According to Condorcet's thinking, he deserved to win.

A ballot for Condorcet voting could list every pair of candidates and ask voters to designate whom they preferred (something like the optician's exam where you're endlessly asked whether *this* . . . or *this* . . . is clearer). A more practical scheme is to use the same ranked ballot as the Borda count. From the rankings it is easy to decide which candidate a voter prefers in each two-way race. Should I rank Edwards number one and Holloway number four, it follows that I would prefer Edwards in a two-way match between Edwards and Holloway.

Today, Condorcet ballots can be easily tallied by computer. In Condorcet's time, the difficulty of tallying ballots was a deal-breaker. Borda's system was a fair amount of work itself.

This may be a good time to pause and ask yourself which system is fairer, Borda's or Condorcet's. Most people would probably say that *both* sound fair. And since both systems are "fair," it might be expected that both lead to the same candidate being declared the winner.

This is not always the case. Condorcet provided an example in a 1788 publication. Imagine there are three candidates running. I'll call them Adams, Bush, and Clinton. We ask the voters to rank them. There are six possible ways of ranking three candidates. The tallies look like this:

a. Adams > Bush > Clinton: 30
b. Adams > Clinton > Bush: 1
c. Bush > Adams > Clinton: 29
d. Bush > Clinton > Adams: 10
e. Clinton > Adams > Bush: 10
f. Clinton > Bush > Adams: 1

Line a means that thirty voters prefer Adams to Bush and Bush to Clinton. This is the most popular ranking. Line c, Bush > Adams > Clinton is nearly as popular, with twenty-nine voters.

In a Borda count, Bush wins. (Do the math, or take Condorcet's word for it.) Yet Adams is the Condorcet winner. Forty-one voters— those in lines a, b, and e—rank Adams ahead of Bush. Forty voters rank Bush ahead of Adams. Consequently, Adams beats Bush 41 to 40. You can also see that Adams beats Clinton 69 to 12.

Bottom line: Bush is the Borda winner, but that's ridiculous, because most voters prefer Adams to Bush. Condorcet thought it ridiculous, anyway.

The Borda count flip-flops. Suppose Clinton pulled out of the race. Recomputing the Borda count with Clinton out of the picture, you find that Adams wins. Whether Bush or Adams wins depends on Clinton. This makes no sense, Condorcet argued. "As long as it relies on irrelevant factors to form its judgments, it is bound to lead to error."

Condorcet was apparently the first to discover the paradox of voting, the one that Arrow would rediscover. A majority may favor candidate A over candidate B; a majority may also favor B over C; *and* a majority may favor C over A. In this unusual case, no one is undefeated, and there is no Condorcet winner. Instead, there's a "Condorcet cycle."

This paradox must have been an affront to Condorcet's belief that pure reason could impose its neoclassical logic on human affairs. A practical method has to be decisive.

The paradox is not a particular failing of Condorcet's voting method. Even if you vote some other way, the weirdness is still there; it just may not be evident. In any case, it is necessary for Condorcet voters to agree beforehand on a method of resolving any cycle that might arise. Condorcet gave this matter some thought and came up with what he considered a rational solution. But as Edward Nanson— one of the few mathematicians who slogged through Condorcet's *Essay*—complained, Condorcet's explanation is "stated so briefly as to be hardly intelligible . . . and as no examples are given it is quite hopeless to find out what Condorcet meant."

Condorcet's concerns about the Borda count were like the early talk of global warming. The cause of the alarm required most careful attention to understand. The remedy offered was neither painless nor certain to work.

It was a more clear and present danger that killed the Borda count. The Marquis de Laplace, famous for his development of calculus, probability, and astronomy, pointed out that the Borda count was easily manipulated.

Imagine a tight race between a Democrat, Kennedy, and a Republican, Nixon. Under the Borda count, you are to rank every candidate running, including minor candidates with no realistic chance of winning. In this race, there is also a minor candidate, Schickelgruber, running on the Nazi Party ticket. Your rankings are:

1. Kennedy
2. Nixon
3. Schickelgruber

There's a sneaky way of helping Kennedy. You move Nixon to the bottom of the list. Instead of the honest ballot above, you submit this one:

1. Kennedy
2. Schickelgruber
3. Nixon

This is called "burying." By moving Nixon to last place, you penalize him in the Borda count. Because every ranking counts, Nixon will lose a point by your rating him third rather than second. There's little downside to this. Though you honestly prefer Nixon to Schickelgruber, the truly abominable Nazi, the latter has no chance of winning.

Laplace realized that this was a serious defect. To give the extreme case, imagine that *all* of Kennedy's supporters cleverly rank Schickelgruber above Nixon, and all of Nixon's equally devious supporters put the Nazi above Kennedy. The few who sincerely support Schickelgruber will put their candidate ahead of both the others. Schickelgruber could win.

A happier outcome is that only *some* of the voters will be underhanded enough to do this. The Nazi will not win. *Whew!* Who does win? It's likely to be the major candidate whose supporters are *less* honest.

When this flaw was brought to Borda's attention, he made a famous reply: "My scheme is intended only for honest men!"

Borda has been judged a woolly-headed dreamer for that line. In all fairness, he intended his system for the French Academy, a collegial group of gentlemen. Ballots were not secret in Borda's time. Academy members were expected to vote in accordance with convictions that were already more or less known to their fellows. They would hardly stoop to crass trickery.

This is what Borda believed, and he was completely wrong. The academicians routinely "abused" the Borda count by "deliberately ranking [their favorite's] most dangerous opponents last," complained Academy member P.C.F. Daunou, a historian and critic. American football fans will recall a similar scandal in 2004. Some of the sportswriters in the AP poll were accused of rigging the Borda count to help or hurt particular teams.

Mathematician Warren D. Smith has his own Borda story: "I was at NEC Research Institute, and we scientists were supposed to hire people. At one meeting, my boss, who will remain nameless, apparently invented Borda voting—right at that meeting. 'Let's do this,' he said, 'we gotta be fair.'

"Well, of course, since everybody there was an arrogant pushy scientist, everybody quickly figured out that the thing to do was to rank your favorite first, then artificially rank all of his perceived major rivals last. There was no incentive to be honest. And in fact, if you were honest and rated A, B, and C at the top of your ballot, then you were an idiot. You were going to be a dozen times less powerful than somebody that rated B and C at the bottom of the ballot. It definitely came out completely crazy. A non-entity was elected. The manager said, 'Hey, this is strange, the ordering is completely different from what I expected it to be.'

"NEC Research Institute eventually collapsed, and nearly all its scientists were fired. This particular meeting, in its small way, was one contribution to its downfall."

Neither Borda nor Condorcet was the first to describe the voting methods bearing their names. The Borda count was used by the Roman Senate in the second century AD. That is perhaps the high point of an otherwise thin résumé. Over a millennium later, both the Borda and Condorcet systems turn up in the writings of Ramon Llull (c. 1235–1315), a Catalonian alchemist, logician, and mystic. Llull's *The Art of Elections* (1299) advocates Condorcet voting for the Catholic Church, where "good elections are greatly needed" in order to fight "sinners, infidels, and schismatics" and to distinguish the church's "faithful sons" from "evil men."

The church took no evident interest. Llull did influence a later medieval thinker, Nicholas of Cusa (1401–1464). In his *De Concordantia Catholica*, Nicholas proposes a Borda count for electing the Holy Roman Emperor. This suggestion also fell flat, though no false modesty inhibited him from touting his procedure. "In fact no method of election can be conceived which is more holy, just, honest, or free," he wrote. "I have myself been unable to find a better method than this even after much effort; and you can safely take it that a more perfect method cannot be found."

Western theorists belatedly discovered that the Borda count was being used in the South Pacific nation of Kiribati—a revelation that scholar Benjamin Reilly called "something akin to finding that an exotic animal long thought to be extinct is actually surviving happily on a remote island." Kiribati had apparently devised the system independently. Reilly reports that the vote was rigged in 1991. The government faction ranked the most serious rival candidate (Tewareka Tentao) in last place, leading to the election of Teatao Teannaki. As one observer wrote, "It remains to be seen just how long such a system will be tolerated which has the effect of eliminating popular candidates through backroom political maneuvering."

America's founders were well aware of the French controversy over voting systems. Thomas Jefferson owned a copy of Condorcet's *Essay* and sent another to James Madison. Whether they trudged through Condorcet's clotted prose or just skimmed it, the Americans may have concluded that democracy was an idea needing a little more work. In his own way, Madison intuited that rational people could be collectively irrational. "Had every Athenian citizen been a Socrates, every Athenian assembly would still have been a mob," he wrote in *Federalist Paper No. 55*. Neither the original Constitution nor the Bill of Rights guarantees Americans the right to vote for president, congressional representatives, or *any* office whatsoever. The democracy that Americans now enjoy is a retrofit.

In March 1800 the French Academy of Sciences got a new member. He was Napoléon Bonaparte, First Consul of France. One of his first actions was to demand that the Academy stop using the Borda count. Napoléon was politician enough to realize that the manipulability of the Borda method was a more serious defect than these gentlemen of science appreciated. The Academy dropped the Borda count, replacing it with a simple majority vote. When none of the candidates for membership received more than 50 percent of the vote, the position was left vacant.

Borda's scheme began its steady descent into oblivion (and the sports pages). An equally obscure fate awaited Condorcet's voting system, imprisoned in a book that almost no one could bear to read.

EIGHT

The New Belfry

The Reverend Charles Lutwidge Dodgson was the most conservative of men, in politics and nearly everything else. When he went on a rail trip, he was careful to map the route and compute exactly how much he would spend on tickets, meals, newspapers, and cab fare. He would put the exact change for each expense in pockets of a multicompartment purse, where it would be ready at hand.

At the theater, the reverend would mentally compile pointers for improving the production. In London, he saw a play in which a character was thrown off a bridge. It bothered Dodgson that there was no splash. "A little bit of realism . . . would be very welcome," he wrote the leading man, appending a sketch of a device for producing a suitable sound effect on cue.

Dodgson was thin because he ate only one meal a day (carefully recording its contents in his diary). One eye, and one shoulder, was slightly higher than the other. A speech impediment caused him to freeze in mid-sentence, unable to get out the next word. This was a serious handicap for a man who was not only a preacher but a mathematics lecturer at Oxford's Christ Church College. His lectures were said to be "dull as ditchwater," and his sermons were undistinguished except for the fact that he sometimes worked himself into tears.

The windows of Dodgson's rooms at Oxford overlooked the gardens of the deanery, the residence of the worldly dean Henry George Liddell, his wife, and his huge family. Liddell, a classics scholar who coauthored the first lexicon of classical Greek, was the polar opposite of Dodgson in many ways, including politics. Liddell supported the Liberal Party.

The new dean, recruited with great fanfare from Westminster School, had scarcely unpacked his bags when he began an ambitious architectural program for Christ Church College. This commenced with a McMansion-style renovation of his own living quarters. (Mrs. Liddell did not move in until it was completed.) The dean then turned his daring eye to the rest of campus. Both the expense and the aesthetics of his new construction became sensitive issues.

Dodgson adored architecture—the older the better. He thoroughly despised the dean's changes. What particularly ticked off Dodgson was the dean's new belfry. The cathedral's bells had long hung in its crumbling spire. The dean moved the bells to a new, temporary wooden structure above the grand staircase of the dining hall. The new structure was a box. Dodgson was appalled.

The Victorian equivalent of blogging was pamphleteering. When one of Oxford's professors got worked up on an issue, he could write a pamphlet, have it printed handsomely on Oxford's university presses, and distribute copies to that ever-so-small circle who might care. Dodgson responded to the dean with a satiric pamphlet titled "The New Belfry," in which he tartly labeled the belfry style "'Early Debased': very early, and remarkably debased." The pamphlet sold for six pence in local bookstores and was a modest success.

Oxford held an architectural competition for a new and more permanent belfry. This entailed committee meetings, parliamentary rules of order, and, above all, voting. Liddell was a charismatic politician, as Dodgson was not. Unable to compete with the dean on those terms, Dodgson turned his rigorously logical mind to something else: What is the fairest and most logical way of voting?

Electoral reform was in the air. The 1872 Reform Act gave British voters a secret ballot for the first time. Dodgson is known to have attended some of the House of Commons debates on this very matter.

"The following paper has been written and printed in great haste," Dodgson began the first of several pamphlets he would write on voting, "as it was only on the night of Friday the 12th that it occurred to me to investigate the subject, which proved to be much more complicated than I had expected."

This pamphlet, dated December 18, 1873, starts by remarking on the "extraordinary injustice" of a plurality vote. Dodgson then proposed a system ("whether new or not I cannot say") that is in fact identical to Jean-Charles de Borda's.

This raises the question of whether Dodgson knew of his eighteenth-century French predecessor. Evidently not. The work of Borda (and Condorcet) had by then been utterly forgotten. In the twentieth century, Kenneth Arrow's rival, Duncan Black, went so far as to examine the 1781 volume of the French Academy proceedings containing Borda's article in the Christ Church Library. The pages were still uncut in the 1950s.

The very day that Dodgson's first pamphlet was published, his (Borda's) system was adopted in the voting for a readership in physics. There were three candidates, and in the tally used, a high score was good. A candidate named Becker got forty-eight points. That was just one point more than the second-place candidate, Baynes. Becker should have won, but because it was so close, they held a second, runoff vote with just the two front runners. This time Baynes beat Becker, 11 to 9. Baynes was declared the winner.

The runoff *wasn't* part of Dodgson's plan, and in his diary he reported, with a trace of disappointment, that "we partly used my method."

The runoff must have shaken Dodgson's confidence. The candidate who won by the Dodgson (Borda) system was revealed to be *less* popular than another candidate in a two-way vote. This possibility had been the nub of Borda and Condorcet's dispute, and it happened the first time Dodgson's voting scheme was used.

Dodgson went back to the drawing board. In 1874 he issued a second voting pamphlet "in the immediate prospect of a meeting of the Governing Body, where matters may be debated of very great importance, on which various and conflicting opinions are known to be held." The matters of great importance included another vote on the belfry.

Nothing more was said of the Borda system. This time Dodgson suggested that they conduct two-way votes of every pair of candidates (belfry designs, actually). The candidate who beats every other candidate in two-way votes deserves to win. This is exactly what Condorcet had said, and again Dodgson apparently came up with it on his own. (The closest copy of Condorcet's ghastly *Essay* was in another Oxford library, the Bodelian. Duncan Black found that that copy had an uncut page in the section on elections.)

This plan was followed at the June 18, 1874, meeting. There were then four proposals for the belfry. In successive two-way votes, George Frederick Bodley's design beat those of Thomas Graham Jackson, Thomas Deane, and George Gilbert Scott. Bodley's design, the Condorcet winner, was chosen.

At the time that Henry Liddell assumed the post of dean, few could have imagined that Charles Dodgson, a minor and peevish mathematician, would one day be among the best-known men in Britain, a man

whose renown would far eclipse that of Oxford's famous dean. This
was the case, and Dodgson's dislike of Liddell was rooted in something
deeper than a difference in architectural taste.

It had to do with Liddell's daughter Alice. Dodgson first met Alice
in April 1856 while photographing Oxford's cathedral, the one whose
belfry would become the point of contention. Just shy of four, Alice became Dodgson's favorite photographic subject. By late 1856, Mrs. Liddell sensed something unwholesome in Dodgson's interest in Alice and
her sisters. She told him to stop taking photographs of her children.

Soon afterward, the dean and his wife went on vacation, leaving the
children in the care of the governess, a Miss Prickett, who let Dodgson
resume seeing the Liddell children. These meetings continued even
after the parents returned.

On July 4, 1862, Dodgson took the three Liddell sisters on a boat
trip, accompanied by a Reverend Duckworth of Trinity College. Dodgson entertained the children with an improvised tale of an Alice who
fell down a rabbit hole. The real Alice begged him to write the story
down. He did so, greatly expanding it in the process.

While Dodgson was in the course of writing *Alice's Adventures Underground*, as he called it, something happened that again caused the
Liddells to ban Dodgson from seeing their children. By the time he
completed his handwritten and illustrated copy of *Alice's Adventures
Underground*, Dodgson was unwelcome in the Liddell home. He sent
the manuscript to Alice as a Christmas present in 1864. There is no in-
dication in Dodgson's generally obsessive diary that the Liddells ever
acknowledged the gift.

In 1865, Dodgson published the manuscript as *Alice's Adventures in
Wonderland*. He used the pen name Lewis Carroll to preserve his pri-
vacy. The book became a sensation and was followed in 1871 by a se-
quel, *Through the Looking Glass*. Most biographers believe that Dodgson
was in love with the real Alice, and Morton Cohen speculated that the
author even brought up the possibility of marriage. Alice was eleven,

and Dodgson was thirty-one. The Liddells would have been outraged, not only by the age difference but by their none-too-high opinion of Dodgson.

The scandal overshadowed Dodgson's later dealings with the family. In Duncan Black's colorful surmise,

we will simply state what appears to us to be the almost inescapable conclusion. It is that by about 1872, when Alice Liddell, a girl of outstanding beauty and charm, reached twenty, surrounded by some of the most eligible young bachelors in England, and Dodgson reached forty without much reputation in Christ Church, he realized that Alice Liddell, who had meant so much to him, was slipping out of his life . . . Dodgson felt frustrated and humiliated. His reaction amounted to the attempt to triumph over Liddell and lower the stature of the Dean. By his pen, the instrument of his genius, he would alter the direction of architectural policy, and college policy, the objects at the centre of the life which he still shared with the Liddells.

In Black's half-plausible reconstruction, Dodgson's interest in voting was motivated by attempts to reconcile his own conflicting feelings about Alice and other child-friends. Not everyone has bought Black's psychoanalysis. One Carroll biographer, Roger Lancelyn Green, wrote Black, "Frankly I think you are barking up a Tum Tum tree." (It's a tree in "Jabberwocky.")

The pages in Dodgson's diary that appear to bear on the break with the Liddells are missing, removed by razor. Elsewhere, the diaries are full of pleas for God's forgiveness of a sin that is never specified. "God help me to lead a new and better life," Dodgson wrote just eighteen days after the river trip that prompted the Alice story (July 22, 1862). Later the same month, he postpones a preaching engagement: "Till I can rule myself better, preaching is but a solemn mockery—'thou that teachest another, teachest thou not thyself?' God grant that may be the last such entry I may have to make!"

That prayer went unanswered. Over a hundred similar admonitions were to follow it in Dodgson's diaries. One of the most anguished is dated June 5, 1866: "Gracious Lord, send Thy Holy Spirit to dwell in this cold love for Thee, to strengthen this failing faith, to lead back from the wilderness this thy wandering sheep, to make real my repentance, my resolution to amend my struggles against the temptations of the devil, and the inclinations of my own sinful heart."

The most important of Dodgson's voting pamphlets was printed in March 1876, days before the publication (on April 1) of "The Hunting of the Snark." It was again occasioned by the ongoing grudge against Dean Liddell. Oxford philologist Max Müller had announced his intention to retire from teaching in order to translate the sacred texts of the Orient. The University of Vienna offered him an appointment that would give him the freedom to do so. Dean Liddell presented a "decree" to keep Müller at Oxford. This proposal would pay Müller's salary and hire a successor at half the usual salary.

Dodgson objected to hiring a new teacher at half price. The Oxford community sided with its dean. Most saw the decree as a referendum on whether to keep Müller at Oxford. "The advocates of the Decree persisted so much in praising Max Müller," Dodgson told his diary, "and ignoring the half-pay of the Deputy that I rose to ask them to keep more to the point."

Liddell's decree was put to a simple vote and won by 94 to 35. A jubilant crowd pressed congratulations on Liddell as he himself walked to Müller's residence to tell him the good news.

Dodgson occupied the next week thinking more about voting. Exactly eight days later, he "spent the afternoon in writing out a *Method for Taking Votes* which I sent to the Press to be set up in slip."

This, Dodgson's third and most original publication on voting, was titled "A Method of Taking Votes on More Than Two Issues." The title page contains the disclaimer "Not yet published" and the author's note:

(As I hope to investigate this subject further, and to publish a more complete pamphlet on this subject, I shall feel greatly obliged to you if you will enter in this copy any remarks that occur to you, and return it to me . . .)

The pamphlet was interleaved with blank pages for comments. "What responses he got, if any, we do not know," Duncan Black wrote, "but it is likely to have been negligible."

Dodgson's pamphlet treats the paradox of voting, going well beyond Condorcet's discussion. His interest in paradoxes is of course evident throughout the Alice books. The story's young heroine is forever encountering authority figures oblivious to the illogic of what they say and do. One episode in *Alice's Adventures in Wonderland*, the "Caucus-Race," may bear on voting. The Dodo

> marked out a race-course, in a sort of circle, ("the exact shape doesn't matter," it said) and then all the party were placed along the course, here and there . . . they began running when they liked, and left off when they liked, so that it was not easy to know when the race was over. However, when they had been running a half hour or so . . . the Dodo suddenly called out "The race is over!" and they all crowded round it, panting, and asking, "But who has won?"
>
> This question the Dodo could not answer without a great deal of thought . . . At last the Dodo said, "Everybody has won, and all must have prizes."

American readers are apt to ask what Alice does—"What *is* a Caucus-race?" *Caucus* was and is a political word on both sides of the Atlantic. In England, it is a derogatory term for factions that vote as a bloc. It is less clear what Dodgson meant by a caucus-race. Critics have assumed that he was lampooning Oxford committees that ran around in circles while getting nowhere.

In his third voting pamphlet, Dodgson presents majority rule as an absurd race that everyone can win. "The majorities may be 'cyclical,'" he wrote, "e.g. there may be a majority for A over B, B over C, and C over A." It was Dodgson who coined the term *cycle* for this situation.

Dodgson described and critiqued several schemes for resolving cycles. He concluded, however, that none of these schemes can be entirely satisfactory. He ended with the dispiriting suggestion that the result of a "persistent" cycle should be "no election." The vote should be tossed out.

This may not be practical. It does show what a provocation a voting cycle is to any reasonable theory of voting.

Dodgson insisted that "The Hunting of the Snark" contain no picture of the title's mythic beast. He did not want to frighten his child-friend readers or dispel the mystery he intended. The point of this book is to *un*mystify Dodgson's (Condorcet's, Arrow's) beast. It is helpful to have a "picture" of a voting cycle, if only to decide how terrified we should be.

You can think of the picture on the next page as a precinct map. The eighteen black dots mark the locations of voters' homes, which cluster in three small towns. The region is voting on the location of a new nuclear power plant. The ballots label the three proposed sites A, B, and C.

In this case, politics is simple. Every voter wants the nuclear plant RIMBY ("right in my back yard"). Everyone hopes to get a job at the plant, and no one likes a long commute.

Start with a vote on whether to put the plant at site A or B. Twelve of the voter dots (in the communities of Springfield and Shelbyville) are closer to A than they are to B. Those twelve would vote for A. The other six voters (in Capital City) would favor B. Site A wins.

Now try B versus C. Twelve of the dots (in Springfield and Capital City) are closer to B. Site B beats C, 12 to 6.

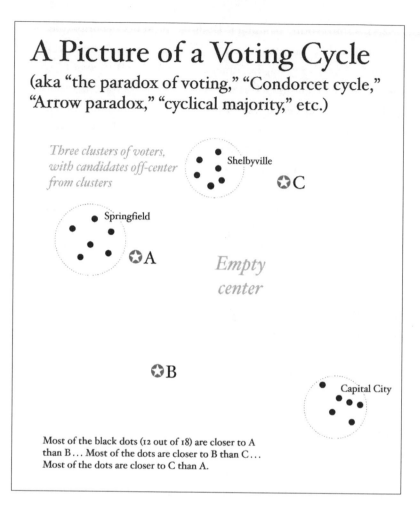

A Picture of a Voting Cycle

(aka "the paradox of voting," "Condorcet cycle,"
"Arrow paradox," "cyclical majority," etc.)

Three clusters of voters, with candidates off-center from clusters

Shelbyville

✪C

Springfield

✪A

Empty center

✪B

Capital City

Most of the black dots (12 out of 18) are closer to A
than B... Most of the dots are closer to B than C...
Most of the dots are closer to C than A.

Finally, let's have a vote between C and A. Shelbyville and Capital City are closer to C (slightly), so C beats A, and again it's by a twelve-to-six margin.

This is a voting cycle. Of course, in the more usual kind of election, the landscape is one of ideology. Each candidate stakes out a position on the issues of the day. Voters tend to favor the candidate whose views are closest to their own. A good voting method minimizes political "distance" between what voters want and what they get.

The diagram is a "trick picture." I had to place the dots carefully. A haphazard scattering almost certainly would *not* be a cycle. That probably means that voting cycles are rare in the real world. The diagram indicates some of the conditions that have to be met for a cycle to exist. Voters must cluster in three (or more) groups that are not in a straight (ideological) line. Some or all of the candidates must be off-center from the clusters. The center is relatively empty of voters *and* candidates.

The overall arrangement creates shifting coalitions. In one vote, Springfield allies with Shelbyville; in another, it joins with Capital City *against* Shelbyville; and in still another, Springfield stands alone.

Many follow Dodgson in saying that a symmetrical cycle like this ought to be declared a tie. ("Circular tie" is another name for a cycle.) This is reasonable provided that two-way votes are the only information we have or can have. This example is different: we know that everyone actually wants to minimize commuting time. Degrees of preference can be measured in miles or minutes saved. So why not figure the total commuting distance (from all eighteen voters' homes) to each site? The site with the smallest total would be "closest" to the voters overall. It's unlikely that *this* would result in an exact tie.

You don't even have to measure. A glance at the diagram shows that site A is the best choice for commuters. It is adjacent to Springfield and reasonably close to Shelbyville. The downside is that A is a long drive from Capital City. The other two sites aren't much better. Capital City commuters aren't going to be delighted with *any* of the three choices.

The worst location is B, way out in the middle of nowhere. You may wonder how it managed to beat C in a two-way vote. The explanation is that B is the lesser of two evils. Being barely closer to Springfield and Capital City than C is, B picks up these communities' half-hearted votes—even though it's not a convenient choice for anybody.

This is the fundamental problem with two-way comparisons. There is no accounting for degrees of preference. Springfield commuters must greatly prefer site A to B. It will save them ten miles, say, each way. In a two-way vote, that counts no more than the fact that choosing site B over C will shave two miles off the Springfield commute. Cycles result from giving equal weight to unequal preferences. In this case, the cycle is all smoke and mirrors. The paradox obscures the fact that the voters really do prefer one option.

Charles Dodgson intended to publish a book on his voting theory. He never did. He was frustrated by his inability to devise a truly satisfactory system. "A really scientific method for arriving at the result which is, on the whole, most satisfactory to a body of electors, seems to be still a desideratum," he conceded in December 1877.

Dodgson died on January 14, 1898. Dean Liddell followed him four days later. Alice Liddell had thirty-six years left. In that time she would lose her husband, two sons, her happiness, and her wealth. Only the Sotheby's auction of the original manuscript of *Alice's Adventures Underground*, the year before the stock market crash, saved her from genteel poverty. "But oh my dear I am tired of being Alice in Wonderland," she wrote toward the end of her long life. "Does it sound ungrateful? It is. Only I do get tired."

Dodgson's voting pamphlets were preserved by Lewis Carroll completists, who scarcely knew what to make of them. Consequently, for the second time, the would-be science of voting was almost completely forgotten. Dodgson's most enduring public legacy was to political cartoonists, who gained an inexhaustible metaphor for the mad tea party of politics.

Reform Party presidential hopefuls Pat Buchanan (as the March Hare), Ross Perot (Dormouse), and Donald Trump (Mad Hatter) in a 1999 Herblock cartoon. *("Said Alice . . . 'It's the Stupidest Tea-Party I Ever Was at in All My Life'" © The Herb Block Foundation)*

NINE

Instant Runoff

Among the many statues and fountains in Boston's Public Garden is a bit of eccentrica worthy of Edward Gorey. The Ether Monument is a forty-foot gothic tower topped with a sculptural group commemorating the first use of anesthetic. The stone figures at the top, by John Quincy Adams Ward, represent the Good Samaritan. To conservative Boston tastes, this was a suitable substitute for the bloody actuality being commemorated, the removal of a tumor from a man's neck by Boston dentist Thomas Morton in 1846. The monument was the peculiar design of architect William Robert Ware (1832–1915). Ware had another idea that is important to our story: an electoral system that is now called instant-runoff voting.

Ware was (like Charles Dodgson) a lifelong bachelor interested in preaching, architecture, and voting. The son of a Unitarian minister, Ware filled journals with critiques of sermons. After graduating from Harvard, he did a grand tour of Europe, followed by a stint in the atelier of Richard M. Hunt, the great architect of Gilded Age New York.

Ware set up an architectural practice in Boston, where his firm designed a number of churches (notably Brookline's High Street Church and the Back Bay's First Church), Harvard's Memorial Hall and Episcopal Divinity School, and a train station for Worcester, Massachusetts. Ware decided his true gift was for teaching. In 1865, at age thirty-three, he accepted the challenge of starting a new architecture school at MIT, where he remained until 1881. He left in a pique over an unpaid bill. (He claimed he had been asked to make drawings for an unrealized MIT building in Copley Square and that the institute had stiffed him.) At MIT and later at Columbia, Ware became known as the father of architectural education in America. In 1902 he had a nervous breakdown, followed by retirement as professor emeritus. He spent the remainder of his days living with his sister, Harriet, in Milton, Massachusetts.

Around 1870, Ware became interested in voting, following news of electoral controversies from across the Atlantic. Britain had begun extending the vote to the working (that is to say, non-landowning) class. This swelled the ranks of the Liberal Party. The Conservatives rapidly lost seats in Parliament. The losses were greater than might be expected. Victorian Britain was a relatively homogeneous nation. It was possible to imagine that the Liberals might win 51 percent of the vote in every district and thereby win every single seat in Parliament. The Conservatives could be shut out entirely, even though they still had 49 percent of the vote.

"Predominant power," warned philosopher John Stuart Mill, "should not be turned over to persons in the mental and moral condition of the working class." *Ouch*. Anyway, there was interest in schemes that would guarantee representation in Parliament in proportion to the parties' overall share of the vote. This went by the name *proportional representation*. Its battle cry was "tyranny of the majority," a phrase Mill plucked out of context from Alexis de Tocqueville's *Democracy in America*. The point of that charged phrase is that majority rule need not be fair. Only proportional representation could guarantee that minority (Conserva-

tive) interests got a fair hearing. The British debate resonated with Ware, whose own politics were conservative.

Finding ways to achieve proportional representation is a challenging mathematical puzzle. It is also a very *different* puzzle from that of finding a fair voting system for a single office. A single-office system is supposed to reconcile the electorate's contradictions and find the most reasonable representative for everyone. Proportional representation strives to reproduce the diversity and contradictions of the electorate on the smaller scale of the legislature. In many ways, the problem of proportional representation is *opposite* to the problem of single-office voting.

The most popular system of proportional representation is now known as the single transferable vote (STV). With minor variations, it dates at least to 1821, when Thomas Wright Hill conceived it. In the 1850s a British barrister, Thomas Hare, and a Dane, Carl George Andrae, independently proposed STV systems.

STV uses a ranked ballot. There might be twenty candidates running for six seats on a school board. Voters would rank all twenty from favorite to least favorite. (Yes, that can be a chore.) The vote tallying is fairly complicated. Unpopular candidates are successively eliminated and their votes transferred to other candidates based on the rankings. The system does a good job of making sure that no one's vote is "wasted."

Now here is the proportional representation part. Suppose that women decide that male legislators are hopeless in representing their interests. Women voters can band together and resolve to consistently rank all the female candidates ahead of all the males. Provided *every* woman does this, it guarantees that about half the legislature will be women. Republicans, Greens, Latinos, evangelicals, college students, Marxists, wealthy white males . . . all could, *if they wanted*, achieve a representation proportional to their share of the population. This is not to say that everyone has to play a partisan/identity politics game. STV lets the voters decide what kind of distinctions matter.

The best argument for proportional representation is ethical. The laws that legislatures pass are binding on everyone. We can't guarantee that every small faction gets its way, of course. We can guarantee that every substantial group has a voice in the legislative debate. That is what proportional representation offers.

STV is not the only possible proportional representation system. Charles Dodgson devised a clever one of his own, with the novel feature that the "eliminated" candidates themselves decide how to redistribute their supporters' votes. In 1884 Dodgson pitched his voting system to Lord Salisbury, leader of the Conservative Party and future prime minister. "How I wish the enclosed could have appeared as your scheme!" Dodgson wrote. "Then it would have been attended to." Salisbury politely replied that it was difficult to make a sweeping change in voting procedures "however Conservative the object."

This brought a quick chiding from Dodgson. "Please don't call my scheme . . . a 'Conservative' one! ('Give a dog a bad name, etc.') . . . All I aim at is to secure that, whatever be the proportions of opinions among the Electors, the *same* shall exist among the Members. Such a scheme may at one time favor one party, at one time another: just as it happens. But it really has *no* political bias of its own."

Dodgson published another pamphlet, "The Principles of Parliamentary Representation" (1884), and sent copies of it to all the members of Parliament. He joined with Hare and sundry Conservative and Liberal members of Parliament to found the Proportional Representation Society (later the Electoral Reform Society, and still active).

Dodgson was not the only celebrity flogging proportional representation. H. G. Wells was a proponent, and John Stuart Mill said that Hare's system "lifted the cloud which hung over the future of civilization."

Hare's system had scant success in Victorian England. It was adopted (under various names and with slight differences) in many Commonwealth nations, including Scotland, Ireland, Northern Ireland, Malta,

Australia, and New Zealand. In America, it underwent a slight change in its DNA.

William Ware knew that the geographic representation of the U.S. Congress was written into the Constitution and would be formidably difficult to change. At that, legislatures play less of a role in American politics than they do in Britain. America gives more power to single-seat offices such as mayor, governor, and president.

Ware realized that it was possible to use the single transferable vote to elect a single candidate. Of course, you can't have proportional representation where there is just one seat to fill. But when used for a single seat, STV has another advantage: it can prevent the spoiler effect.

The single-seat form of STV is now called instant-runoff voting (IRV). As the name promises, IRV is much like an open election followed by one or more runoffs among the most popular candidates. The runoffs, if needed, are immediate.

Imagine counting ballots by hand (it's easier to explain that way). Ballots are collected and placed in stacks, one for each candidate. Each stack contains all the ballots where a given candidate is ranked number one. Should one candidate get a clear majority of first-place votes, that candidate wins immediately.

Otherwise, you pick up the shortest stack. This represents the candidate with the fewest number of first-place votes. That candidate is eliminated. You sift through the eliminated stack and use the second-place choices to redistribute the ballots to the remaining stacks. Again you check to see whether any candidate now has a majority of votes. If so, that candidate wins. Otherwise, you continue eliminating candidates and redistributing ballots until one candidate achieves a majority.

This solves the spoiler effect. At least, it does when you have two major candidates and a few minor ones. In such an election, the votes for third-party candidates are successively transferred to the major-party candidates, and one of the latter wins. You could vote for a minor candidate (as your number one choice) and also have your vote count toward the major-party candidate of your choice.

More good news: IRV can avoid the Borda count's sneaky strategizing problem. A Republican has nothing to gain by ranking Democratic candidates last, and vice versa. That's because ballots ranking one of the two front-running candidates first are not going to be redistributed. The lower rankings don't matter unless you've voted for a minor candidate.

Ware did not publish his voting system or embark on a grand campaign to promote it. He seems only to have used his position at MIT to lobby for its adoption there. MIT began using the system for university elections, and still uses it. IRV spread to Harvard and to the city of Cambridge. Ware's system offered one-stop shopping. You could use IRV for single offices and the very similar STV for proportional legislatures. Over the following decades, IRV and/or STV proportional representation became widely adopted in American cities and especially at universities.

"Instant runoff is an improvement over our current plurality vote, no question," UC Irvine voting theorist Donald Saari told me. "It's bad, though. Let me give you an example. I believe it was in 1991 in the state of Louisiana."

David Duke was not a typical spoiler. He was the second most popular candidate. What *would have* happened under IRV is probably the same as what *did* happen under Louisiana's open primary. Buddy Roemer, being in third place, would have been eliminated and his votes transferred to second-place choices. Edwin Edwards probably would have won under IRV.

Like the plurality vote, IRV places a lot of emphasis on first-place rankings (since they determine the all-important order of elimination). The usual rationale is that these first-place rankings are important because they measure voter conviction. "IRV elects candidates with both strong core support and also broad appeal," says a pamphlet distributed by the Center for Voting and Democracy, an IRV advocacy group. By

"strong core support" they mean candidates who inspire passion, as true leaders need to do.

No one would object to that. The trouble is that ballot rankings are not a foolproof way of measuring this core support. First-place rankings are funny things. You might be impressed if I told you I was number one in my class. You'd be less impressed if I told you I was home-schooled, and I'm an only child. "Number one" is meaningful only in context. It depends on how much competition you've got and what kind of competition.

IRV is subject to something called the "center squeeze." A popular moderate can receive relatively few first-place votes through no fault of her own but because of vote splitting from candidates to the right and left. The moderate will likely be eliminated early on. The center squeeze can lead to unpalatable, Wizard-or-Lizard dilemmas.

When Betty was the only ice-cream vendor on the beach, everyone rated her stand "the best." Then Alan moved in, positioning his stand six feet to the left of Betty's, and taking away nearly half of Betty's business. Then Christine moved in, with a stand six feet to the right of Betty's. Christine got nearly all of Betty's remaining business. Christine's stand is the first-place choice of everyone on the right side of the beach, Alan's stand is the favorite of everyone on the left side, and practically nobody goes to Betty's stand anymore. It's the old "center squeeze." Does this mean that Alan's and Christine's ice cream is superior to Betty's? No, they all get their ice cream from the same wholesaler! Does it mean Betty is in a bad location? No, it *wasn't* a bad location before the competition stole her territory. All it means is that "first-place choices" aren't a good way of judging how people feel about Betty's ice cream.

IRV is excellent for preventing classic spoilers—minor candidates who irrationally tip the election from one major candidate to another. It is not so good when the "spoiler" has a real chance of winning.

———

A 1977 article carried the pointed title "Single Transferable Vote: An Example of a Perverse Social Choice Function." The authors, Gideon Doron and Richard Kronick, showed that it is possible for a voter to make an IRV candidate lose by ranking him *higher*. Huh?

This is known as the "winner-turns-loser paradox." Thirty-four percent of the voters are for Edwards, 32 percent are for Duke, and 27 percent are for Roemer. (For simplicity, I'll ignore the lesser candidates in the actual 1991 race. The totals, therefore, won't add to 100 percent.) Since Edwards does not have a majority, the lowest-ranking candidate will be eliminated. That's Roemer. Roemer's votes are transferred to the remaining two candidates, giving Edwards an easy victory over Duke (as actually happened in 1991).

Okay. Now say that Edwards decided to court the Duke vote just before the election. He gave speeches or ran ads or spread rumors, with the result that a few Duke voters (6 percent of the total electorate) switched their votes to Edwards. They ranked Edwards first, ahead of Duke.

The resulting numbers are now 40 percent for Edwards, 26 percent for Duke, and 27 percent for Roemer. See what happens? Duke is now in third place. It's Duke who is eliminated. The runoff is between Edwards and Roemer. Most of Duke's archconservatives rank moderate Roemer ahead of liberal Edwards. Therefore, the Duke vote is transferred primarily to Roemer, who beats Edwards by up to 13 points. This outcome is in line with the perception that Roemer would have beaten Edwards in a two-way contest.

For the 6 percent who switched, voting for Edwards instead of Duke caused Edwards to *lose*. This is through-the-looking-glass politics. It is even crazier than the spoiler effect.

One feature that IRV shares with Borda and Condorcet voting is the ranked ballot. It can be a hassle to rank a large number of candidates. In the 2003 recall election for California's governor, there were 135 candidates.

Inevitably, most voters have never heard of many of the candidates in a highly contested race. How would you rank these candidates?

Charles Jay (Personal Choice)
Earl Dodge (Prohibition)
Gene Amondson (Concerns of People)
Stanford Andress (Independent)
Leonard Peltier (Peace and Freedom)

These are not made-up names. All ran for president of the United States in 2004.

There are various ways of dealing with this problem. In Australia, which uses IRV, voting is mandatory. Any citizen who fails to rank the candidates is required to pay a fine. There is, however, an option called "above-the-line" voting. By choosing this option, the voter accepts a party's default choices.

It's rarely necessary to rank all the candidates on an IRV ballot. In San Francisco, which began using IRV in 2004, ballots have three columns for voters' first, second, and third choices. That's easy to live with and works fine as long as a "major" candidate is among your top three choices. (Otherwise, your three picks could all be eliminated, and it would impossible to transfer your vote to anyone still in the race.)

The logistics of tallying IRV ballots are relatively complex. There is no way of knowing how the votes are going to be transferred until you do the tally. That means it may be necessary to transmit every ballot or its data to a central counting place or computer. Just for the record, you don't have to do that with plurality, Borda, Condorcet, or range ballots. Precinct totals, rather than every ballot's complete ranking, are enough.

"In IRV, every time there is a near-tie among two no-hope candidates, we have to wait, and wait, and wait, until we have the *exact* vote totals for the Flat-Earth candidate and for the Alien-Kidnapping candidate . . . before we can finally decide which one to eliminate in the first round," explains mathematician Warren D. Smith. "Only then can we proceed to the second round."

San Francisco's election board was realistic enough to call its system "ranked-choice" voting. They didn't want people expecting an instant result. In the city's first IRV election, in November 2004, "software problems" were blamed for delaying results for several days.

TEN

Who's Afraid of the
Big Bad Cycle?

Abraham Lincoln's firstborn son, Robert Todd Lincoln, is remembered best for a morbid coincidence. Robert was present at the assassinations of two American presidents (Garfield and McKinley) and had almost seen his own father shot, too. (The younger Lincoln decided not to go to Ford's Theatre that night.) After the McKinley assassination, Robert Lincoln was all too aware of his reputation as the executive branch's angel of death. He thereafter refused all invitations to meet a president.

There was another strange thing about Lincoln. In his old age—he lived until 1926—he did not like to be around black people. His father's role in history was only half the irony. Robert Todd Lincoln had made a successful career for himself as president of the Pullman Company. The firm supplied "Pullman porters" for railroad cars and was the largest employer of blacks in the post–Civil War era.

Lincoln spent his last years in Vermont. When he felt like an evening out, he would have his chauffeur drive him to the Equinox

House for dinner. No sooner had the car arrived than a flurry of black hands would rush out to open the door of Lincoln's Rolls-Royce. Lincoln would furiously beat them away with his cane. The management of the Equinox House was forced to devise a way to prevent further unpleasantness. The "whitest" boy on the staff was a youth from Harlem with curly, almost golden hair. The management paid him an extra ten dollars a week to open the door of Mr. Lincoln's car. Lincoln knew nothing of the arrangement. He was so pleased that he tipped the boy a silver dollar each time.

The "white" boy was the future New York congressman Adam Clayton Powell, Jr., and this was only the beginning of a long career gaming race relations. Powell came of age during an unprecedented wave of interest in proportional representation in America. This enthusiasm had been building since the 1870s and included such influential figures as President James Garfield. Some believe that had Garfield lived longer, he might have made proportional representation the law of the land. (Four months into his term, he invited a couple of cabinet members to accompany him on a train trip. Secretary of War Robert Todd Lincoln arrived just in time to hear the gunshots that mortally wounded the president.)

A score of American cities adopted the single transferable vote in the early twentieth century, including Cleveland (in 1921), Cincinnati (1925), and New York (1936). This being politics, there was the usual hidden agenda. In New York it was the Republicans who wanted the new system. They were a minority and thought they could use proportional representation to secure seats on the City Council in proportion to their strength, rather than seeing practically all the seats go to the Democrats' Tammany Hall machine.

The trouble with this plan was that the Republicans were not the only minority in New York. It had been effectively impossible for a black man to be elected to public office with the plurality vote. Adam Clayton Powell, Jr., saw the city's new voting system as a way of launching a political career. He was already a well-known figure, having inherited his father's pulpit at Harlem's Abyssinian Baptist Church. Powell knew Malcolm X and, like him, segued easily from religion to community activism. In 1941 Powell convinced a coalition of Harlem churchgoers, labor interests, and socialists to vote for him. He thereby became the first African American elected to the New York City Council.

"I consider PR [proportional representation] the most un-American, most diabolical system ever yet devised to hoodwink the voters," wrote Rita Casey, a Democrat on the City Council. Democrats had reason to worry. Before proportional representation, the Democratic Party commanded 91 percent of the seats. Afterward, that figure plummeted to 68 percent.

The Republicans weren't cheering. Their 9 percent of the council seats rose only modestly, to 13 percent. The real beneficiaries were ethnic minorities, the American Labor Party (which got more seats than the Republicans), and the Communist Party (which got 5 percent of the seats).

"P.R. Is a Godsend to Commies," thundered *The New York World Telegram,* asserting that the new system was "complicated, trying the voters' patience, tiresomely long and costly to count, apt to play straight into the hands of alert and sinister Communist-led minorities." Apparently, some voters were left with the impression that their votes got mysteriously "transferred" to the Communist Party. The *Brooklyn Daily Eagle* warned that "there is among the PR groups a refusal to recognize the fact that in Germany it produced Hitler, and in Italy Mussolini."

To this day, Adolf Hitler is the poster boy for opponents of proportional representation. The German Reichstag used proportional representation, and it led to a profusion of fringe parties winning seats. One of them was the National Socialists. Had it not been for proportional representation, the argument goes, Hitler would have been a "third-party" candidate who never won anything. Hindenberg would not have appointed him chancellor, and Hitler would not have been able to have himself voted dictator.

Maurice Duverger, a twentieth-century French sociologist, noted that in countries with the plurality vote, a winner-takes-all system, there tend to be two major parties. In countries with proportional representation, there are many parties. If nothing else, this makes politics more interesting. In Italy, porn star Ilona Staller was elected to parliament as a Radical Party candidate. Staller flashed her left breast at rallies, continued making hardcore films while in office, and offered to sleep with Saddam Hussein if it would achieve peace in the Middle East. She didn't have to worry about offending the easily offended, just about getting enough supporters to rank her above the more conventional politicians.

You might question whether it's good to have fringe viewpoints like Hitler's or even Staller's in a legislature. But proportional representation doesn't invent nutty factions. It just turns a mirror to the electorate. The real problem in Germany wasn't that proportional representation gave a voice to an angry minority in the Reichstag; it was that the single-seat post of chancellor was filled by *appointment*. It's hard to blame proportional representation for that.

New York's Democratic and Republican parties *did* blame proportional representation for Hitler, and for communism, too. "The whole effort ran into the buzz saw of the post–World War II era," said Rob Richie, founder of the Center for Voting and Democracy. "There was the Red scare and less tolerance toward dissent." Tammany Hall and the GOP instructed New York voters to repeal the "'Stalin Frankenstein' Project" of proportional representation. A ballot proposition did that in 1947. Other cities followed suit. "By 1960 there was only Cambridge and Hopkins, Minnesota, left," said Richie, "and Hopkins got rid of it, too."

Adam Clayton Powell, Jr., made the most of his window of opportunity. He used his time on the City Council as a springboard to a 1944 bid for Harlem's recently created congressional seat. Powell won both the Democratic and Republican primaries, ran unopposed, and won. His congressional career ran twelve terms. An expert logroller, he was by far the most influential African American in Congress. Perceived (accurately) as that lowest of life forms, the slick politician, Powell did not fit the heroic mold of other civil rights movement figures. Yet it was he more than anyone who leveraged Martin Luther King's words into political action. Unlike Malcolm and Martin, Powell survived the sixties, barely. He spent much of his later years cloistered on the Bahamian island of Bimini, missing important committee meetings, neglecting to file income tax forms, and dodging mistresses, ex-wives, and a warrant for his arrest in New York. The Democrats shunned Powell when he came up for reelection in 1970. He could not even make the ballot as an independent.

Powell's political gamesmanship unintentionally put him at the center of a debate over the meaning of Arrow's impossibility theorem. How pessimistic should we be over Arrow's result?

Okay, voting isn't "perfect." But it was still possible to hope that it worked well enough, most of the time. The exceptions, such as the paradox of voting, could be hothouse rarities, unlikely to be encountered in real politics.

Scholars were discovering that the author of *Alice's Adventures in Wonderland* had weighed in on this very issue. Duncan Black republished Dodgson's voting pamphlets in 1958. In a real sense, Dodgson entered the modern conversation *after* Arrow. In his third voting pamphlet, after describing the paradox of voting, Dodgson defensively wrote,

> I am quite prepared to be told, with regard to the cases I have here proposed . . . "Oh, that is an extreme case: it could never really happen!" Now I have observed that the answer is always given instantly, with perfect confidence, and without examination of the details of the proposed case. It must therefore rest on some general principle: the mental process being probably something like this—"I have formed a

theory. This case contradicts my theory. Therefore this is an extreme case, and would never occur in practice."

He then argues that cycles can happen when people vote strategically. In the following, Dodgson's word *division* is Victorian English for a vote, referring to the practice of having assembled voters literally divide themselves into groups.

Suppose *A* to be the candidate whom I wish to elect, and that a division is taken between *B* and *C*; am I bound in honour to the vote for the one whom I should really prefer, if *A* were not in the field, or may I vote in whatever way I think most favourable to *A*'s chances? Some say "the former," some "the latter." I proceed to show that, whenever [no candidate has a clear majority of first-place votes] and there are among the electors a certain number who hold the latter course to be allowable, the result *must* be a case of cyclical majorities.

Dodgson thereby derives an all-purpose Machiavellian rule for succeeding in politics. "This principle of voting," he wrote,

makes an election more of a game of skill than a real test of the wishes of the electors, and as my own opinion is that it is better for elections to be decided according to the wish of the majority than of those who happen to have most skill in the game, I think it desirable that all should know the rule by which this game may be won. It is simply this: "In any division taken on a pair of issues neither of which you desire, vote against the most popular."

Dodgson's basic idea is as familiar to any politician as breathing. In 1995 Bill Clinton ran a TV ad attacking the Republican stand on cutting Medicare. The spot needed an unflattering sound bite from a prominent Republican, either Senator Bob Dole or Representative Newt Gingrich. According to Clinton consultant Dick Morris, they made a calculated decision to use Gingrich because they didn't want to hurt Dole. Dole was expected to run against Clinton in 1996, and they believed that he would be easier to beat than another, possibly stronger Republican. They therefore didn't want to do anything that might hurt Dole's chances of being nominated.

Same principle, different Clinton: in 2006 evangelist Jerry Falwell told supporters that he hoped Hillary Clinton would be the Democratic presidential candidate in 2008 because she would motivate conservatives to oppose her more than Lucifer himself would.

And as I've already remarked, a 2006 California congressional race had Democrats paying for ads to help an "unelectable" Republican (Randy Graf) beat a more popular Republican rival. This is Dodgson's rule in action. You might say it's a restatement of the Middle Eastern proverb "The enemy of my enemy is my friend."

One person who took Dodgson's point to heart was William H. Riker. Riker (1920–1993) was an important nexus in the reception of Arrow's theorem. He was a political scientist of conservative leanings who studied at Harvard and taught at Lawrence College and the University of Rochester. In the 1950s, Riker discovered game theory and concluded that it was the key to understanding the mysteries of politics. He quickly assimilated the work of von Neumann, Morgenstern, and Arrow, and began teaching them in his political science classes at Lawrence. Riker's approach became known as "positive political science." At a time when enthusiasm for game theory was cooling in defense planning and economics, Riker helped make it the hot new trend in political science.

Riker believed he had found an example of Dodgson's trick—and a real-life voting cycle—in the so-called Powell amendment. In 1956 the postwar baby boom created unprecedented demand for new schools. The House of Representatives considered a Democrat-sponsored bill to provide federal funds for school construction. There was strong bipartisan support. No one could deny that the schools were needed and that they would have to be built with somebody's tax money. Both parties were eager to score points with parent-voters.

Adam Clayton Powell, Jr., introduced an amendment to the bill that stipulated that the federal money be given *only* to states with desegregated schools. Two years previously, the Supreme Court's decision in *Brown v. Board of Education* had ruled segregated schools unconstitutional.

Powell's state, New York, was in compliance with the Supreme Court decision. The South, however, was still dragging its feet. Southern congresspeople had loved the original school-aid bill. It would rake yet more federal money south of the Mason-Dixon Line. Under Powell's amendment, the segregated South would get *nothing*. Either that, or the South would have to scramble to integrate its schools. The southern Democrats who had supported the original bill opposed Powell's amendment.

Under parliamentary law, a vote must first be taken between the amendment and the original bill. The winner of this two-way contest is then voted against the status quo. The winner in that contest prevails. You can think of the amendment, the bill, and the status quo as three candidates. The amendment will be passed only if it is a Condorcet winner (assuming everyone votes honestly).

In the first role call vote, the Powell amendment prevailed 229 to 197 over the original bill. The Powell-amended bill was then put up for vote against the status quo. It lost 199 to 227. Consequently, Congress rejected federal funding for schools. That was indeed a paradox, for most congresspeople had supported the original bill.

In 1958 Riker identified the Powell amendment voting as a Condorcet cycle contrived for political reasons. He was not saying that Powell, or anyone else in Congress, had even heard of a Condorcet cycle. The only math they needed was counting votes. Everyone knew that Powell's amendment would capsize the school-aid bill's chances of passage. Consequently, diehard Republicans who were against any federal spending supported Powell's amendment on the first vote. On the second vote, these same Republicans voted for the status quo.

In a letter to Congress, former president Harry Truman wrote that the Powell amendment

> has been seized upon by House Republican leadership, which has al-ways been opposed to Federal aid to education, as a means of defeat-ing Federal aid and gaining political advantage at the same time. I think it would be most unfortunate if the Congress should fall into the trap which the Republican leadership has thus set . . . The result would be that no Federal legislation would be passed at all, and the loser would be our children of every race and creed in every State of the Union.

There were 97 flip-floppers who voted for the Powell amendment before they voted against it. All 97 were Republican. Riker reported that at least 12 of the 97 voted *against* civil rights amendments in other bills that came to a vote shortly afterward. This suggests that they were no fans of the civil rights movement and that they voted for the Powell amendment for strategic reasons. It was Dodgson's rule, and it worked.

William Riker was the Joe McCarthy of Condorcet cycles. He made lists of them. He believed them to be lurking around every corner, in-sidiously attacking American values. To Riker, identifying a congres-sional vote as a cycle was a discovery imbued with hidden significance. It was like a conspiracy theory where everything is connected. Each new piece of the puzzle had true believers nodding their heads.

At the heart of it all was the impossibility theorem. "The main thrust of Arrow's theorem and all the associated literature is that there is an unresolvable tension between logicality and fairness," Riker wrote. "No adequate resolution of the tension has been discovered, and it ap-pears unlikely that any will be." Riker concluded, therefore, that the impossibility theorem "consigns democratic outcomes—and hence the democratic method—to the world of arbitrary nonsense."

Riker presented democracy as a shell game. The "marks" (voters) put up with voting only because they *believe* it's a fair game. The smart operators who run the show know how easily it's rigged. Every "paradox" of voting is an opportunity for insiders to force the outcome they desire.

This notion has been the great theme of the more noir phase of social choice theory. Elections are determined by the details of voting (to which few pay attention) as much as by the public will. Whoever sets the agenda can produce the "democratic" outcome desired. "I don't care who does the electing," cracked "Boss" Tweed, "so long as I get to do the nominating."

The apotheosis of this idea must be the notorious challenge issued by contemporary theorist Donald Saari: "For a price, I will come to your organization just prior to your next important election. You tell me who you want to win. I will talk with the voters to determine their preferences over the candidates. Then, I will design a 'democratic voting method' which involves all candidates. In the election, the specified candidate will win."

The offer was a joke, Saari assured me. Not everyone was laughing. "I don't want to identify who, but I've had senior staff people from several congressmen and at least two, maybe three senators, and from the president of one country contact me and ask for advice. And I've had several politicians running for office call."

Riker's grand obsession was crystallized in an influential, sometimes delirious 1982 book, *Liberalism Against Populism*. His thesis was that much of American history has been shaped by shrewd operatives manipulating the ambiguities of voting. According to Riker, Abraham Lincoln became president because of a voting cycle. The Depew Amendment, the Wilmot Proviso, and many another half-familiar

"THAT'S WHAT'S THE MATTER."

Boss Tweed. "As long as I count the Votes, what are you going to do about it? say?"

New York Democratic Party boss William Tweed, as seen by Thomas Nast. Such cartoons caused Tweed to demand, "Stop them damned pictures. I don't care so much what the papers say about me. My constituents can't read. But, damn it, they can see pictures!"

phrase from history class are, under Riker's discerning reappraisal, cases of manipulated voting. A leitmotif is that slavery and its never-ending legacy are often the source of electoral paradox.

Riker's publications helped frame the debate on Arrow's theorem. Arrow's seminal paper is a work of prim mathematical logic. Terms are defined, axioms laid out. *Liberalism Against Populism* is fast-moving revisionist history. It was read by political scientists and political consultants. In it, Riker uses the intellectual mystique of Arrow's theorem to advance an essentially philosophical point. Personal freedom and majority rule are *both* part of the American tradition. Americans have always existed in denial of the potential conflict between the two. We would like to think that a democratic majority would never vote to stone all left-handed accountants to death—but what if they did? Riker comes down on the side of individual rights and "liberalism"—or libertarianism, we might say. Riker was willing to take Arrow's mathematical conclusion at face value. Democracy is not such a good thing after all.

Riker's classroom examples, collected in *The Art of Political Manipulation* (1984), have influenced generations of political strategists. I'll give one tale that's not in Riker's books. One day a *U.S. News and World Report* reporter contacted Riker saying the magazine was planning to run a feature on the top American grad schools for political science and was asking department chairs such as Riker to rank the top schools. Riker had assembled a first-rate political science program at Rochester and took due pride in this achievement. Eliciting the fact that the magazine's published ranking would be determined by a Borda count, he naturally buried Rochester's most serious rivals at the very bottom of his list.

In some of the details at least, Riker was wrong. One of his juiciest claims was that the popular vote in the 1860 presidential election was a Condorcet cycle. This was the type of election that might be expected to yield a cycle. There were four strong candidates and two political dimensions, namely slavery versus abolition and Democrat versus Republican/Whig. Riker believed that Stephen Douglas would have beaten Abraham Lincoln in a head-to-head match . . . that Lincoln would have beaten John Bell . . . and that Bell would have beaten Douglas. (The Southern Democrat, John Breckenridge, was not part of Riker's cycle.)

In a 1999 study in the aptly named *Journal of Theoretical Politics*, Alexander Tabarrok and Lee Spector convincingly refuted Riker's claim. Remember first of all that the official 1860 vote counts do not contain enough information to say whether a cycle existed. You have to guess the second- and third-place choices of long-dead voters. Riker (who had himself died in 1993) made his own guesses. He was not an expert on the Civil War period. Tabarrok and Spector surveyed prominent historians who were. They got thirteen historians to estimate the rankings, and they averaged these values. The historians' figures said there was no cycle. Douglas would have beaten Lincoln (as Riker claimed and everyone believed), but Lincoln and Bell would have been virtually tied, and Bell would have lost to Douglas (refuting Riker). This means that Douglas would have been a Condorcet winner.

Further theoretical studies implied that cycles must be rare. Candidates have incentive to move to the middle, the "empty center" of the diagram on p. 158. By presenting herself as a compromise choice, a candidate could become a Condorcet winner and destroy the cycle. A cycle therefore requires not only an unusual distribution of voter opinion but also candidates unwilling to help themselves by assuming a more popular stance.

The few believable cases of strong cycles involve legislative votes. Adam Clayton Powell, Jr., was apparently more interested in rattling the cage of the segregationists (and making a point for the voters back home?) than in seeing his amendment pass. He devised an amendment creating shifting coalitions of three very partisan factions (northern Democrats, southern Democrats, and Republicans). No one could immediately rush in with a more viable amendment. Congress had to vote on the present amendment first. Hence the implicit cycle (that Riker rather creatively reconstructed).

The changed tone of the room was summed up in the title of a 1992 paper, "Who's Afraid of the Big Bad Cycle?" Authors Scott L. Feld and Bernard Grofman examined thirty-six elections in British and Irish professional societies conducted using ranked ballots. All thirty-six elections had a Condorcet winner. Feld and Grofman then broke down the election results into groups of three candidates in the same election. Of the 14,270 triplets of candidates, only 71 formed cycles. This means that, for a given set of three candidates, the chance of a cycle is about 1 in 200.

"We have not exorcised the paradox of cyclical majorities," Feld and Grofman wrote; "we have, we hope, put its importance for ordinary political choice into perspective."

Today just about everyone would agree. The cycle is a mathematical rarity hardly worth losing sleep over. In a larger sense, though, Riker was probably right. Voters and candidates can be expected to exploit the ambiguities that exist with any method of voting. This must be considered in evaluating voting methods, and in understanding politics.

Arrow's proof did not address manipulated ("strategic") voting. Subsequent theorists have devoted much attention to the topic. In Riker's time, the major theoretical developments reinforced the dark thoughts and quashed any optimism. Is it possible to devise a voting system in which no one has an incentive to misrepresent his or her true preferences? The answer (given certain reasonable-sounding assumptions) is regrettably no. This, too, has been demonstrated with unarguable mathematical certainty. The proof, independently devised by the University of Michigan's Allan Gibbard (1973) and Northwestern University's Mark Satterthwaite (1975), is now called the Gibbard-Satterthwaite theorem. It shows that, like the Republicans in the Powell amendment vote, voters may get what they want by pretending to want something else. No voting system can prevent such manipulation.

Such melancholy findings inspired Amartya Sen to pose this amusing allegory of social choice:

> "Can you direct me to the railway station?" asks the stranger. "Certainly," says the local, pointing in the opposite direction, towards the post office, "and would you post this letter for me on your way?" "Certainly," says the stranger, resolving to open it to see if it contains anything worth stealing.

Voters, too, don't always tell the truth. The momentous decisions of free societies arise from this mutual con game we call voting.

ELEVEN

Buckley and the Clones

Oskar Morgenstern learned something that no egotistical economist ever should. He somehow found out how much money his colleagues were making. Morgenstern was shocked. He could not believe how high the salaries of the other economics professors were, and how low his own salary was in comparison. For someone with Morgenstern's self-esteem (and belief in market valuations), this finding was impossible to accept. He did not accept it. In 1970 he severed ties with Princeton and took a professorship at New York University.

Once again, Morgenstern was more or less cast adrift by fate. At NYU he met a young political scientist named Steven Brams. Brams revered Morgenstern as a living legend, and Brams's wife, who happened to be Austrian, charmed the elderly economist. The couple socialized with Morgenstern—until he became too ill to socialize with anyone. Brams visited Morgenstern on his deathbed. Shortly before his death, Morgenstern passed on to Brams something he might be able to make use of: a description of a new way of voting.

The voting method was the creation of George A. W. Boehm (1922–1993), a Columbia University–trained mathematician, editor, and writer who worked for such publications as *Newsweek*, *Fortune*, and *Scientific American*. Boehm was also an avid bridge player, known for popularizing the card game's so-called Lebensohl convention. Boehm never published the voting system he invented. He got only so far as writing a short description (1976) and passing mimeographed copies to a few friends. The description was titled, "One Fervent Vote Against Wintergreen."

This is a dated reference to a 1931 Broadway musical, *Of Thee I Sing*, a political satire by George S. Kaufman and Morris Ryskind with music by George and Ira Gershwin. The protagonist is John P. Wintergreen, an airhead opportunist who bumbles his way to the White House. That is all you need of the plot to understand Boehm's title. Boehm thought that voters should be given the option of voting *against* Wintergreen rather than *for* their favorite candidate. He called this a "negative vote."

A negative vote is not a veto. (You obviously can't grant veto power to each of millions of voters.) It is simply a less-than-zero vote, to be deducted from Wintergreen's total of regular, positive votes. By casting a negative vote for Wintergreen, you diminish the chance that he will win. Under Boehm's system, each voter can decide whether he's better off casting a positive vote for his favorite candidate or a negative one for his least-favorite.

Brams thought the idea had merit. In the summer of 1976 he attended a workshop at Cornell where he met a young game theorist named Robert J. Weber. Each told the other about his pet project. Weber was working on something he called "approval voting." They quickly realized that Weber's approval voting was closely related to Boehm's negative voting.

Weber had been inspired by a problematic Senate race in New York. On June 6, 1968, an assassin gunned down New York senator Robert F. Kennedy in Los Angeles. It fell on New York's liberal Republican governor, Nelson Rockefeller, to appoint a replacement. Rockefeller exercised his prerogative to replace Kennedy with a very liberal Republican, congressman Charles Goodell.

New York's Republicans were less delighted than they might have been to gain a Senate seat. Goodell was critical of the Vietnam War and of the newly elected Republican president, Richard Nixon. As the sixties came to a close, the war and Nixon became even more polarizing issues. In the Senate, Goodell edged further left.

The Kennedy/Goodell Senate seat came up for reelection in November 1970. Goodell was determined to cement his appointment with a victory at the polls. He had a lot going for him. He was a reasonably popular incumbent with the nomination of Rockefeller's GOP and New York's Liberal Party.

The Conservative Party felt that Goodell was Republican in name only. They decided to run a candidate of their own. Their dream choice, unquestionably, would have been William F. Buckley, Jr. Founder of the *National Review*, Buckley had run for New York City mayor as a Conservative in 1965 and had charmed even the liberal press with his wit. (Asked what he'd do if he won, he replied, "I'd demand a recount.") The campaign had helped launch Buckley's career as host of a PBS show, *Firing Line*. By 1970, Buckley was the conservative king of all media. The last thing he needed was more publicity. Nor did he relish another political race he could not possibly win. He did, however, have a brother.

James L. Buckley was two years older than William F. He was also Yale-educated, personable, and intelligent. He had managed his brother's mayoral campaign, so he knew politics. If less famous and witty than his brother, James had the Buckley surname, and that was solid gold to right-wing America. James agreed to run for the New York Senate seat. He took his race more seriously than his brother had, spending a then-astonishing $1.8 million. To almost everyone's surprise, he won.

He won because of vote splitting. In the jargon of social choice theory, "clones" are candidates so similar to one another that they split the vote. Two classic examples are Buckley's opponents, Republican Charles Goodell and Democrat Richard Ottinger. There was hardly much ideological space between them. Both were antiwar activists. Even their biographies were similar. Both had served in the air force. Ottinger was Harvard Law School class of '53; Goodell was Yale Law School, '51. Both were multiterm New York congressmen.

The early polls pointed to a win for Ottinger. Inertia gave the Democrat an advantage over his Republican "clone," and the true conservatives favored Buckley. Then Nixon's vice president, Spiro Agnew, made a trip to New York.

Agnew was a hard-line conservative. He had traveled to New York not to talk up the embattled Republican candidate Goodell but instead to blast him as a "political Christine Jorgenson." (Jorgenson was the most famous transgendered person of the time.) The result was a massive sympathy spike in Goodell's numbers. Agnew's attack helped Goodell and hurt Ottinger.

There are two theories about this. In one, the Nixon administration is smart; in the other, it's dumb. The smart theory is that Nixon and company intended what did in fact happen. They knew that loutish, anti-intellectual Agnew was anathema to liberal New Yorkers. Anyone Agnew hated would instantly look cool. By damning Goodell, Agnew would help him steal votes from Ottinger. This would diminish the Democrat's chances. The winner would be Goodell (or Buckley), either preferable to the Democrat.

The dumb theory is that Nixon simply couldn't bear a Republican who spoke against him and his unpopular war. He lashed out at Goodell, via Agnew, regardless of the political consequences.

I suspect that the dumb theory is closer to the truth. Nixon was unerring in remembering and sticking it to his enemies. James Buckley won with just 39 percent of the vote. Ottinger had about 37 percent, leaving Goodell with only 24 percent. That meant that 61 percent had voted liberal and antiwar, yet an archconservative won.

Buckley's victory illustrates a paradox noted by economist Claude Hillinger: "the worst candidate can win." This is not a dig at Buckley. It simply reflects the fact that, of the three major candidates, Buckley was the *least* in tune with New York's liberal electorate. He was a "Condorcet loser." This is the opposite of a Condorcet winner. Buckley would have lost a two-way match with *either* of his major opponents.

The race's outcome disturbed Robert Weber. "Why shouldn't supporters of Charles Goodell and Richard Ottinger, who represented similar political philosophies, be able to vote for both?" he wondered. "It didn't make sense that the best approach to winning an election was to hope for multiple similar opponents who would split the vote."

Negative voting could have solved the clone problem. New York liberals could have cast a negative vote for Buckley. This would have been a way of saying, "I don't much care which of the liberals wins because they're so similar; the important thing is to make sure Buckley *doesn't* win."

Negative voting is less appealing when there are more than three candidates. In 1971, the college town of Ithaca, New York, held an election for mayor. It was a free-for-all, with two Democrats and three Republicans running against one another. The winner was a Democrat who achieved a mere 29.1 percent plurality. Making this even more ridiculous was the fact that the front-running Republican got 28.9 percent.

It gets worse. The three Republicans collectively got 60.7 percent of the vote. Ithaca voted overwhelmingly Republican and got a Democrat.

Weber, then a Cornell grad student, discussed these elections with others at Cornell. His field of study, game theory, takes as its operating assumption that everyone is ruthless, selfish, and backstabbing. Game theory does not assert a particularly cynical view of human nature; it only asks what is possible under the conditions that it takes as axiomatic. The surprising thing is that there are ways for completely distrusting parties to get along.

A familiar example of game-theoretic thinking is the way two children divide a cake. One child cuts the cake into two "equal" pieces, and the other gets first choice of pieces. The cutter would like to cut herself a bigger piece. However, she expects that the chooser will pick the bigger piece for himself, provided there is a bigger piece. The best the cutter can do is to make the pieces as equal as possible. The *selfishness* of both parties enforces a Solomonically fair outcome. (There is now an academic subspeciality of fair-division schemes, and Steven Brams is one of the field's experts.)

Voting systems often penalize voters for being honest. Had all of Goodell's supporters "lied" and pretended to like Ottinger best of all, casting their ballots for him instead of for Goodell, Ottinger would have won with 61 percent of the vote. Instead, much of New York's liberal majority voted honestly and paid a price for it.

Obviously, it's a bad thing to reward dishonesty. Voting systems cannot read voters' minds. When ballots express something other than sincere feelings, the already "impossible"(!) task of finding a fair winner becomes all the more hopeless.

Weber devised an amazingly simple voting scheme that struck him as notably honest. It can be described in two sentences: Let people vote for as many candidates as they like. The candidate who gets the most votes wins.

That's it. I might add that you are allowed to cast only one vote per candidate. This means, for instance, that New York liberals could have cast one vote for Ottinger and one vote for Goodell. Diehard conservatives probably would have voted for Buckley alone. Ithaca Republicans in 1971 could have voted for all three Republicans, while Democrats could have voted for both Democrats. This way, the majority could have gotten its way. One of the liberals would have won instead of Buckley; a Republican would have been Ithaca's mayor instead of a Democrat. Weber called his system approval voting. Roughly speaking, you vote for candidates you approve of.

Some people's initial reaction to Weber's idea is "Isn't that unfair?" With approval voting, one voter may cast *five* votes. Another may cast only one. Isn't the single-vote guy cheated?

The short answer is no. For one thing, everyone has an equal opportunity to cast multiple votes. If you think there's an advantage in voting for five candidates, go for it.

You will discover that there is no automatic benefit to casting lots of votes. Should you vote for every candidate on the ballot, your votes will cancel out. That is, your votes will merely add one to every candidate's total and cannot possibly be decisive. It's as if you stayed home and didn't vote at all.

A meaningful ballot must approve at least one candidate and must *not* approve at least one. As with cake division, the voter has the incentive to be neither too stingy nor too generous with approval votes.

Approval voting is a handy way for a group to decide on a restaurant or a movie. This can be a tough decision in the big city, where there are likely to be more options than there are people in the group. Everyone could have a different choice. What then?

This can lead to passive-aggressive excuses about why someone can't stomach Korean food or a Brazilian film with subtitles. One way of breaking the deadlock is to run through the list of choices, with everyone giving a thumbs-up or thumbs-down for each option. The choice that gets the most thumbs-up votes wins. (This is another form of approval voting. You don't need to count the thumbs-down votes, just the thumbs-ups.)

The result of a thumbs-up vote might look like this:

👍 Red Snapper Thai Grill

👍👍 Indian Tampura

👍👍👍👍 Williams Bar-B-Que

👍👍 Star of Bombay

👍👍👍 Charro Mexicana

There are two Indian restaurants on the list. With a simple plurality vote, that would be unfair to the Indian food lovers. The two choices would split the Indian food vote, making it less likely that either Indian restaurant would win. With approval voting, the people who like Indian food can vote for both Indian places. This does not cheat the people who want Mexican or Thai. It just levels the playing field by ensuring that vote splitting neither hurts nor helps the Indian restaurants.

Four out of five people gave the barbecue place a thumbs-up. It might have been only one person's *first* choice, but practically everyone is happy enough with it to give it a thumbs-up. No other choice has broader support. With approval voting, the barbecue place wins.

When there are exactly three candidates, approval and negative voting are equivalent. Casting a negative vote for Buckley has the same effect as casting approval votes for Goodell and Ottinger (and not for Buckley). When there are four or more candidates, as in the 1971 Ithaca election, there is a difference, and approval voting is more flexible. You can vote for three of five candidates, say. Both Brams and Weber agreed that approval voting was better.

It was an odd coincidence that two people had come across nearly the same idea at nearly the same time and then crossed paths at Cornell. The coincidence was bigger than Brams and Weber realized. At least three other people or groups independently described approval voting at about the same time.

John Kellett and Kenneth Mott published a 1977 article on the problem of choosing candidates in presidential primaries. Vote splitting is a big problem there; Kellett and Mott proposed an approval voting scheme to select the party's nominee. Richard A. Morin also came up with the idea and published it in a 1980 book, *Structural Reform: Ballots*. Of the group of coinventors publishing in the mid-1970s, Guy Ottewell apparently holds the distinction of being the first to come up with the idea of approval voting. British-born Ottewell is a polymath best known for publishing an astronomical calendar popular with amateur astronomers. He says he got the idea for approval voting in the early 1960s. The 1968 presidential election—where George Wallace was seen as a potential spoiler—provoked Ottewell to write up his system in an essay, "The Arithmetic of Voting," in February 1968. He showed the manuscript to a few friends in Los Angeles, but did not publish it until 1977. His article concluded, "This form of voting is the second simplest after one-person-one-vote. It is time to give this costless reform a conspicuous trial."

Approval voting *is* simple, as long as you don't think about it too much. Once you start asking questions, it gets more complicated.

How does an approval voter draw the line between the "good guys" to approve and the "bad guys" to disapprove? There has been a lot of cross talk on this issue. Approval voting's inventors and promoters have offered at least three answers. You might call them the totally honest, the semi-strategic, and the strategic approaches.

The totally honest approach says that approval voters should vote for every candidate they "approve" of. An election is therefore like an opinion poll to determine a candidate's "approval rating." The ballot amounts to a set of simultaneous approval-rating polls.

Because this is a nice, simple explanation, it gets rehashed in press accounts of approval voting. Okay, "approving" of someone is a vague concept. Maybe that doesn't matter. Approval-rating polls tell us *something*, after all. Pollsters do not explain what it means to "approve" of someone, no one polled gives much thought to his or her answer, and some people must answer the way they do for silly reasons. As long as you interview enough people, the noise cancels out. You are left with a decent index of how the public feels about a particular politician. This index can be useful for comparing one politician's popularity to another's, or for tracking one politician's popularity over time.

In an attempt to make the vague sound precise, it's sometimes said that you should approve anyone who rates better than halfway on your scale of political appeal. There is a catch to this. Maybe you think *all* politicians are crooks. On a scale of 0 to 100, nobody rates higher than a 2. That would mean you approve nobody. This might be fine on an opinion poll. It would send the message that they're all bums. Voting for office is different. You are trying to help decide which of the "bums" is going to run the country. By approving no one you disenfranchise yourself. A voter who is easy to please, and who approves *all* the candidates, is equally disenfranchised.

In politics above all, "acceptable" is on a sliding scale. We grade on the curve and do it so naturally we don't realize it. This leads to the second, semi-strategic way to mark an approval ballot. You approve any candidate who's better-than-average *of the group that's actually running for that office*.

The semi-strategic approach is a shade less honest. You sometimes "pretend" to like a candidate (by approving her) when all you mean is that she's the least of the ballot's evils. (You order the best thing on the menu, even though all the food's terrible.) There are other occasions when you pretend to dislike a candidate (by not approving him) because there are a wealth of better choices. It's generally expected that approval voters would do this. No one's going to be so brutally honest as to disenfranchise himself.

The third and optimally strategic way to mark your approval ballot was described in detail by Robert Weber, Warren Smith, and others. Ask yourself why you vote in the first place. The answer is that every vote increases (ever so slightly) the chance that the candidate you vote for will win. You are hoping that your vote will be the one that makes the difference.

The *only* reason to approve *any* candidate is because you rate the prospect of that candidate's winning higher than you rate the expected outcome of the election. This "expected outcome" is a weighted average. Think of a game show where you can take either a sure thing or an unknown prize behind a door. Behind door number one is your next president. It may be Clinton, Bush, or Perot, with probabilities equal to your best-informed estimates of who's going to win. Would you rather take your chances on door number one, or trade it for the sure thing of having Perot as the next president? Say yes, and you should approve Perot. Say no, and you shouldn't approve Perot.

It makes no difference whether Perot is your first choice, second choice, or tenth choice. It makes no difference how many other candidates you're voting for. All that matters is whether Perot is better than the outcome you can reasonably expect—whether it would be good news to turn on the TV and learn that he had won.

We rarely have a clear idea of the probabilities of the various candidates' winning. Instead we have polls. These usually allow us to identify the race's two front runners with confidence. A handy shortcut, close to optimal, is to approve the front runner you prefer; disapprove the front runner you like less; and approve any candidates you like *more* than your preferred front runner.

There is one important qualification with these rules. Pollsters must ask subjects which candidate(s) they intend to approve and then report candidate standings *by approval votes*. This makes sense. If approval voting were actually in use, opinion polls would naturally want to reflect what was likely to happen on Election Day.

To its proponents, approval voting is a uniquely honest way of voting. This claim may appear puzzling. The approval voter is restricted to a yes-or-no verdict. Politics is more nuanced than that!

Of course, the opportunity of saying a lot does not guarantee candor. Are long after-dinner speeches more honest than short ones? Sometimes it's a case of "ask me no questions, I'll tell you no lies."

With any system, a strategic voter divides the list of candidates into those she intends to help and those she intends to hurt. All approval voting asks of a strategic voter is, *Whom do you want to help?* There is no cause for a strategic voter to be dishonest about this.

A nice feature of approval voting is that no one betrays a favorite. The voter can always vote her conscience. Jackie loves Ralph Nader, will settle for Al Gore, and definitely doesn't want George W. Bush. She can cast an approval vote for Nader, confident that it will not boomerang and cause Bush to win instead of Gore.

In order to have any realistic chance of affecting the outcome, Jackie will also have to approve Gore as well. But she doesn't have to forgo voting for Nader, or to pretend she likes Gore better than Nader.

Approval voting thus appears to solve the problem of vote splitting simply and elegantly. What does the impossibility theorem have to say about *that*?

In the strictest sense, the answer is "nothing." The impossibility theorem deals only with ranked voting systems. Approval voting is a "rating" system where each candidate is given a score (of approval or disapproval) that is independent from the other candidates' scores. When voters are completely honest (as Arrow's proof assumes), approval voting meets all of Arrow's conditions.

You might think that this would have been a major selling point for approval voting. It wasn't. Few even articulated this fact.

The timing of Arrow's Nobel Prize, in 1972, probably affected the reception of approval voting. Like many Nobels, Arrow's was to some extent a lifetime achievement award. The Nobel proclamation mentions the impossibility theorem only incidentally as part of a litany of

Arrow's achievements in economic theory. The prize nonetheless had an outsize impact on the small community of voting theorists. Arrow's theorem "created this kind of aura," Warren D. Smith explained. "The fact that he did it, and the fact that they gave him the Nobel Prize" cemented the perception that the impossibility theorem was "the last word on the subject. Good voting systems don't exist. There's no such thing as a best voting system."

Besides, it was clear that approval voting wasn't "perfect," either. When people vote strategically, approval voting fails to meet independence of irrelevant alternatives (important because Arrow said it was important). You may well feel that the spirit, if not the letter, of Arrow's theorem applies.

Like the Borda count, approval voting has been discovered, forgotten, and rediscovered a number of times. The Serene Republic of Venice used approval voting from 1268 through 1789, the age of Venice's greatest economic and military power. When a doge (leader) was to be elected, an extravagant ritual selected forty-one patricians to serve as the *Quarantuno,* Venice's electoral college. The number forty-one was chosen to prevent a tie. These electors were confined to the Ducal Palace, eating dorm-style in the "Room of Four Doors" and sleeping in a hospital ward of a space—in their own beds, transported by servants from their palaces.

The details of the vote varied over five centuries of use. A typical procedure used numbered boxes, one for each candidate. Each box was divided into two partitions. The forty-one voters received one ball per candidate, placing it in the box's left partition for "si" (yes, approval, or thumbs-up) or the right partition for "no" (disapproval, thumbs-down). After all had voted, a youth recruited from the piazza opened the boxes. A candidate needed twenty-five "si" votes to win (61 percent approval) and of course had to have the *most* votes should more than one candidate meet that threshold. When no one got the required twenty-five votes, there was more debate and further round(s) of voting.

Venice was one of the most durable republics the world has seen. Its doges are remembered more for their portraits by Bellini and Titian than for the dirty politics that fills history books. Historian Robert Finlay concludes his *Politics in Renaissance Venice* (1980) with the assessment:

> The patrician republic gave Venice five hundred years of domestic peace and stability. Violence was kept from politics, electioneering and voting engendered collaboration and dedication, political behaviour was conventional and restrained, pervasive corruption made for civic concord. A commonplace, entirely unexceptional political life thus gave birth to the extravagant and hopeful notion that at least one society had transcended the difficulties and dangers inherited by other political communities. Not all republics have been so fortunate.

Venice used approval voting up until its conquest by Napoléon (who thus bears responsibility for quashing two allegedly brilliant voting schemes).

The Venetian example probably inspired the use of a similar system for electing popes from 1294 through 1621/1622. A mirror-image form of approval voting was used in the last days of the Soviet Union. Voters were given a slate of candidates and allowed to cross off any they *dis*approved. Today, approval voting is used by only one political body of note. The United Nations employs it to elect its secretary-general.

Could approval voting work in modern-day America? The system began getting wide attention after the 1983 publication of a book, *Approval Voting*, by Steven Brams and Peter Fishburn of Bell Labs. Brams and Fishburn argued that approval voting would not only prevent spoilers but also increase voter turnout and diminish negative campaigning. Brams did some legal research and concluded that approval voting does not violate U.S. state constitutions. It would require only a statute to put it into force.

In the 1980s, Brams launched a public campaign to get approval voting adopted. Brams is a soft-spoken man with the earnest quality of a sitcom father. More used to the intimate confines of a classroom, he became a minor public figure with his campaign, testifying before the legislatures of New York, New Hampshire, and Vermont; writing editorials; and appearing on *Good Morning America*. The press reaction was largely positive. Here was a voting system that solved the spoiler effect, promoted honesty, and perhaps freed voters from some of the more pernicious effects of parties and political consultants. To those who knew of Arrow's disconcerting theorem, approval voting offered a ray of hope.

"I was at a conference in Minnesota in 1984," mathematician Donald Saari recalled, "and I ran into Steve Brams. And Steve said, 'Don, with your new techniques, why don't you look at approval voting?'" Saari agreed to do so. "I knew I'd find flaws because with this method you find flaws in anything. But I also expected I'd find a lot of virtues. And in a couple of days I was discovering that approval voting was *horrible*. Very, very bad."

It took only a few days for Saari to conclude that approval voting was about the worst, most dangerous system ever invented.

TWELVE

Bad Santa

Donald Saari looks enough like Santa Claus to have played that role in twenty years of departmental holiday parties. Now in his sixties, he is to be sure a trim Santa, with Kris Kringle beard and neatly thinning white hair. An actor in his school days, Saari deftly punctuates his speech with theatrical emphasis. His surname is Finnish American, and he hails from a region of Michigan's upper peninsula so far north, he says, that its winter-weary residents used to seek relief by driving down south to Minneapolis.

To some of his colleagues, Saari is the bad Santa of voting theory. He is a natural gadfly with a particular talent for finding flaws in other people's ideas. This has embroiled him in a long, at times barely civil academic dispute. Steven Brams says that he and Saari have had to "agree to disagree" about approval voting.

I recently sat with Saari in his sun-filled office at UC Irvine as he explained how he became convinced that approval voting was one of the worst ideas ever conceived, and why he and Brams can't talk about it anymore. I began by mentioning one twist in the story that I'd already heard from Brams: once upon a time, Saari had *liked* approval voting.

"Oh, isn't that *funny!*" he said. "Yes, that was before I did any serious research."

Like many people in the field, Saari came to voting theory indirectly. In graduate school at Purdue he became absorbed in one of the most famous unsolved problems of astronomy, the "n-body problem." It is easy to calculate the orbit of the moon around the Earth, or the orbit of Mars around the sun. When there are just two objects involved, the laws of motion are simple. Add a third object, and things become chaotic. As Saari would later realize, voting too is simple with two candidates and extremely complicated with three or more.

While on the math faculty at Northwestern University, Saari followed Chicago politics and acquired a dark fascination with the city's political bosses. Voting was "a hobby, looked at on weekends and weeknights." Then Len Edwards at Northwestern "was telling me about Arrow's theorem, and I said, 'Ah, that can't possibly be true.'" Of course it was true. "Like an addiction, it took over. After a while I began to realize that this was my academic research area."

In November 1983, Northwestern needed to vote on a search committee for a new president. Saari was the chair of the math department. "They asked me what voting method we should have. I didn't know much about it, but I said, this thing called approval voting is very good."

He had read Steven Brams's and Peter Fishburn's publications on the subject. On Saari's recommendation, the faculty adopted approval voting. Soon afterward, the chair of the history department called Saari.

"Do you see that stupid method they're using?" the historian asked.

"I said, 'Sure. Let me hear *your* views on why it's bad.'"

The historian said that with approval voting, his department and the math department could together determine the committee. "They choose three, we choose three, we all vote for six, and we win."

Northwestern was using approval voting to elect a committee rather than a single official. You won't lose too much by ignoring that complication. Essentially, the historian was saying that the history and math departments should make a pact to vote alike in order to get something they both wanted. This would be like Goodell and Ottinger's supporters coming to an explicit agreement to approve each other's candidates, in order to defeat Buckley.

"I'll leave it to your imagination" whether we manipulated the election, Saari said, doing a jolly North Pole laugh.

He began to have doubts about approval voting. After the meeting with Brams in 1984, Saari investigated approval voting at length. The results were, as Saari judged them, appalling.

"Well, now there's a quandary," he told me. "A friend asked me to investigate something. Intellectually, you've got to report. But I don't have to have an article *just* on approval voting, do I?"

To soften the blow of his findings, Saari says, he embedded them in a survey of a larger class of voting systems. He submitted the paper to the journal *Public Choice*. The paper was then sent out to anonymous referees, who would naturally be experts on voting theory.

"Brams and Fishburn objected to the paper," Saari said. "One of them, I don't know which one. There were four referee reports, three praising it, and one of them says this was a horrible paper." The editor decided to publish Saari's paper with a dissenting commentary by Brams, Fishburn, and Samuel Merrill III.

Saari's article, cowritten with Jill Van Newenhizen, was titled "The Problem of Indeterminacy in Approval, Multiple, and Truncated Voting Systems." "We began our analysis of approval voting with the expectation that, in some sense, it is an improvement over most other systems," wrote Saari and Van Newenhizen. "But we found that it has several disturbing features that seem to make it worse than even the plurality voting system. Indeed, *these properties appear to be sufficiently bad to disqualify approval voting as a viable reform alternative*."

These words were mild compared with what was to come. Brams, Fishburn, and Merrill's rebuttal took issue with the "bizarre cases" in the Saari–Van Newenhizen article. The rebuttal was forwarded to

Saari and Van Newenhizen for a counter-rebuttal, and then back to Brams, Fishburn, and Merrill for a rebuttal to the counter-rebuttal. The testiness ratcheted upward with each iteration.

In the counter-rebuttal, Saari and Van Newenhizen asserted that "AV [approval voting] is much worse than our original essay implies." Approval voting "inherits the vices of all systems." "A more accurate title for AV is the Unsophisticated Voter System (UVS)." The authors used that abbreviation in the rest of the paper.

As the pièce de résistance, Saari and Van Newenhizen conceded that approval voting may have a place in the world, just not in the civilized world.

> It may make good sense to use the UVS, or AV, for a society newly experimenting with voting and democracy. But for any organization where the voters understand distinctions, the UVS is inappropriate . . . In our view this includes all "Western" as well as many "Third World" countries.

Saari's daughter was later a student of Brams's at NYU. One day Brams's class discussed approval voting. That night the daughter called Saari and asked incredulously, "Dad, did you ever write a paper called 'Is approval voting an unmitigated evil'?"

The answer was yes. Saari assured her that "Steve's a good person. He's absolutely wrong on this approval voting, but that is just one aspect of the man."

Saari and other critics of approval voting see at least three major problems. One is the fear that approval voters will mark their ballots casually or capriciously. Dubious judgments about who's "good enough" to approve could swing the outcome of an election.

I have already mentioned another problem, which must occur to everyone who hears about approval voting. The all-or-none nature of approval voting is a ham-handed way of characterizing politics and politicians. There might be cases where the "wrong" candidate is elected because voters couldn't express themselves properly.

A third problem is strategic voting. Approval voters are allowed to decide how to vote based on how they think other people will vote. Those other people will be voting based on how they think *you'll* be voting. It becomes a hall of mirrors. Who knows what will happen?

To understand these matters better, it helps to get some flavor of Saari's approach to voting. It is founded on symmetry. "The connection between mathematical symmetry and what is ethically right may be closer than has been recognized," Duncan Black wrote. He meant that our notions of fair play amount to statements of symmetry. A rich person and a poor one should be treated the same before the law; do unto others as you would have them do unto you. Democracy is a highly symmetrical enterprise. Every vote counts the same, no matter who cast it.

The symmetries of voting are hard to perceive in tables of election results. Over the years, Saari has devised geometric models of elections to render the symmetries visible. Take one of those rubber erasers in the form of a cube. Neatly slice off two opposite corners to form an eight-sided solid where every face is a triangle. This oddly endearing shape is one of Saari's electoral models. Mutilated cubes, dissected triangles, and n-dimensional polyhedra make visible the complexities of voting. In these models, each voter is a point in space, the position encoding the way in which that voter ranks the candidates.

Saari has used these models to catalog the paradoxes that can arise in voting and to ask what causes them. His answer is a "breakdown of symmetry." In order to be decisive, voting systems sometimes impose a choice that's not in the vote tallies. One of Saari's classroom examples is the not-so-uncommon case of a husband and wife, one Republican and one Democrat. "Hey, why do we bother to vote?" Max asks Maxine. "Our votes cancel each other out!"

They do in any race where the Republican and Democratic candidates are the only serious contenders. Husband and wife could just as well make a pact not to vote.

Here's a slightly trickier example, a three-way race. Max prefers Edwards to Roemer and Roemer to Duke. Maxine prefers Duke to Roemer and Roemer to Edwards—the exact opposite ranking. They are the only two voters. Which candidate should win?

You might say it's a two-way tie. Max will vote for Edwards, and Maxine will vote for Duke. Roemer will get no votes. This is the way the plurality vote works.

Saari's answer is that it should be a *three-way* tie between all three candidates. Since Max's and Maxine's views are the exact opposite, they ought to cancel each other out completely. Their equal and opposite rankings ought not to favor *any* of the three candidates. Saari calls this principle "reversal symmetry."

You may or may not agree. Since most of us have experience with plurality voting only, it may take some thought to appreciate Saari's point. Look at the Borda count, a system that does guarantee reversal symmetry. Max's ranking gives two points to Edwards, one to Roemer, and none to Duke. Maxine's Borda ballot gives no points to Edwards, one to Roemer, and two to Duke. Overall, each candidate gets two points. Middle candidate Roemer does just as well as love-'em-or-hate-'em candidates Edwards and Duke.

Does the approval vote observe reversal symmetry? No, says Saari. Max will certainly approve Edwards, and Maxine will approve Duke. It is impossible to say, from the rankings alone, whether Max and Maxine will approve their middle choice, Roemer. Roemer might get no approval votes, or one, or two. That makes a big difference in this two-voter election. It's possible that Roemer could get two votes and win. It's also possible to have a three-way tie among all the candidates, or a two-way tie between Edwards and Duke. Almost any outcome is possible, even when the voters' rankings are known. This is a point well illustrated in Saari's geometric diagrams. With ranked voting systems, an election's outcome is a single point in space. With approval voting, the point bloats into a polygon or polyhedron, signifying that a whole range of outcomes is possible.

Saari calls this "indeterminacy," meaning that the voters' rankings of candidates do not suffice to determine the winner. The winner also depends on these fuzzy judgment calls about who's "good enough" to approve.

No one knows how real approval voters will decide, Saari maintains. Even the system's proponents have sent mixed messages about how they think people should, would, or could vote. "While the behavioral assumptions may sound nice over a cup of coffee, they may not have anything to do with how people behave," Saari says. "And I find that to be very dangerous."

Approval voting is about good guys and bad guys, with no shades of gray. Saari and Van Newenhizen offer this example of how that can go awry. There are 10,000 voters and three candidates, A, B, and C. Candidate A is the clear favorite of 9,999 of the 10,000 voters. These people all believe that A is superb, B is mediocre, and C would be a disaster.

The lone oddball voter has the exact opposite preferences. He loves C, hates A—and again judges B to be Mr. Mediocre.

With plurality voting, A would win, 9,999 to 0 (for B) to 1 (for C). Candidate A would also sweep a Condorcet, Borda, or instant-runoff vote. No surprise there: The voters are practically unanimous! How can A *not* win?

The answer is, by using approval voting. It is possible, Saari and Van Newenhizen point out, that the 9,999 A supporters will all cast approval votes for B because he's at least okay and a lot better than that dreadful C. It is also possible that the lone C supporter will cast a vote for B as well as C.

The votes will then total 9,999 for A and 1 for C—and 10,000 for B. Candidate B is elected *unanimously*.

That's ridiculous. Everyone except one "nut" wants A. Everyone *in-*

cluding the nut agrees that B is only mediocre. "Although excellence is the clear choice of these voters," Saari and Van Newenhizen wrote, "AV selects mediocrity."

The underlying problem, as Saari and Van Newenhizen diagnose it, is that *all* of B's 10,000 votes are really "second-place" votes. They shouldn't count as much as A's 9,999 first-place votes. In approval voting, they do.

"Indeed, these problems are sufficiently serious [for us] to wonder whether we should recall AV from the public market, to await a more careful examination," Saari and Van Newenhizen wrote. "We have a growing suspicion that AV will turn out to be an attractive idea that just did not pan out."

Brams, Fishburn, and Merrill did not directly rebut this example in their accompanying article. The 9,999-voters scenario occurs in Saari and Van Newenhizen's rebuttal to a rebuttal, and in Brams and company's rebuttal to *that* (a single paragraph that reads as if it had been written with gritted teeth), the authors limit themselves to repeating, very slowly, what they have already said.

Mr. Mediocre was not about to go away. He was about to run for president of the United States.

In the early days of electricity, Thomas Edison and George Westinghouse fought bitterly over the virtues of direct and alternating current. Edison found Westinghouse's advocacy of alternating current misguided, irritating, and unprofitable—for Edison's new company, General Electric, was promoting direct current. In the interest of an informed public, Edison arranged demonstrations in which a dog was placed on a metal plate charged with direct current. The dog was unharmed. Then Edison showed the same dog on alternating current. It was instantly electrocuted. In the war over approval voting, "President Perot" is that dog.

"Let me give you a real-world example I've used with Steve Brams

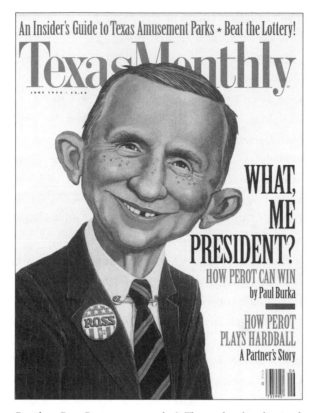

An Insider's Guide to Texas Amusement Parks ⋆ Beat the Lottery!

Texas Monthly

WHAT, ME PRESIDENT?

HOW PEROT CAN WIN
by Paul Burka

HOW PEROT
PLAYS HARDBALL
A Partner's Story

President Ross Perot: scary or what? The media elite dismissed Perot's candidacy as an intelligence test that twenty million American voters had flunked. The very *possibility* of electing Perot became a serious charge in the debate over approval voting. *(Texas Monthly)*

in the room," Saari said to me. "Let's look back at the Clinton/Perot/Father Bush election. Now let's suppose that your preferences were Clinton > Bush > Perot. How many would you vote for, one or two? You're not going to vote for two because you know that Bush or Clinton is going to win. You vote for both, and you're throwing away your vote. And if you [prefer] Bush > Clinton > Perot, you're not going to vote for Clinton. And the Perot voters, trying to make their point, are going to vote only for Perot. So the only people with some rational motivation to vote for two candidates would be those who had Perot ranked second. In that case, we would have had President Perot."

Ross Perot has become the living, breathing embodiment of Saari and Van Newenhizen's "mediocre" bogeyman. Saari may not have been first to accord Perot this dubious honor. In 1994 Brams and Samuel Merrill III published "Would Ross Perot Have Won the 1992 Presidential Election Under Approval Voting?" Their answer was an emphatic no. Perot likely would have received twice as many votes under approval voting as he did, they claim, but he still would have come in third place, behind Bush. Despite the article's mild, scholarly tone, the authors do not appear to hold a high opinion of the "authoritarian and conspiratorial (his enemies would say paranoiac)" Perot.

This provoked a 2001 article by Alexander Tabarrok, who is firmly in the Saari camp on approval voting. Tabarrok charges (italics his) that *"Clinton could have come in last and Perot first under approval voting."*

Perot embodies Saari's worst nightmare of approval voting, that an unqualified candidate in the middle of the political spectrum could get enough approval votes to win. The 1992 presidential race differed from Saari and Van Newenhizen's original example in that the lopsided 9,999-to-1 majority was replaced by a nearly even split between Clinton and Bush. The point of similarity is that a lot of Clinton and Bush supporters probably would have rated Perot second out of three.

It is easy to see that Perot could have won with approval voting *if* everyone who ranked him second had approved him *and* no one who ranked Clinton or Bush second had approved them. Perot could potentially have won by an approval-vote landslide, not just a single vote. Tabarrok concedes that such scenarios are unlikely, but he finds the possibility alarming nonetheless.

"Indeterminacy, like inconsistency, may sound disconcerting, even loathsome," Brams, Fishburn, and Merrill write. They then argue that indeterminacy is a good thing, a badge of how responsive approval voting is to the nuances of voter opinion.

They believe that voters would have used intensity of feelings ("cardinal utilities") to decide whether to approve Perot. Voters who liked Perot almost as much as their first choice would have approved him. Voters who thought Perot unqualified would *not* have approved him. The Perot vote becomes just what it ought to be, a referendum on whether it's a good idea for Ross Perot to be president of the United States. Perot *could* win—in a world in which he had near-universal appeal and the Clinton and Bush people were polarized into mutually hating camps. And Perot could lose, if people saw him as egotistical, paranoid, and scary.

"President Perot" is the flip side of Buddy Roemer. Both were moderates sandwiched between a pair of more ideologically extreme candidates. We want a system that doesn't *automatically* exclude such candidates from winning. We also want a system that doesn't make it easy for any goof who calls himself a moderate to win. Roemer was running against two of the most character-challenged opponents in his state's history. Perot, on the other hand, looked like a dicey choice next to his more polished competition. With approval voting, the voters make judgment calls about which middle choices are good enough to approve. Brams takes the position that voters can do that just fine. Saari fears they will fail at it. To some extent, the math and the diagrams are ways of talking around more and less optimistic views of the human condition.

Most have heard the familiar advice on buying kitchen cabinets. Have the cabinetmaker come out and take measurements. Then it's *his* responsibility to make sure the cabinets fit. The not-so-good way to buy cabinets is for the homeowner to measure and give the cabinetmaker the measurements. Then, if the cabinets don't fit, it's the homeowner's fault.

Voting can also be broken into two parts. There's a measurement part, where voters get their feelings down on ballots, and a tallying part, where votes are counted. Saari holds approval voting responsible for both parts of voting. That makes just as much sense here as it does with kitchen cabinets. Saari is saying that, should anything go wrong with either part of approval voting, we should hold the voting system accountable.

To compare approval voting to other schemes, you need to hold those other systems responsible for getting the complete job done. Voters also exercise a great deal of freedom in marking ranked ballots. Asked to rank obscure candidates, a voter may do so arbitrarily or simply leave those candidates unranked (a "truncated ballot"). Voters may purposely misrepresent their rankings for strategic gain. Here, too, small changes in the ballots can make big, "indeterminate" differences in the final outcome.

Saari takes voters' rankings of candidates as a given, like measurements submitted to a cabinetmaker. (Any errors are the customer's responsibility!) This is the working assumption of Arrow's proof, followed by most of the subsequent literature on social choice. It is only a useful fiction, though. You cannot look inside every voter's head and find a little list ranking the candidates. Rankings do not exist until the voter invests some thought into determining them. (The same goes for approval choices, of course.) The rankings on ballots are not necessarily honest ones.

What's truly a "given" is the voters. A system succeeds or fails by how well it works with people the way they are. Whether average citizens are better able to fill out a ranked or approval ballot is an important issue little addressed.

Much of the debate boils down to one oft-repeated standoff. If lots of voters approve Perot, Saari says, Perot will win, and that proves what a lousy system approval voting is. No, Brams and Weber counter, if lots of voters approve Perot, that proves how much the voters like Perot. This rebuttal can sound a little like "wherever you go, there you are." Of course, "wherever you go, there you are" happens to be true.

———

To many, the most worrisome thing about approval voting is the strategy issue. In deciding whether to approve "middle" choices, the approval voter is allowed to consider how others will vote. The analysis becomes complexly self-referential. Saari quipped that the approval voter has to be strategic in order to be sincere. It wasn't just Saari who thought so. This bothered Robert Weber, one of the system's inventors. "The primary challenge one could raise to approval voting was that, in the presence of polls, it might fall apart," Weber said.

In our intensely polled age, the voter is a chameleon on a mirror. Polls sample public opinion, and then the published results *change* that opinion. Poll numbers shift candidates' views and the spin their campaign places on them. The process of polling and reacting to polls continues until the final poll on Election Day.

Strategic concerns are not unique to approval voting. With the plurality vote, people flock to or desert a candidate based on changing perceptions of the candidate's chances of winning. This is the familiar "bandwagon effect." In the 1998 race for Minnesota governor, Democrat Skip Humphrey had an early lead over Republican Norm Coleman. The Humphrey people insisted on including Reform Party candidate Jesse Ventura in the debates with Coleman. Democratic advisors believed that Ventura's fiscally conservative stance would take votes away from the Republican. Even the lifestyle targeting was right. Ventura, a former TV wrestler and Navy SEAL, connected with hunters, sportsmen, and gun owners, who are usually Republican. Therefore, anything that legitimized Ventura as a serious contender was bad for Coleman and good for Humphrey. It didn't work out that way. As more voters concluded that Ventura had a real chance, more decided they were willing to vote for him. Ventura won the election (with a slim 37 percent of the vote). It's believed that he took more votes from Humphrey than from Coleman.

Weber was concerned that some of the elections he had viewed as paradigms of approval voting's benefits could be problematic. In the

1970 New York Senate race, the state's liberal majority had reason to fear that vote splitting would lead to a victory for a conservative. The liberals could have prevented this outcome by casting approval votes for both of the liberal candidates, Goodell and Ottinger. Fine. Then a poll is taken. It reports that Goodell and Ottinger are way ahead because most of the liberal voters are approving both. It's a virtual tie between the two.

Hearing that, Joe Liberal goes into the voting booth. "I'm a Democrat, and I prefer Ottinger," he thinks. "If I approve him *and* Goodell, I'm wasting my vote. What I should do is to vote just for Ottinger. That will increase the chance that Ottinger rather than Goodell will win. I don't have to worry about Buckley. The polls say he's way behind."

If *all* the liberals vote just for their favorite, Buckley will win!

This type of paradox is familiar to game theorists. It is similar to a "prisoner's dilemma," the all-too-common situation where narrow self-interest subverts the common good. Weber aired these concerns at a lunchtime seminar at Northwestern's Kellogg School of Management. One of those present, Roger B. Myerson, saw a clever way of treating the problem. Myerson and Weber ended up collaborating on a 1993 article, "A Theory of Voting Equilibria." In Weber's words, "This is the paper that, I believe, makes the strongest theoretical case for approval voting."

The publication invokes another idea with roots in the cold war, the "Nash equilibrium." As a RAND consultant, mathematician John Nash (of *A Beautiful Mind* fame) proposed a particular kind of solution to the "games" of nuclear deterrence or voting or anything else. A Nash equilibrium is an outcome where everyone is satisfied with his or her decision, *given what everyone else did*. No one has any regrets about doing what he did.

In the case of voting, this means that all the voters are happy with the way they voted (though not necessarily happy with the election's outcome). No one would choose to change the way he voted, if given the chance, after learning how everyone else voted.

Spoilers and vote splitting lead to outcomes that are *not* Nash equilibria. If I cast a plurality vote for Nader, thinking that Gore is sure to win, and then Bush wins because of my vote and I kick myself for not having voted for Gore, my vote would *not* be part of a Nash equilibrium.

It goes without saying that 99-plus percent of voters have never heard of a Nash equilibrium. No matter; opinion polls tend to herd voters into equilibrium outcomes. What worries Saari is roughly this. I go into the voting booth believing that the race is between Bill Clinton and George H. W. Bush. I cast an approval vote for whichever front runner I like better. Then there's Perot. Something about the little guy appeals to me. Maybe I want to protest inside-the-Beltway thinking by voting for Perot. Since Perot has no chance whatsoever of winning, I vote for him along with my favorite. So do millions of other voters, and what the hey—Perot wins?!

Saari implies that Perot's election would come as a complete surprise. That is almost impossible with polls. Let's say that an early poll showed that Perot is leading in approval votes. Clinton is second, and Bush is third. That would be a wake-up call for everyone intending to approve Perot. *Be very, very sure that President Perot is what you want.*

Not everyone changes his or her mind based on a poll. Not everyone even learns of a given poll. But over many polling and reporting and re-assessing cycles, the electorate tends to zero in on a Nash equilibrium. By Election Day, voters have a reasonably accurate picture of how the vote is going to go and what they should do to best further their own interests. There are no bad surprises, and no "President Perot"—unless that is what the voters, upon careful reflection, truly want.

Many of Saari's horrible examples (such as the 9,999 voters story) are cast from the same mold. They entail large fractions of the electorate voting for *both* front runners (front runners in the approval vote, of course). The implausibility of this is concealed by the fact that we tend to think of polls as giving people's first-place choices. That is what polls do today because only first-place choices count with the plurality vote. Were it approval votes that counted, polls would report intended approval votes. "President Perot" would not come out of nowhere.

A similar analysis bears on Saari's tale of the "manipulated" committee election at Northwestern. The history and math departments made a pact to approve each other's candidates. Isn't it bad that approval voting makes such things possible?

Look at it this way. The only pacts that make sense are those in the mutual interest of both parties. I may say I'll approve your candidate *if* you approve mine. With a secret ballot, you'll never *know* whether I did. A pact is credible only when both sides can assure themselves that no one has an incentive to violate the pact—in other words, when it's a Nash equilibrium. In that case, you don't need a pact. Everyone can be expected to vote in his own best interests anyway.

Myerson and Weber treat a hypothetical race similar to Buckley v. Goodell v. Ottinger. Preelection polls would help voters decide which of the two "clone" candidates is stronger. Say it was Ottinger. The Nash equilibrium outcome would then be for Ottinger's supporters to approve *only* Ottinger, for Goodell's supporters to approve both Goodell *and* Ottinger, and for Buckley's supporters to approve Buckley alone. Ottinger would get about 60 percent approval vote, easily beating Buckley's 40 percent or so, and also beating Goodell.

This means that the Goodell people are sacrificing their own candidate's chances in order to help Ottinger. Ottinger's people are *not* returning the favor. Why are the Goodell people being so noble? Because they don't have any better option, given the way the other people are voting. Should many Goodell supporters try to single-vote for Goodell, it would switch the outcome from Ottinger to Buckley, *not* to Goodell. They are better off with Ottinger.

Myerson and Weber conclude that strategic approval voters should often vote only for their favorite (a practice called "bullet voting"). This has long been a point of confusion. There is a widespread misconception that it is somehow "cheating" to cast an approval vote for one candidate only. Saari tells a couple of stories on this theme. Pennsylvania's

Democratic State Committee tried using approval voting for a straw vote of presidential contenders in 1983. In a letter to Saari, former North Carolina governor Terry Sanford reported, "The great weakness, it seemed to me, was that most voters . . . are inclined to cheat a little and 'single shot' if it suits their purpose, which it generally does. I was present for the Pennsylvania straw vote, helped explain it, and was not surprised when very few who voted for [candidate A] voted for anyone else, although surely there were other acceptable candidates."

Sanford evidently felt that every "acceptable" candidate is entitled to your approval vote. And it was Sanford who helped coach the delegates on how to fill out an approval ballot. It's telling what happened. The delegates ignored Sanford's explanation and voted strategically.

Steven Brams convinced the Society for Social Choice and Welfare to use approval voting in an election. Saari gets the laugh out of this tale, so let him tell it:

"They had three excellent candidates. Any one of the three would have made an excellent president. Now, I told some of the people that I thought that since there were three solid candidates, that people would vote strategically. How do you vote strategically? Strategically, you're going to vote for one candidate rather than two. And I made the outrageous statement that 60 percent of the voters would vote for one candidate. Sixty percent, that's a high number. I was wrong . . . Steve Brams is the *only* person who voted for two people. Everyone else voted for one, to be strategic."

Weber's position is that casting multiple votes is a *feature* of approval voting, like the airbags in your car are a feature. That doesn't mean that the airbags have to deploy every time you run to the mall. You don't have to cast multiple votes in every race. In a typical American election with two major candidates, most Republicans and Democrats would probably vote exactly the way they do now, for their party's candidate and no one else. It would be Greens, Libertarians, Constitutions, and other minor-party supporters who would have reason to vote for more than one candidate.

No one knows with certainty how masses of real-world, twenty-first-century approval voters will act. Myerson and Weber have shown that approval voting works well when voters are the perfect Machiavellians of game theory. That is an important distinction, for other voting systems are seriously compromised by strategic voters. However, no one expects all voters to be so calculating, or for all elections to be Nash equilibria. Many voters are altruistic, uninformed, misinformed, or apathetic. The polls necessary for strategic calculations can be wrong. Atwater-style smear campaigns are often launched immediately before an election, to provoke an emotional response unmediated by polls, journalism, second thoughts, or a calm reappraisal of the evidence.

Some real-world cases suggest that Saari's concerns are not overblown. One of the most interesting is known as "Burr's dilemma." In America's first few presidential elections, the electoral college used a system that was somewhat like approval voting. Each elector was required to vote for exactly two of the candidates. The candidate with the most votes became president *provided he had a majority*. The runner-up became vice president.

In 1800 the Democratic-Republican Party's vote was split between two candidates of intense ambition and roughly equal appeal, Aaron Burr and Thomas Jefferson. The party needed to rally behind one in order to achieve a majority. Otherwise, the election would have been decided by the House of Representatives, controlled by the rival Federalist Party. The Democratic-Republican Party failed to settle on a "stronger" candidate. The electoral vote was tied with seventy-three votes for Burr *and* for Jefferson. (Jefferson eventually won in the House of Representatives, on the thirty-sixth ballot.) It may not be so easy for people to arrive at strategically optimal outcomes, even when they have strong incentive to do so.

THIRTEEN

Last Man Standing

In 1979 Orange County, California, named its suburban airport after the recently deceased Western movie star John Wayne. Three years later, the facility dedicated a larger-than-life bronze statue of "The Duke." The bronze Wayne now saunters past a Dodge City of car-rental stands. His eyes stare down an imaginary adversary as his right hand eases back toward his pistol, a careful replica of an 1873 Colt .45.

Donald Saari often sees the Wayne statue when he travels to conferences on voting theory. For Saari, the statue is an ambiguous symbol, not of American machismo but of some very wrong ideas about voting. Or maybe the two are related. "That's the Condorcet winner!" Saari told me. "It's part of our culture to believe the best duelist should be the best. 'I'll take on anyone at all—gotcha! I'll be the last man standing!' It takes a while to understand that there's more subtle issues, that we're throwing away valuable, *valuable* information."

In March 2001, Saari's travels took him to San Antonio, home of the Alamo, for the meeting of the Public Choice Society. The still-recent victory of Texans Bush and Rove was much on the minds of the assembled group. A highlight of the conference was dual (and dueling) presentations by Donald Saari and Kenneth Arrow. Both speakers discussed independence of irrelevant alternatives. Arrow had no trouble defending the intuitive reasonableness of his condition. A race between A [Gore] and B [Bush] should not be decided by C [Nader]. This was the heart of Condorcet's philosophy of voting. Saari challenged this. He maintained that both independence of irrelevant alternatives and Condorcet voting were overrated concepts. He extolled the properties of the Borda count—a system that many, if not most, in attendance regarded as absurdly impractical. One of those there, Iain McLean, characterized the meeting as a "dialog of the deaf."

You would have to be deaf not to hear Saari loud and clear on the evils of Condorcet voting. "I find the Condorcet winner to be a lousy concept full of dangers," he wrote with characteristic candor. "Pairwise voting is a mess!"

These are boom times for Condorcet voting. For two centuries, no one used Condorcet's system because it was too time-consuming to count ballots. Now software can tally electronic votes in nanoseconds. The Linux operating system deserves much credit for the revival of Condorcet voting. Linux is the collective work of hundreds of opinionated contributors who rarely meet face to face. The several Linux organizations have styled themselves as global-village nation-states with "constitutions," "social contracts," and democratically elected leaders. There are often many candidates for a leadership post, and there are no political parties to vet them. The Linux community appreciated that plurality voting is particularly troublesome under these conditions. In that watershed year 2000, the Debian Project, one of the Linux groups, commissioned a study to determine the best system to use for its internal voting. Three years later, Debian adopted a form of Condorcet voting.

The voters fill out a ranked ballot. The software then conducts virtual two-way matches. It essentially asks, if Gore and Bush were the only two candidates running, who would win? It determines the answer by checking how many ballots have Gore ranked higher than Bush and vice versa. The software runs through every possible two-way match-up, even seemingly pointless ones like Nader v. Bush or Buchanan v. Browne. With luck, one candidate beats all others in two-way matches. This candidate is the winner.

Otherwise, there's more work to do. When there is no Condorcet winner, there must be a scissors-paper-stone cycle. A tiebreaker method is used to decide which candidate wins. The one used by Debian was devised by German theorist Markus Schulze in 1997. It often goes by a name that only a coder could love: cloneproof Schwartz sequential dropping. That's CSSD for short. ("Schwartz" refers to another social choice theorist, Thomas Schwartz.)

Condorcet voting, often the CSSD variety, has been widely adopted by other online communities. Among them is the online reference Wikipedia, which uses approval voting as well. Wikipedia founders Larry Sanger and Jimmy Wales dealt with issues that do not exist as acutely with Linux. A Linux contributor has to know how to write code. A Wikipedia contributor can be totally ignorant. "Trolls" is the term for Wikipedia contributors who can't accept criticism and keep reversing edits and reposting articles that others have deleted. In some ways, Wikipedia is a scary, *Animal Farm* vision of democracy gone feral.

In May 2005, Wikipedia contributors debated the etiquette for supplying formal titles in biographical entries. Do you say *Her Majesty* Queen Elizabeth II or *Dear Leader* Kim Jong Il? This is a style-manual issue that another organization might settle by, well, looking it up in a style manual. Wikipedia voted. They had five written-by-committee ballot options.

1. Yes. As a matter of Wikipedia policy, in all cases where a formal style is known, it must be used to begin the biographical article.

2. Yes, with exceptions. In certain cases of controversy, the formal style may be provided in the body of the article after the name is provided.
3. No. The formal style of address should always be provided in the introductory paragraph of the article, but only after the name is provided, and not otherwise prefixed.
4. No, but we should follow a different convention than that prescribed in Alternative 3.
5. None of the above.

If you can understand these choices at first reading, you're way ahead of most people. The Wikipedia voters had to not only understand the options but also rank them in order of preference. Seventy-three people did that. None of the five options was a Condorcet winner, it turned out. There was a cycle where option 3 beat 1, 1 beat 4, and 4 beat 3. CSSD kicked into tiebreaker mode and declared option 3 the winner.

The archived postmortem discussion is laced with the sarcasm endemic to online discourse. ("Forgive me for having a 'personal project' to improve Wikipedia. Would you prefer if I delegated this issue to a committee comprised of you and jguk? You can have a CSSD vote on it.") A recurring complaint was that partisans of "experimental" voting systems were trying to foist them on the Wikipedia community in order to prove that they worked. "This is not the purpose of WP," wrote one contributor, "and we should not encourage the development of ever more complicated and ever more theoretical voting methods."

Gripes aside, online projects *have* become de facto proving grounds for new voting systems. Condorcet voting is starting to make the transition from cyberspace to the so-called real world. Facilitating this is the Condorcet Internet Voting Service (www.cs.cornell.edu/andru/civs.html), created by Andrew Myers of Cornell's computer science department. This is a free site allowing any group or organization to hold a Condorcet vote. It doesn't have to be "important." A third-grade class can vote on names for the class hamster. All that's required is an e-mail address for each voter.

In 2002, Washington state representative Toby Nixon began pushing for Condorcet voting in state elections. There are growing networks of Condorcet supporters fretting over issues such as the system's gallic name. (You supposedly lose red staters at the first hint of French.) Names such as "true majority voting" and "instant round-robin voting" have been proposed as better tailored to the American market.

Maybe the biggest hitch with Condorcet voting is the simplicity issue. Condorcet supporters talk up the populist appeal of the John Wayne, last-man-standing premise. Soccer moms and NASCAR dads will nod their heads to that. The thing is, it's impossible to explain Condorcet voting any further without talking about cycles and "beat-paths" and "cloneproof Schwartz sequential dropping." This is where the android's mask falls off and it's all wires and microchips inside. Non-Ph.D.s run screaming for the exits. So far, Condorcet voting has tended to appeal to the kind of people who can write Javascript code for it.

One of those people is Ka-Ping Yee. Yee is a software engineer, Berkeley computer science grad student, and former IBM fellow. The 2004 presidential election got Yee interested in voting. He knew that the Help America Vote Act, passed after the Florida vote-counting debacle in 2000, mandated a phase-in of electronic voting machines. As a specialist in computer security and interface design, Yee found this premature. The machines were running Microsoft Windows CE, a consumer operating system that was vastly more complicated (and buggy) than needed for voting. Any public-minded citizen wanting to verify the security of Windows was out of luck. Microsoft wouldn't release the code. The voting machines did not print paper receipts as backup. When a machine crashed, votes might be lost. Worse, there was no way of telling *whether* votes had been lost. This provided an easy way to "lose" votes someone didn't want counted. Yee believes there were "suspicious numbers" in some areas of the 2004 counts.

Yee read up on Arrow's theorem and on voting systems. He became particularly enthusiastic about approval voting. Resolving to act locally, he introduced a motion to use approval voting at his Berkeley residence, Kingman Hall. Kingman had semiannual elections for house manager and half a dozen other posts. Yee's motion was put to a vote and failed to get the needed two-thirds majority.

After the motion failed, several residents asked Yee about Condorcet voting, a system he had also mentioned. The Kingman residents *liked* the idea of ranking choices. Yee was mildly surprised that the more complicated system had more traction than the simpler one. But he thought Condorcet voting was a good idea, too. A motion to adopt it at Kingman was presented, and it passed in April 2005.

Yee wrote the software used to tally the ballots. When I spoke with him, two elections had been held with the new system. Kingman Hall's residents take pride in what they see as a particularly enlightened form of voting. And according to Donald Saari, they are woefully mistaken.

What's so bad about Condorcet voting? Well, like all systems, it can be manipulated. The Wikipedia vote on formal titles "suggests to me that it is, indeed, possible to 'game' Condorcet given the peculiarities of voting on Wikipedia," wrote contributor TreyHarris. "You can't make it more likely for your preferred choice to *win* by voting insincerely. But when you can see everyone else's vote and change your vote, and you see your preferred option is losing, you *may* be able to vote in such a way as to make a Condorcet cycle more likely."

This is how "burying" works with Condorcet voting. Dropping your favorites' rival to the bottom of the list can't hurt him any more in the crucial two-way matchup with your favorite. Sometimes, however, it prevents the rival from being a Condorcet winner. This may work to your advantage. (It's especially easy to do in Wikipedia, which lets voters change their votes *after* seeing posted interim results.)

Burying is most likely to work in a race with three or more strong contenders, such as Edwards v. Roemer v. Duke. Suppose that a Condorcet system had been used in Louisiana and that you were an Edwards supporter. You know Edwards is going to lose because the polls say Roemer is the Condorcet winner. Nothing you can do will make Edwards the Condorcet winner. (You're already ranking him number one.) You can sabotage Roemer's shot at being the Condorcet winner by ranking him last, under Duke. Provided enough Edwards supporters do this, Duke will beat Roemer. He will have the sincere support of his own followers and the fake support of many of Edwards's followers.

That will create a cycle. Roemer beats Edwards, Edwards beats Duke, and Duke beats Roemer. What happens next depends on the rule used for breaking a cycle. Burying would be most attractive if Edwards's supporters could predict that Edwards would be declared the winner of a Roemer-Edwards-Duke cycle. Failing that, burying is a way of getting a second spin when your favorite is sure to lose otherwise. By manipulating the vote, Edwards's supporters might succeed in electing him (in which case they'd be better off), electing Roemer (in which case they're no worse off), or electing Duke (then they would be worse off).

This tactic would have been a poor gamble for most of Edwin Edwards's supporters in 1991. In other cases, the gamble could be worth it. Had Edwards's supporters believed that Roemer was virtually as "bad" as Duke, they would have had little to lose by manipulating the vote.

There are problems even with honest Condorcet voting. Donald Saari discovered that sometimes the "wrong" candidate is the Condorcet winner.

Suppose that the 1992 presidential election had asked voters to rank the candidates, and the results looked like this:

Clinton > Bush > Perot (thirty million voters)
Bush > Perot > Clinton (thirty million)
Perot > Clinton > Bush (thirty million)

These preferences create a perfectly symmetrical, scissors-paper-stone cycle. Everyone beats someone else by the same 60-million to 30-million landslide. It would be ridiculous to say that *any* of the three candidates deserves to win over the other two. Agreed?

Saari therefore says that all these votes should cancel one another out. Now suppose a recount turns up one additional ballot marked "Bush > Perot > Clinton." This breaks the deadlock. Bush is now the logical winner.

He is, but he wouldn't be a Condorcet winner. Clinton still beats Bush 60 million to 30,000,001. The "spin" of the massive Condorcet cycle overwhelms the new, uncancelled ballot.

It can get worse. Suppose that instead of one extra ballot, we add thirty-five million new ballots, looking like this:

Bush > Clinton > Perot (twenty million)
Clinton > Bush > Perot (fifteen million)

These additional ballots favor Bush by a wide margin. Bush obviously ought to win. When you add the new ballots to the old, you get this:

Clinton > Bush > Perot (forty-five million)
Bush > Perot > Clinton (thirty million)
Perot > Clinton > Bush (thirty million)
Bush > Clinton > Perot (twenty million)

Clinton *still* beats Bush. (Seventy-five million ballots rank Clinton higher than Bush, versus fifty million ranking Bush higher than Clinton.) And now Clinton beats Perot (sixty-five million to sixty million) because *all* the new ballots rank Clinton above Perot. Clinton is the last man standing, the Condorcet winner. But he doesn't deserve to win.

This example can be criticized as unrealistic. It requires that much of the electorate be locked in an "invisible" cycle, and we have reason to believe that cyclical preferences are rare in the real world. Saari's demonstration nonetheless takes much of the luster off of Condorcet voting. For two centuries, almost everyone thought of the Condorcet winner as a gold standard. Common sense tells us that a candidate who beats every rival ought to win. Well, here's another case where common sense is wrong. There is not even an apparent cycle to warn us that something funny might be going on.

Saari is one of the few defenders of the Borda count. He knows that many find his affection for Borda odd. "Manipulative behavior is important," he concedes in his 1995 book, *Basic Geometry of Voting*, "but it must never be the deciding factor in choosing a system. As an analogy, we can prevent 'carjacking' by driving a beat up, rusted, uncomfortable automobile wildly belching smoke, but few people do so." Because all voting systems can be manipulated, "*all procedures join the BC in this hall of shame.*"

It is hard to pin down Saari on whether he is proposing that the Borda count actually be used in public elections. "I'm not interested in advocating one system over another," he said, adding, "If people ask me which one's the best, I will tell them, from a mathematical perspective." He does report that committee elections in his own academic department have used the Borda count successfully. One of his tales concerns a 1991 talk he gave to a class of fourth-graders in Pittsburgh, as part of Mathematics Awareness Week. He posed the problem of a group of children having to decide what TV show to watch. To his surprise, the children instantly grasped the unfairness of a plurality vote. They gravitated to a Borda count as the fairest way of deciding. "Kids wanted to write Congress on why their voting procedure was wrong," Saari recalls.

Unlike Brams or some Condorcet supporters, Saari has not launched a public campaign to promote Borda count elections. He said that this would be premature. "I think the field is maturing fairly rapidly, and five to ten years from now might be the best time" to consider a change in American elections.

What about the idea that the Borda count is absurdly easy to manipulate?

"I thought for sure [this idea] was correct," Saari said. "In fact, I tried to prove it. To my surprise, the Borda count turned out to be the *least* manipulatable system."

This is where some colleagues heave a deep sigh. Saari's claim is true in the way that he chooses to define it. To manipulate a vote, you need a near tie where just a few votes can change the outcome. "The Borda count, because of its symmetry, has the least surface area where you can change from one outcome to another," Saari said. "It's highly counterintuitive, against standard belief."

Oxford political scientist Iain McLean prefers to put things this way: The Borda count is "the easiest to manipulate of all ranking rules."

In McLean's view, large fractions of the electorate will be tempted to manipulate virtually every Borda count election. The same simple trick works in every close election. (Democrats, rank the Republicans last! Republicans, rank the Democrats last!) This is what Laplace and Napoléon were concerned about; what happened in Kiribati and with the sportswriters in the 2004 AP poll.

Saari counters that this large-scale manipulation is unlikely to occur because it requires three things: First, it demands "wide-spread prior knowledge of 'who are the real competitors.'" Second, it requires a "coordinator to ensure that the correct number of voters vote strategically." Otherwise, the fringe candidate(s) you're using as pawns might actually win. Third, there has to be a "way to impose discipline so that the designated strategic voters obediently carry out the planned action."

Saari's critics say that "wide-spread prior knowledge" of the front runners is easy to come by. It's in the news, right? Formal "coordinators" and "discipline" might not be necessary. It's probably safe to assume that only a minority of voters would manipulate. That could be enough to tip a close election.

In 2000, everyone knew it was a tight contest between Bush and Gore. With a Borda count, Bush voters would have been tempted to rank Gore last, under Nader. Would they have been worried that Nader would win? Not likely—that would have taken practically *everyone* ranking Nader second. Ditto for Gore people ranking Bush below Buchanan.

Under Borda, the sneakier party would have the advantage. This would be a particularly demoralizing fact. After every close election, the loser could complain that he lost only because the winner's supporters were more manipulative.

"Saari is clearly right that Borda does the most with the least," said McLean. "The Borda rule beats all other ranking systems by its simplicity and elegance, and its superiority can be shown axiomatically in many ingenious ways, as Saari and his associates have done. But that cuts both ways . . . The very suitability of Borda as a theoretical choice procedure rules it out absolutely as a practical choice procedure—at least, for humans."

Arrow jump-started the field of voting theory with his attempt to find a system meeting a few simple, commonsense properties. This approach is still influential. The literature is full of discussion of properties with names such as "favorite betrayal" and "monotonicity" and "clone independence." The vague hope is that it might be possible yet to find a set of desirable, commonsense properties that are compatible. This would point us to the best way of voting. So far, it hasn't happened. "You start getting into these debates which never end about how important different properties are," explained Warren Smith. "It never *did* end for fifty years. It just led to a kind of permanent pointlessness."

"There are *billions* of properties," Saari concedes. "I mean, I'm guilty. I have papers where I point out the properties of this and the properties of that."

This ongoing lack of expert consensus has been the biggest obstacle confronting those who would reform American voting. It is easy enough to convince people that the plurality vote is deeply flawed. *If only* the experts agreed on what system should replace it, reform would have a fighting chance. But somebody has something terrible to say about every voting method. When the media does features on voting systems, they often interview Donald Saari and Steven Brams, as *Discover* magazine did the month of the 2000 election. They got comments on the horrible defects of approval voting (from Saari) and the ruinous faults of the Borda count (from Brams). The reportage can leave the impression that (a) the plurality vote is really bad, and (b) so is every other system.

"Academics probably are not the best sales people" Brams and Peter Fishburn wrote wistfully, as "they squabble among themselves. Because few if any ideas in the social sciences are certifiably 'right' under all circumstances, squabbles may well be grounded in serious intellectual differences. Sometimes, however, they are not."

FOURTEEN

Hot or Not?

"Ever hang out with your friends drinking and come up with a totally crazy idea based on something someone said? Well, that's exactly what happened."

This is James Hong's account of the origin of the website hotornot.com—pronounced *hot or not*. It's yet another networking site, something along the lines of MySpace or Facebook. The difference is that it's all about voting. Go to hotornot.com and you will be presented with a succession of photographs of mostly college-age men and women. Site visitors are asked to rate each picture on a scale of one to ten. Ten is HOT, and one is NOT.

The site requires visitors to rate the current photo in order to view the next one. Each time a new photo pops up, you learn the average rating of the person you've just rated. It will read something like: "Official Rating 6.1 based on 271 votes."

There's a not-to-be-denied curiosity about how your rating compares to everyone else's. Gene-survival means spotting the most suitable mate (quickly! from a distance!!). This is the sexual version of a shooter video game. The photos are an uncurated museum of vernacular photography. Many subjects hold a cell phone up to a bathroom mirror. There are cars, exes, children, pets, and tattoos.

Hot or Not makes speed dating seem slow. A few clicks let you zero in on the age, gender, and geographic locale of your choice. Should you see someone you want to meet, there's a place to click. Provided the person also likes your picture, the site connects you up. (This costs money.)

The site is a hungry meme. In order to keep going, it must persuade its voyeurs to turn exhibitionist. It takes an interesting blend of courage and masochism to submit a picture. Anyone who does is hooked. On the left of the browser window, beneath the small picture of the last-rated person, is a telling statistic. "You rated her: 9," the caption may say. "She checked her score: 3 hours ago."

That is roughly the median. *They can't go three hours without checking.* With heroin, they would have gotten eight hours easy time between fixes.

The idea for hotornot.com originated when a friend of Hong's named Jim Young commented that a girl he'd met at a party was a "perfect ten." "We live in Silicon Valley, where we think about websites all the time," Hong explained. "We actually had a whiteboard in our living room. So we said, wouldn't it be funny if there was a website where you could see if someone is a 'perfect ten'?"

Jim Young coded the site in just a few days. In October 2000, Young and Hong sent e-mails to friends telling them about the site. Pictures poured in, and site visits grew exponentially. On the eighth day, the site got 1.8 million hits. By early 2001, NetNielson listed it as one of the top twenty-five sites for Web advertising. It was soon being written up in Slashdot and *Playboy*. By adding the matchmaking feature, the site went commercial. Hong, now the site's CEO, reports that about a marriage a day results from people who meet on the site. More than twelve billion votes have been cast. That is more than four times the votes cast in every presidential election in the history of the United States.

The type of voting used on Hot or Not is called range voting, and it has become the favored voting method of the Internet. YouTube and Amazon allow users to rate videos and books on a five-point scale. The Internet Movie Database (IMDb) has ten-point ratings of movies. In each case, the rating you see is simply an average of all the ratings submitted by site visitors.

Range voting is much older than the Internet. Grade point averages amount to a range vote (of students, by teachers). A class valedictorian is the range-vote winner. Consumer surveys and *Consumer Reports* ratings use a five-point scale of "poor" to "excellent." The star ratings of restaurants in the Michelin, GaultMillau, and Zagat guides are range votes, too. Range votes are often taken seriously. The reliability ratings reported by *Consumer Reports'* subscribers affect the prices paid for used cars. In 2003 French chef Bernard Loiseau shot himself in the head after GaultMillau downgraded his establishment from nineteen to seventeen points out of twenty.

Range voting works best when the same group of people rates all the candidates. That's rarely possible on the Web. You have to have seen a movie or read a book to submit a meaningful IMDb or Amazon rating. This makes it hard to compare the ratings of a small independent film and a Hollywood blockbuster. It's a different, self-selected group rating each film.

Range voting would probably work better in a public election. There every voter would rate all the candidates. The ballot could look like that on the next page. This assumes a scale of one to five. The numbers are printed in the circles for reference. All the voter had to do was blacken one dot for each candidate. This voter liked Edwards, so he gave him a five, the best score permitted here. Filling in a range ballot is vastly more informative that simply putting a check by Edwards's name. The scores tell us that this voter greatly dislikes Duke, thinks

Holloway and Roemer are somewhat better than Duke and about equal to each other. A conventional plurality ballot robs us of all the information about how voters feel about the candidates other than the one voted for.

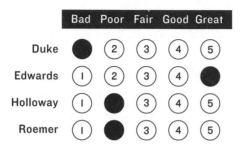

Internet polls express the results of range votes as averages. That's one way to do it. Another is to add up the total points awarded. Either way, the candidate with the highest score wins.

Range voting solves the problems of spoilers and vote splitting. In the ballot above, there are three Republicans and one Democrat. Anyone who likes all three Republicans can give them all high scores. Edwards, the lone Democrat, therefore does not have an arbitrary advantage because the Republican vote is split.

Range voting offers a kind of "independence of irrelevant alternatives." If IMDb users rate *The Seventh Seal* higher than *Wild Strawberries*, this will not be affected by the release of a new Jennifer Aniston movie. And why should it? The Aniston movie is irrelevant to the ratings of the Bergman films. By allowing voters to score rather than rank the candidates, a voting system can meet the intuitive underpinnings of all of Arrow's conditions.

The trouble with ranking candidates is not hard to understand. Look at why teachers score student performance (with a letter or number grade) rather than rank the students from best to worst. It might be there are two equally good straight-A students. With a ranked system, the teacher would have to arbitrarily rank one first in the class and the other second. That's not fair. It might be that all the students are flunking and deserve Fs. A ranked system would still have one student as number one, giving a false impression that that student is doing well. Ranked systems work best when each ranked student/candidate/option is better than the one that follows by the same degree. Otherwise, ranked systems scramble the message an honest voter is trying to send. This leads to serious problems, as Arrow demonstrated.

Range voting captures voter sentiments admirably when everyone is completely honest. The surprising thing is that it also works well when people "cheat." An author can go on Amazon and award five stars to his own book. (Not that *I'd* do that, of course. You hear of such things.) A film buff can give zero points to an "overrated" blockbuster just to pull it down a notch.

This kind of manipulation doesn't have as much effect as you might think *provided each person can vote only once.* Suppose that everyone "cheats" by giving a movie the maximum-allowed rating (a ten on IMDb) or the minimum (one). Then the survey essentially becomes a yay-or-boo vote. The film's rating is determined by the *percentage* of people giving it a ten.

That's not so bad. In fact, it's equivalent to an approval vote.

More likely, you'll have some people voting honestly and others trying to manipulate. I can "cheat" only when I believe the current rating is wrong. I may go on IMDb and find that *Mr. Smith Goes to Washington* has a rating of 7.0 points out of 10. Should that concur with my honest assessment, I have no incentive to manipulate. But let's say I really believe the film is an eight. Sneaky devil that I am, I realize I can make my vote count more by giving the film a ten. And let's say that I, along with a lot of other conniving Frank Capra fans, succeed in pulling the rating up a little higher than it should be. This will increase the number of subsequent voters who feel the film is now overrated. There will be fewer people motivated to manipulate the rating upward, and more who will have reason to manipulate the rating *downward* by giving the film a one. This tug-of-war between strategizers tends to keep the rating about where it should be.

In an election for public office, range voters can be as honest or as strategic as they like. The "honest" way to fill out a range ballot is to give your favorite candidate the maximum score and your least favorite the minimum score. Then scale the other candidates' scores to that range.

Here's a more strategic approach. Say you learn that Roemer and Edwards are way ahead of the other candidates. One of those two is going to win. You can increase your ballot's power by maxing out the difference between the two front runners. Give Edwards the maximum score and Roemer the minimum. Use that scale to assign the other candidates' scores. (In the sample ballot shown, Duke and Holloway would also get the minimum score.)

The key figure in the reappraisal of range voting is Warren D. Smith. Born in Cleveland in 1964, Smith has a midwestern twang, a Mark Twain sense of deadpan humor, and very little reverence for his predecessors in voting theory. "Arrow's Nobel-winning 1951 'impossibility theorem' misdirected the entire field of voting systems for 50 years," Smith commented casually in a 2005 paper. Elsewhere: "Arrow's theorem is not nearly as important as it at first seems."

This may sound like a biologist saying that evolution isn't all that. Smith's candor may have something to do with the fact that he is an outsider to voting theory. He took his Ph.D. at Princeton under the legendary mathematician John Horton Conway. Smith did postdoctoral work at Bell Labs, then spent a dozen years as a research scientist at NEC Research Institute (where he had an interesting experience with a Borda vote). Since 2000, Smith has been on the math faculty at Temple University. He is best known for his investigations of the physical limits of computation, in which he probes such questions as whether it is possible for a computer to fully simulate the complexities of the physical world. (The short answer is "no.")

Smith holds or has applied for patents covering such exotica as a computer made out of DNA, theft-proof credit cards, a 3-D vision process, and a magnetic catapult that could be used for launching satellites. In December 2000, with the Supreme Court deciding a bitterly contested presidency, Smith completed an article purporting to demonstrate the superiority of a system that no one had taken seriously, range voting.

He began with an idea for comparing the merits of different voting systems, using a measure called Bayesian regret. The "Bayes" part refers to eighteenth-century English mathematician Thomas Bayes, a pioneer of probability theory. "Bayesian regret" is a statistical term that Smith defines as "expected avoidable human unhappiness."

In other words, Smith tried to gauge how voting systems fail the voters by electing candidates other than the one who would have resulted in the greatest overall satisfaction. To do this, he ran a large series of computer simulations of elections. In each of his simulations, virtual voters were assigned utilities (degrees of happiness, measured numerically) for simulated candidates. In some of the simulations, the utilities were assigned completely at random. In others, voters and candidates were assumed to exist in a "space" of issues. Voters favored the candidates who were closest to them on the issues.

The advantage of Smith's approach is that it bypasses the interminable arguments over paradoxes and properties. Instead of debating how *bad* the winner-turns-loser paradox is, and then debating how *common* it is, Smith's program computes how well IRV performs in millions of randomly generated situations and compares that to how well other systems perform. Every reasonably common paradox can be expected to turn up in the simulated trials and is given its proper due— no more, no less. This includes paradoxes that haven't yet been discovered or named.

The baseline for Smith's studies is a "magic" best system that unerringly elects whichever candidate makes the voters happiest overall. Imagine that brain scans are built into every voting booth. The voters are flashed video of the candidates as a noninvasive scan probes the neurons of their limbic systems to measure how happy each voter is with each candidate. The system outputs a series of high-precision happiness scores, and the candidate with the highest total score wins. This type of system is defined as having a Bayesian regret of zero.

Every other, more realistic voting system has a larger-than-zero regret. This reflects the fact that every practical system will sometimes fail to elect the "best" candidate.

Smith was not the first to use this approach, he later discovered. However, the earlier studies had been inconclusive, finding that the "best" practical voting system varied with the number of voters, with the way utilities were assigned, and with other details of the simulation. None of the earlier studies had tried range voting. Smith's did. Each reported data point was averaged from at least ten thousand random trials. Smith's simulations used from two to five candidates and five to two hundred voters. He considered both honest and strategic voting. In response to a discussion with Steven Brams, he also added an element of voter "ignorance." He assumed that the voters sometimes didn't know enough about the candidates and thus voted "incorrectly."

In every one of Smith's 144 simulations, using a wide variety of parameters, range voting did the best of any practical voting system, having the lowest regret (next only to "magic" best).

One message of Smith's simulations is the surprising value of honesty. Every system produced less regret when voters were honest. In most cases the improvement is dramatic. The sample chart here shows the results of a simulation with two hundred voters, five candidates, and two ideological issues. The bars show Bayesian regret. The left side of each bar indicates the regret figure when everyone votes honestly. The right side gives the regret when everyone votes strategically. Remember, this works like a golf score: lower is better.

Which Voting System Is Best?

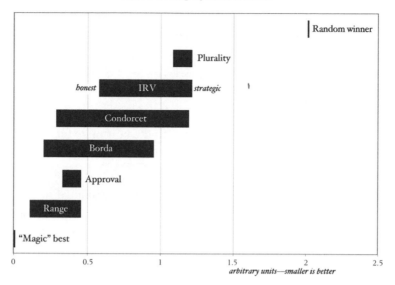

In reality, some people will vote honestly and some strategically. Thus each bar in the chart indicates the range of expected regret for each system. With the ranked systems and range voting in particular, honesty makes a huge difference.

For comparison, the chart also shows a "random winner" system. This is one where votes are ignored and the winning candidate is chosen randomly. All reasonable voting systems are much better than that, as we'd hope.

Whenever you see a graph intended to convince you of something, you should be concerned about cherry picking. Did I choose this particular simulation just to make range voting look good? How different are the 143 simulations I'm not showing?

I chose this simulation because it strikes me as Smith's most realistic scenario overall. It has the most voters that he considered (two hundred: adding voters eats up processor cycles) and the most candidates (five). I suspect that the two-dimensional utility used here is a better approximation to American political reality than Smith's other alternatives.

These variables don't affect the overall shape of the results much. Nearly all of Smith's three-or-more-candidate simulations would look very similar to this chart. The main difference is in the degrees of bar overlap. It is not always the case that the *worst* value for range voting is better than the *best* value for IRV, as it is here. Sometimes the range and IRV bars overlap.

In the simulations where Smith didn't use the ignorance factor, the best value for range was always better than the best value for any other system. The worst value for range was always better than the worst value for any other system (except approval, with which it was tied). In a few of the simulations, Smith cranked up the "ignorance" factor to the point where simulated voters were almost choosing randomly. Range voting still came out best overall, though the differences between the various systems was much less. The superiority of range voting is robust.

Smith's results make some interesting points about the other systems, too. IRV can perform much better than plurality voting *provided there are many honest voters*. (In the unlikely case that everyone votes strategically, the two systems are tied.) Condorcet offers more improvement yet. The results offer at least some vindication for Donald Saari's affection for the Borda count. When everyone votes honestly, Borda outperforms IRV, Condorcet, *and* approval (though not range voting).

One thing that Smith's simulations do *not* address is how systems may encourage honest voting. Many believe that Borda voters would tend to be less honest than Condorcet or IRV voters. If so, the average regret figure for Borda would skew to the right of the chart's bar.

The left side of the approval voting bar represents the "totally honest" approach where people approve only those candidates they rate higher than the midpoint of their imaginary scale. Honest approval voting achieves less regret than the fully strategic kind, where voters factor in poll information to maximize the impact of their votes.

The right (strategic) sides of the approval and range voting bars co-incide. This is because they are really the same thing. The strategic range voter rates every candidate a perfect ten or a zero (or whatever the maximum and minimum scores are). You can think of approval voting as the *strategic* form of range voting, or as the *simplest* kind of range voting, where the possible scores are limited to zero and ten (or whatever).

Based on these results, Smith believes that full-scale range voting is better than approval voting. He is under no illusion that all voters will be honest. He says only that such honesty as we can get is worth having. There must be some voters who are willing to fill out an honest range ballot. Why discard useful information? The more people who vote honestly, the better a result we might expect.

It is not hard to understand why range voting fares so well. For those voters who choose to be honest, range voting lets them express their feelings more precisely than rankings or approvals can. When voters are strategic, all you can hope to learn from a ballot is which candidates the voter is trying to help. This is precisely the information that strategic range/approval voting elicits. Equally important, it uses this information in a way that continues to make sense when voters are strategic. The candidate whom the greatest number of voters are "scheming" to help must be the one that the greatest number *sincerely* want to win. And with range/approval voting, that candidate wins.

It is much more difficult to reconstruct the intentions behind a strategic ranked ballot. Burying scrambles information (as the Republican pretends to like the Communist more than the Democrat). Consequently, the way Borda and Condorcet tally votes often makes no sense when ballots are marked strategically. It's a case of garbage in, garbage out.

Smith believes that his Bayesian regret figures translate directly into good governance. Pay particular attention to the bars for "random winner," plurality, and range voting. A hereditary monarchy is at worst a "random winner" election, Smith says. (It may be slightly better than that, as monarchs were "trained from birth to rule.") By switching from monarchy to democracy, in the form of a plurality vote, we approximately halved the regret. There is still plenty of room for improvement. Smith concludes that "switching to range voting would be a larger improvement in 'democracy' than the entire invention of democracy."

Nobody knows who invented range voting. It is one of those simple ideas that is invented and reinvented all the time, in many cultures and contexts. You will not learn much by Googling "range voting." Smith coined that term for his 2000 paper. He believes that range voting is older than the human race. He claims that the way honeybees decide on a new nesting site amounts to a range vote. Each spring, swarms of bees send out scouts to explore potential sites for a new hive. When they return to the old hive, the scouts report on the site by performing a dance. The length and emphasis of this dance conveys their rating of how desirable the site is.

This dance causes other bees to check out the site for themselves. They return and perform their own dance. Over several cycles, this ensures that the most touted sites are the most visited and most touted again. This has the effect of focusing attention on the site with the highest average rating. That is the site chosen for the new nest.

Smith estimates that there have been something like 10^{16} (ten thousand trillion) bee "elections" over the history of the bee family. Finding an optimal nesting site is important to a hive's survival. That it has persisted through millions of years of Darwinian struggle is evidence that no simple alternative does the job better. As Smith remarks, evolution never invented IRV.

Range voting solves many of the problems (or alleged problems?) of approval voting. Take Saari and Van Newenhizen's Mr. Mediocre: 9,999 out of 10,000 voters believe that candidate A is great (honest range score: ten), B is barely better than average (honest score: six, let's say), and C is terrible (honest score: zero). One lone voter has virtually the opposite opinions. He also rates B a six. Saari and Van Newenhizen are afraid that, in the absence of accurate polls, all 10,000 voters will approve Mr. Mediocre. That will give him a 10,000 to 9,999 victory over the all-but-unanimous favorite, A.

This won't happen with range voting as long as there are at least three honest voters. The honest voters will give B a score of six rather than ten. That will be enough to ensure that mediocre B loses to popular favorite A, as he should. It takes only a tiny fraction of honest voters to prevent this sort of contingency.

The same goes for "President Perot." Range voters who feel ambivalent about Perot can give him a middling score and be done with it. They don't have to do a strategic calculation about whether it's "safe" to approve him. Should Perot win, no reasonable person could complain that his votes were only "half votes." The election results (broken down by how many voters gave each candidate each allowed score) would show exactly why and how Perot beat his opponents.

Robert Weber devised approval voting partly to solve the problem of clones. Not everyone is sure it does, when voters are poorly informed or irrational. Suppose that the last preelection polls show that Goodell and Ottinger each have exactly 30 percent of the vote, with Buckley having 40 percent. A liberal will win *provided* every Goodell voter approves Ottinger, and vice versa. Each liberal is tempted to bullet-vote for his own favorite.

This is a case where the normally strategic voter might want to consider honesty. A Goodell voter may feel that Goodell is a ten, Ottinger is a nine, and Buckley is a zero. Why not vote that way? This prevents Buckley from winning (if every liberal follows a similar course), and it allows him to send the message that he prefers Goodell to Ottinger.

Don't want to be that honest? Here's another option. Give Goodell ten, Ottinger four, and Buckley zero. Provided every liberal gives the other guy at least one third of the maximum score, Buckley cannot win. This way of voting helps Goodell (over Ottinger) as much as possible without risking a Buckley victory.

How many range voters would vote honestly? At one time or another, most of us have reflected that the chance of *my one vote* deciding a large, important election is fantastically slight. Smith notes that, if there is a one-in-a-billion chance of your vote's deciding the election, and if it costs you one dollar in lost time or transportation expense to vote, then voting is irrational unless you place the value of your candidate's winning at one billion dollars. Those who think they are "selfishly" voting their pocketbook aren't—not when you figure in costs this way.

So why do people vote, anyway? This puzzle has earned a name: the voter paradox (not to be confused with the "paradox of voting"). We need lots of people to vote in order to perpetuate the democratic process. Yet it's in no one's personal interest to do so.

The voter paradox is similar to other problems studied by game theorists. They go by such names as the "tragedy of the commons," the "volunteer's dilemma," and the "free-rider dilemma." These describe situations where everyone shares a benefit *provided* enough people volunteer to perform an altruistic act . . . but the shirkers get the same benefit as the volunteers.

More-or-less rational people vote for many reasons. For some, it is a matter of guilt. They have been programmed to feel guilty when they don't vote. For others, voting is a symbolic or quasispiritual act. They vote to feel part of the political process, to be connected to something bigger than their own petty concerns. For whatever reason we vote, narrow self-interest plays little role. Given this fact, it may not be so incredible as partisans (economists, game theorists) think for some people to do the noble, decent, upright thing and fill out an honest ballot.

In his 2000 paper, Smith guesstimated that maybe 10 percent of voters would cast honest range ballots. On Election Day 2004, Smith, Douglas S. Greene, and Jacqueline N. Quintal conducted exit polls in which they asked voters how they would have filled out range and approval ballots. They were surprised to find that most voters cast apparently sincere range ballots in their poll. This probably isn't predictive of behavior in an election where range voting really counted. Still, as long as some people vote honestly, range voting has an advantage over approval voting.

One of those who came across Smith's paper is Jan Kok. He observed that range (and approval) voting can be run on every voting machine presently in use in America. This point is important because voting machines are expensive. Such systems as IRV and Condorcet require new or modified machines. ("There is no machine in the United States that will, on delivery, let you run an election with ranked ballots," reports the website of the Center for Voting and Democracy.)

Kok realized that, with approval or range voting, each candidate can be treated as a "plurality election" between the permitted scores. The machine's overvote check makes sure that the voter gives only one score to each candidate. The drawback is that ballots are longer because you've got X number of options per candidate rather than just one. X is two with approval voting. It can go up to one hundred or more for the really precise forms of range voting. That might be reason to keep the number of permitted scores small. The problem isn't too bad with optical scan machines (the most common type in the United States at present). It's more of an issue with old-fashioned lever machines, where it might be necessary to allot two or more machines per voter.

Smith proposes that range voters have the option of casting a "blank" vote when they don't know enough about a candidate to rate him. There is (or should be) a difference between saying, "I'm giving this candidate a zero because I hate his guts!" and "I haven't a clue who this guy is."

The blank vote idea requires that election results be expressed as average ratings, like an Internet poll. A blank vote is not averaged into a candidate's score. Hence a zero (or minimal) score lowers a candidate's rating, while a blank vote has no effect.

It has generally been assumed that range or approval voters would, by default, give a minimal score to candidates they hadn't heard of. This works against candidates who fail to get media attention and/or who can't afford big TV campaigns. Successful candidates have to appeal to wealthy special interests and are beholden to them. In that sense, Smith's blank vote serves some of the same ends as campaign finance laws.

On the other hand, you can argue that it's a candidate's job to present himself to the people. A candidate nobody's heard of has failed an important part of that job. The real drawback is the "cult film effect." A candidate could be like a small indie film that gets a high rating on IMDb. The few who've seen the film love it. It's hard to tell whether it would play in Peoria.

Suppose I get on the ballot for mayor. I don't campaign, I refuse all media requests for interviews. I won't even say what I stand for. On Election Day, practically everyone gives me a blank, as they well should. Seven friends each rate me a perfect ten (as I've instructed them to do). That gives me an unbeatable *average* score of ten, and I win.

Smith's fix is to require that a candidate get a qualifying percentage of the voters giving him a nonblank score. You might say that you need 50 percent as a threshold. In practice, the media would probably tend to iron out a cult-film effect. Polls would identify any dark horse with a chance of winning, and the media would be all over him. By Election Day, everyone would have heard of the candidate and be able to rate him.

Perhaps the most surprising thing about range voting is that no one seems (yet) to have found anything dreadfully wrong with it. The main concern you hear is that it is *difficult*. Range voting is "unnecessarily complicated," wrote a poster on the Tacoma, Washington, *News-Tribune* electronic bulletin board, calling it "something only math geniuses at MIT would dream up for a populace in which many can't balance a checkbook." This is Steven Brams's main reservation regarding range voting. Many voters don't know who the vice president is, Brams told Smith. Maybe there is something ridiculous about asking such people to supply numerical scores.

It is worth noting that what sold Hot or Not creators James Hong and Jim Young on range voting was its speed. They wanted site visitors to rate photos as fast as possible. That way the site would collect many votes for each picture, giving the scores credibility—"a wisdom of crowds thing," Hong said. "We found that anything that made it harder to vote was a bad thing."

They considered having visitors pick their favorite of two on-screen photos. A photo would win points for each time it was preferred over another, random photo. This would loosely simulate a Borda count. (In a true Borda count, a candidate wins a point every time a voter ranks her above a rival. No Hot or Not voter could rank all the millions of pictures on the site, of course. The aggregate effect of random visitors ranking random pairs would be similar.) However, when shown two photos that happen to be of roughly equal attractiveness, "people will look at the pictures and not know," Hong said. "They have a harder time deciding."

Hong and Young also considered a simple "hot" or "not" vote on a single picture. This would be an approval vote. There it was "average" Joes and Janes who slowed things down. People would have to ponder whether to click "hot" or "not." Range voting was faster. It seemed to require *less* thought. "Sometimes people can't even express the number," Hong explained, "they just have a feeling and like having that bar: 'ah, it's kinda like here.'" They position the cursor where it feels right and click.

There have been complaints that Hot or Not is silly, superficial, and sexist. No one thinks it's hard to understand. The ratings on YouTube, Amazon, and all the other sites do not seem to bother people, either.

Olympic judging provides another demonstration that scoring is easier than ranking. The numbers that judges hold up on cards (in cartoons, anyway) are range votes. These are just for the judges' reference. The scores are converted to rankings, and it's the rankings alone that count (and that produce occasional flip-flops). The judges give preliminary scores because scoring can be done on the fly. With rankings, you have to keep adjusting your numbers so that there's only one athlete or candidate of each rank. This can be devilishly complicated when there are many competitors.

I suspect that what's really behind the perception that scoring is "hard" is number phobia. A check mark is simple. Numbers are difficult. The bigger the numbers involved, the more difficult it seems.

When simplicity is paramount, approval voting is hard to beat. Even so, the Zenlike simplicity of approval voting has not been the selling point its proponents imagined. The experience of people such as Ka-Ping Yee at Berkeley is that early adopters of voting systems like being able to express themselves. Range voting provides more flexibility than approval voting or ranked systems.

The type and number of allowed scores on a range ballot make a big perceptual difference. Some might prefer giving candidates report-card letters (A, B, C, D, F) rather than numbers. Amazon and IMDb downplay the numerical aspect of rating. You sweep your cursor to add to a row of stars. It's a *gesture*.

In the 2004 exit poll, Smith and Greene asked voters to rate the candidates on a whole-number scale of zero to one hundred. That is about the largest range that anyone is seriously proposing. "Before we started," Smith reported, "some self-appointed critics informed us that selecting the range 0–100 was silly; they thought 0–10 or 0–5 was much 'simpler' but yet provided sufficient expressivity." Smith and Greene found that most voters limited themselves to even multiples of ten. This suggests that most would be happy with a zero-to-ten scale. A minority of voters did use the full resolution. One voter gave Ralph Nader a one out of one hundred, for instance.

A three-valued system called "evaluative voting" has been proposed by D. S. Felsenthal, Claude Hillinger, and Mike Ossipoff. This allows just three choices, usually designated −1, 0, and +1. Mathematically, this is no different from allowing votes of 0, 1, or 2. Some like the psychic satisfaction of casting a negative vote for Wintergreen. eBay lets online buyers and sellers rate one another after each transaction. The three allowed choices are called positive, negative, and neutral. (This is not quite evaluative voting, as eBay ignores the neutral votes in computing the ratings. It's really approval voting with an option to abstain.)

Smith quotes Albert Einstein: "Everything should be made as simple as possible, but no simpler." The choices we make in every election are important. They deserve a little extra effort, if that's what it takes.

You may now have noticed something extremely odd. It took Nobel Prize–level work to devise the impossibility theorem. Yet James Hong and Jim Young (re)invented range voting while tossing back a few drinks. Range voting is an omnipresent part of pop culture, as familiar as perfect tens and five-star restaurants.

How is it that such a *simple* solution was overlooked by generations of the best and brightest voting theorists?

FIFTEEN

Present but Not Voting

In the fictional documentary *This Is Spinal Tap* (1984), the also fictional rocker Nigel Tufnel (Christopher Guest) says his band is the loudest in Britain. He credits this to his Marshall amplifier. The amplifier's volume controls go up to eleven rather than the usual ten.

"Does that mean it's louder? Is it any louder?" asks the ostensible filmmaker Marty DiBergi (Rob Reiner).

"Well, it's one louder, isn't it?" Nigel says.

"Why don't you just make ten louder and make ten be the top number, and make that a little louder?"

(Significant pause.) "These go to eleven."

The *Spinal Tap* fiction has commingled with reality. Marshall began selling amplifier faceplates with the volume controls going up to eleven. In 1990, the company introduced a new model with controls that go up to twenty. *Spinal Tap*'s actors have played occasional concert dates in character. Marshall sent "Nigel"/Christopher Guest a special amplifier with a control that goes up to infinity.

The *Spinal Tap* "eleven" joke encapsulates the controversy over range voting and the impossibility theorem itself. It is all about *dynamic range*. Every voter wants his voice to be heard the loudest. Strategic voters shout into megaphones cranked to maximum volume (introducing distortion). Self-assigned "loudness" numbers are meaningless . . . or are they?

Actually, both ranked and scoring systems give voters the freedom to assign to candidates whatever numbers they choose. Yet people seem to have assumed that there is more scope to "lie" with numerical scores than with rankings. Self-assigned scores just seem too slippery-slidey.

Despite that, numerical scores have a long history in economic philosophy. In the late 1970s, Amartya Sen, then at Charles Dodgson's old home of Oxford, had occasion to sketch the history of voting theory. He found two distinct sources, each about two hundred years old. One was the chain of thinkers on ranked voting, from Borda and Condorcet to Dodgson to Arrow. The second source was utilitarianism, the philosophy promoted by Englishman Jeremy Bentham (1749–1832).

Bentham was another liberal light of the Enlightenment, championing much the same set of individual freedoms as Condorcet did. Bentham's utilitarianism asserts that the best choices for society are those that lead to the greatest overall happiness. Ideally, said Bentham, you would add up the happiness of every citizen and use that to decide what policies are best.

Though Bentham had some interest in voting methods, he did not explicitly describe what is now called "utilitarian voting." Each voter writes a number indicating how happy she is with each candidate. The scores are added up, and the candidate with the highest score wins.

In theory, utilitarian voting is the best system anyone could ask for. In practice, it's something else again. Voters would be reporting their happiness scores on the honor system. You can guess how well that would turn out. The election would become a contest to write the biggest number on the ballot.

The obvious fix is to limit the happiness scores to a range. We can tell voters that the lowest score allowed is zero, and the highest allowed is ten. No elevens allowed! This of course is range voting. But until the 1970s, a vital piece of the puzzle was missing—approval voting.

Strategic range voters will cast what amounts to an approval ballot. That's okay. Approval voting is the best system for strategic voters, and it remains an attractive choice for honest voters. That means there is no cause to fear that range voters will strategize. If they do, fine, and if they don't, all the better.

Bentham's dying wish was that his body be preserved for posterity as a model to future students. You may see it today in a glass cabinet at University College, London. (The head is wax. The real one was damaged during embalming.) Bentham is occasionally carted to university meetings, where the roll lists him as "present but not voting."

And Bentham's silent presence has loomed over centuries of economic theory. "No approach to welfare economics has received as much support over the years as utilitarianism," Amartya Sen wrote. Bentham's philosophy has become the credo (articulated or not) of secular societies around the globe. Conservatives and liberals alike justify their policies by promising they will create the greatest public good.

Despite that, utilitarianism fell from favor in the academic world of the twentieth century. You may detect a cryptic hint of this backstory at the beginning of the second chapter of *Social Choice and Individual Values*. Arrow wrote, "The viewpoint will be taken here that interpersonal comparison of utilities has no meaning. The controversy is well-known and hardly need be recited here."

Arrow is alluding to Lionel Robbins (1898–1984), a hugely influential economist at the London School of Economics. In 1932, Robbins published *An Essay on the Nature and Significance of Economic Science*. This was an attempt to defend market economies against the rising call for central planning. Robbins adopted some intellectual gymnastics to do so. He took the position that economics should be a study of behavior *and nothing else*.

Example: I'm selling a collectible Manga lunch box on eBay. I say it's worth a thousand dollars. The highest bid is thirty-seven cents. How much is the lunch box really worth? Robbins would say that we have to look at actions, not words. A seller will exaggerate value, and buyers will lowball. It is only when a transaction occurs that we learn anything. Should you offer fifteen dollars and I say, "Deal," we learn that I prefer having fifteen dollars in my pocket to having the lunch box. We learn that you prefer the opposite. We don't learn who's happier with the deal, or how much happier, or whether anybody's really happy deep down. *Happiness* is the kind of fuzzy value judgment that Robbins wanted to expunge from economic thought. Economists should concern themselves with preferences only: "I prefer A to B." Comparing degrees of happinesss is, in economist-speak, "interpersonal comparison of utilities." *That* was to be forbidden.

Robbins's book became "a kind of bible on methodology" for a generation of Western economists, said Claude Hillinger of the University of Munich. Robbins's modus operandi combined hardheaded empiricism with a dash of trendiness. Transactions only (the ground truth of a market economy) would be used to predict future transactions. There was no need to probe deeply into consumers' and producers' heads. The trendy part was that Robbins linked economics to the latest avant-garde developments in other fields. Like behaviorism in psychology or even the new quantum theory in physics, Robbins denied "hidden variables" that might make good old-fashioned sense of it all. These intellectual positions, arising at about the same time for very different reasons, each entailed a pose of fashionable agnosticism over matters previously held to be common sense.

This new economics also proved useful in the debate over collectivism. The central planners of left and right were making essentially utilitarian arguments. It's *obvious* that a dollar spent on welfare programs benefits the poor more than a dollar in extra taxes hurts the rich. Or *we know better than the people do* that the budget should be spent on guns, not butter. Robbins offered an intellectually respectable way to say, "Not so fast, nobody knows what makes people happy."

Robbins said nothing about voting. And in one significant way, his approach could be judged inapplicable to voting. The preferences expressed in transactions are almost always sincere. I wouldn't sell my lunch box for fifteen dollars unless I truly preferred the fifteen dollars. Voting is different: It really can be a bottomless pit of insincerity. A sneaky Borda voter who ranks a Nazi above a Republican is not obligated to live under the Nazi. In fact, as a strategic voter, she is presumably very confident that *won't* happen.

Arrow was perfectly aware that there are other approaches to voting besides ranked ballots. In fact, he devotes a couple of pages to range voting (not under that name) in *Social Choice and Individual Values*. This is an idea he wrestled with—and rejected.

Arrow proposes "assigning the utility 1 to the best conceivable alternative and 0 to the worst conceivable alternative" with the scores of other alternatives scaled to that 0 to 1 range. This qualifies as range voting. "It is hard not to see that the suggested assignment of utilities is extremely unsatisfactory," Arrow wrote.

Suppose there are altogether three alternatives and three individuals. Let two of the individuals have the utility 1 for alternative x, .9 for y, and 0 for z; and let the third individual have the utility 1 for y, .5 for x, an 0 for z. According to the above criterion, y is preferred to x. Clearly, z is a very undesirable alternative since each individual regards it as worst. If z were blotted out of existence, it should not make any difference to the final outcome; yet, under the proposed rule for assigning utilities to alternatives, doing so would cause the first two individuals to have utility 1 for x and 0 for y, while the third individual has utility 0 for x and 1 for y, so that the ordering by sum of utilities would cause x to be preferred to y.

This one passage must have discouraged generations of social choice theorists from exploring the range voting path. It left the impression that Arrow had already been there, done that. He showed that range voting is susceptible to "irrelevant alternatives," just like ranked systems. But Claude Hillinger sees in this passage "a fundamental blind spot in the work of Arrow and in collective choice theory that followed in his footsteps."

On closer inspection, the flip-flop that Arrow describes is innocuous compared to the ones I've been describing in this book. Two "good" clones (x and y) are nearly tied. There's also an "evil" third candidate whom *nobody* likes (z). In a situation like this one, we normally worry that the clones will split the vote, leading to the election of the unpopular candidate. That doesn't happen. Range voting passes the clone test with flying colors.

Arrow's point is something else. Initially the voters optimize their ballots to ensure that the despicable z doesn't win. When z drops out of the race, there's a whole new political reality. All three voters strategically adjust their votes to help their favorite. The rejiggering causes clone x to win instead of clone y. The winner flip-flops *even though no one has changed his ranking of the candidates*.

True enough. However, all three voters have changed their *scores* for the candidates. It's scores, not rankings, that count in range voting.

This is why Hillinger and Smith feel we need a new version of "independence of irrelevant alternatives" for range voting. The revised condition would say that the electoral outcome for x and y depends only on the scores the voters give x and y, and not on anything else. Range voting *does* obey this rule. Had the voters left their scores for x and y unchanged after z dropped out, the winner would have been unchanged.

What Arrow's x, y, and z really demonstrate is that strategic voting can change the outcome of a range vote. This observation is equally true of ranked systems, of course. Arrow conceded that "the above result appears to depend on the particular method of choosing the units of utility. But this is not true, although the paradox is not so obvious in other cases." Paul Samuelson echoed this thought in a 1967 symposium, saying, in effect, that an Arrow-style impossibility theorem can be proved for range voting.

Samuelson must have been thinking of a proof involving Arrow's original, ranking version of irrelevant alternatives. That said, it's *easy* to show that range voting meets all of Arrow's conditions with the reasonable tweak I just mentioned. "The conditions follow trivially from the definition" of range voting, says Hillinger.

Warren Smith contends that Arrow's original independence of irrelevant alternatives (IIA) *shouldn't* always be obeyed. It is like a ballot proposition that sounds like it's about something everyone wants but that has hidden consequences. We are told that IIA outlaws the spoiler effect. Who could be against that? Read the fine print, and you see there's more to IIA than spoilers. When you say that whether A beats B can depend only on how voters rank A and B, it means we have to ignore all degrees of desire that go beyond rankings. Sometimes this restriction makes no sense at all.

Two scholars with close ties to Arrow, Amartya Sen and John Harsanyi (both Nobel laureates themselves), championed the necessity of interpersonal comparisons of utility. One of Sen's examples is Nero's burning of Rome. Whatever pleasure the emperor gained by setting decadent Rome ablaze can't possibly have outweighed the misery of the masses. Everyone seconds this assessment, and yes, it involves "interpersonal comparison of utilities." How can anyone say we *shouldn't* make comparisons like that?

In the 1950s John Harsanyi devised a modern formulation of utilitarianism, an alternative to Robbins's framework. "Harsanyi's axioms were abstract and his discussion moved on an equally abstract philosophical level," Claude Hillinger wrote in a 2006 article. "He did not discuss any application. To me the application to voting was clear. The voter must be given a numerical scale . . . As in any ordinary measurement process, there should be no restriction on how the voter distributes the values permitted by the scale over the alternatives; specifically, he must be free to assign the same value to alternatives that he values equally."

Sen describes Arrow's theorem as showing that "conditions satisfied comfortably by utilitarianism . . . cannot be fulfilled by any rule whatsoever that has to base the social ordering . . . on individual orderings." Coming from one of the most important social choice theorists, these words should have caused the discipline to look more closely at scoring systems.

They had little visible effect. Nearly all of voting theory had been built around ranked systems and the study of their defects. It was almost like the old joke about dermatology. It's a great field because the "patient" never dies and never gets better. "To admit a simple solution," Hillinger suggests, "would undermine the raison d'être of the discipline."

Range voting is still largely a samizdat enterprise on the fringes of social choice theory. The most glaring example must be Smith's pivotal 2000 paper. It has never been published in a journal. Smith posted the paper on his home page, along with computer code so others could replicate his simulations. The article has reached a wide audience and helped to spark a grassroots range voting movement. Yet the paper has probably convinced more people outside of academic voting theory than in it. Donald Saari "always cuts me down and calls me an idiot," Smith dryly reports. (Not much love is lost there: "Saari kind of lives in a mathematical universe," Smith says, "but it's not the same as our universe.")

"At first I tried to publish in journals devoted to collective choice," Claude Hillinger said of his own writings on range voting. "It was hopeless. The referees just rejected the paper without even making contact with its contents. I then gave it to *Homo Oeconomicus*. That journal was started by a former student of mine, Manfred Holler. He and the current editor made a great effort to guide it through the refereeing process. They told me that some referee reports were so vituperative that they were not forwarded to me. One that was forwarded and that I found rather amusing said that I should read the classic introductory text by Luce and Raiffa [*Games and Decisions*, 1957] in order to find out what the field was all about!" The one exception was Steven Brams: "He was very friendly and helpful."

Hillinger's "The Case for Utilitarian Voting" did make it into print in 2005. The small literature on range voting, virtual and otherwise, has produced a diverse group of converts. Mike Ossipoff and Forest Simmons, both prominent in online discussions of election methods, have endorsed range voting. "I can see that Range Voting takes the same basic idea [as approval voting] and improves it, into something that would be history's first thoroughly accurate and fair way of measuring an electorate's wishes," Guy Ottewell wrote. But Ottewell, too, is an outsider with no standing in the social choice theory community.

"The profession dealing with collective choice is just about completely dysfunctional," Hillinger said, "from the point of view of dealing with the social problem that they are ostensibly dealing with." That "social problem" is of course making our elections fairer. To have any chance of solving the problem it is necessary to recognize the gaping chasm between what Arrow's theorem *says* and what people *thought it meant*. The impossibility theorem is poised on the knife's edge of truth. Frame the problem exactly the way Arrow did, and rational democracy is "impossible." Drop the obsession with ranking, and life becomes a lot easier.

So what does the impossibility theorem mean? Smith's and Hillinger's answer could hardly be more different from the pessimistic interpretations that have prevailed. The message of the impossibility theorem is: don't use ranked voting systems.

"There is an open door to social choice," Hillinger says, "and another one . . . that is closed. One would have expected choice theorists to pass through the open door; they chose instead to bang their heads against the closed one."

THE
REALITY

SIXTEEN

The Way Democracy Will Be

Days before the 2000 election, Steven Brams told *The Chronicle of Higher Education*, "In a way, I secretly hope that the 2000 presidential election will produce a result that makes a lot of people unhappy. It would show the fragility of our system."

Brams got his wish. It didn't do much for approval voting, or for range voting, either. "People are happy with plurality voting until a problem arises," Robert Weber said. "By then, it's too late to fix the current problem—and the winners are content to let the short-term furor die down."

That was the double-edged sword. Only the blue half of America was willing to listen to talk of fixing the spoiler effect. And if 2000 did not get people interested in a new voting system, Brams asked me, what would? He left the question hanging.

In March 2001, John Flanigan of the University of Hawaii mailed copies of Guy Ottewell's approval voting manifesto, "The Arithmetic of Voting," to all the U.S. senators and congresspeople. Flanigan's brother

Mike had been a congressional aide. He warned John that congress-people were not in the habit of paying attention to brilliant ideas unac-companied by large donations. "We received immediate answers from our own Senators' offices—from assistants, of course," reported Flani-gan. "The one from the aide of Sen. Akaka was polite; Sen. Inouye's assistant had read the booklet, commented on it, and promised to mention it to the senator." And nothing happened.

The fallout from the 2000 election *has* advanced the cause of one voting system. This is due largely to the efforts of Rob Richie and the organization he cofounded, FairVote: The Center for Voting and Democracy.

Richie is that Washington rarity, a man born inside the Beltway (in 1962). Voting reform was in the family. Richie's great uncle was George H. Hallett, director of the now-defunct Proportional Represen-tation League. Hallett resided in New York, backed that city's adoption of proportional representation in the 1930s, and lived long enough to see the proportional representation movement wither in the cold-war era.

After studying philosophy at Haverford College, Richie worked on the congressional campaign of Jolene Unsoeld, a liberal Democrat rep-resenting a blue-collar part of Washington state. There Richie and fel-low campaign worker Cynthia Terrell (now his wife) founded a group called the Citizens for Proportional Representation. This appeared a propitious time for reviving the idea in the United States. In 1991, Cincinnati, another city that had once used proportional representa-tion, then dropped it (in 1955), put proportional representation on the ballot. Richie and Terrell traveled there to work on that campaign. Though the referendum failed, it led to a June 1992 conference on proportional representation in Cincinnati. Richie and Terrell joined forces with several other advocates to create a national organization, also called the Citizens for Proportional Representation. Richie was named the director. Former congressman and presidential candidate John Anderson was appointed head of the advisory board.

The organization had a baptism by fire. In 1993, Bill Clinton nominated Harvard professor Lani Guinier for the head of the Civil Rights Division of the Department of Justice. Guinier advocated proportional representation, specifically a form called cumulative voting. Of Jamaican and Jewish American parentage, Guinier argued in her writings that proportional representation would better serve ethnic minorities.

Some conservatives went ballistic. Clint Bolick, writing in *The Wall Street Journal*, called Guinier a "quota queen." As in the schoolyard, it is tough to talk your way out of a memorable nickname. Guinier was specifically *against* quotas. When she protested the misrepresentation of her views, the *New York Post* wrote, "Unbelievably, the woman known as the 'quota queen' claimed she did not believe in quotas."

Proportional representation probably got more press during the Guinier controversy than it had in decades. Almost all of it was negative. That Republicans had once supported proportional representation was long forgotten. Even Democrats assumed that Clinton was having one of his liberal relapses. There was speculation that his new consultant David Gergen (a Republican) would advise him to withdraw the Guinier nomination, and fast. Clinton did just that.

Richie's organization had just opened a steak house in the middle of a mad cow epidemic. Even before the Guinier nomination, "we had to change the name," he explained, "because people said, 'Oh, we know exactly what you're for and I don't like it.'" The organization began calling itself the Center for Voting and Democracy. They have lately appended to that the shorter name FairVote.

The new names permitted a broader focus. Richie shifted more of his energies to other reforms such as a direct popular vote for president, a constitutional right to vote, universal voter registration, and instant-runoff voting. "IRV was sort of there from the beginning as a side issue," Richie recalled. "John Anderson had a piece in *The New York Times* in 1992 about IRV and the presidential race with Perot. And then, as we talked more about IRV, it resonated with people. They said,

'Oh, I want to do something about that.' By 1997 or 1998, we found that this is something that can really move in state legislatures. In 1999 the New Mexico state senate passed IRV eighteen months after first hearing about it in an op-ed."

Then 2000 happened. "I thought that Al Gore was well positioned to win the presidency while losing the national popular vote," Richie said. "And if that happens, you've got Republicans willing to change the system, Democrats might go along, and we might actually see movement on a constitutional amendment" for a direct popular vote. "I was worried that they would push a plurality constitutional amendment."

Richie was of course completely wrong. Gore won the popular vote while losing the election. The election became the perfect IRV sales pitch (for Democrats and Greens). With IRV, the Nader votes (and all the third-party votes) would have been redistributed to Gore and Bush, as specified on the ballots. This very likely would have elected Gore. Richie became an omnipresent talking head on CNN, Fox, and C-SPAN. He and other Center staff were quoted in *The Wall Street Journal*, the *Los Angeles Times*, and *Congressional Quarterly*.

"I think it's helped us but made it more partisan," Richie says of the publicity blitz. "That can help us get IRV passed in Tacoma Park [Maryland], Berkeley, and Burlington [Vermont], but when we want to win in Pierce County, Washington, Kansas, or wherever, we need to have a broader set of stories to tell."

The Center's funding had tended to skew toward liberal (George Soros's Open Society Institute and the Stewart R. Mott Charitable Trust were early supporters). The 2000 publicity brought in more money from the left, allowing a modest expansion in staff. FairVote: The Center for Voting and Democracy now has an informative, frequently updated website containing late-breaking news, staffer blogs, and an online feature showing the Muppets using IRV to select a CEO. The Center has collected a number of impressive endorsements for IRV. Senator John McCain praised the system in a campaign to adopt it in Alaska; former Vermont governor Howard Dean endorsed it during his run for the Democratic nomination; and Senator Barack Obama introduced an IRV bill in Illinois.

IRV has also been backed by the League of Women Voters; Lani Guinier; the Sierra Club; *USA Today* and *The Harvard Crimson*; the Republican party of Alaska, the Reform Party, the Green Party, the Libertarian Party, and the Democratic parties of California, Colorado, Maine, and Massachusetts. Even Ralph Nader has given IRV the nod, which is something like a spirochete endorsing penicillin. "I'm in favor of trying it," he told *Time* magazine in 2002, "but nobody knows whether it will really work."

That's a little unfair. IRV is working all over the world. The Center declared 2001 "the biggest year yet for IRV." Legislation to adopt it was introduced in Congress and in twelve states. In most cases it was Center staffers who organized grassroots efforts. Among the Center's most important victories to date was a 2002 referendum adopting IRV for San Francisco's civic elections. The year 2004 saw IRV adopted in Berkeley, California; Burlington, Vermont; and Ferndale, Michigan. And 2006 was another boom year. North Carolina governor Michael Easley signed into law a bill providing for a phase-in of IRV in state and local elections. In fall 2006, the Center backed IRV referenda in Minneapolis, Oakland, California, and Washington's Pierce County, plus a proportional representation vote in Davis, California. All four measures passed (Oakland by an impressive 69 percent of the vote).

There are already moves to adopt IRV nationally. Congressman Jesse Jackson, Jr., an Illinois Democrat, introduced the Majority Vote Act of 2004, which would have required all states to conduct general elections for federal office using IRV. Inevitability is part of the pitch. FairVote uses the slogan "The Way Democracy Will Be." IRV is cool, futuristic (and kind of liberal)—the Prius of voting systems.

Ivan Stang wrote, "A heretic is someone who shares ALMOST all your beliefs. Kill him." This is not a bad way of characterizing the reaction of many voting theorists to Rob Richie and his Center. Practically every theorist believes IRV is a genuine improvement, but hardly anyone believes it's the *best* way to vote. So kill him.

"They grabbed onto something," says Donald Saari—he means Richie's Center, and IRV—"and they've got their reputation tied onto something." Try Claude Hillinger: "I find it disturbing that, on an issue so vital to the functioning of democracy, snake oil [IRV] sells better than a genuine remedy." He reported that on the Center's website "I could not find any argument in favor of IRV that had intellectual or scientific substance."

Then there's the money issue. Richie has some, and the academics don't. "I'm trying to get money, although so far I haven't gotten any," Warren Smith said of his efforts to promote range voting for public elections. "Because our opponents, this Center for Voting and Democracy, have like half a million dollars a year to push their nonsense."

To hear many of the theorists talk about it, Richie is Richie Rich, the poor little nonprofit boy, rolling in money to promote the "wrong" voting system. Even the tactful Steve Brams and Peter Fishburn concede, with a twinge of envy, that Richie's Center "does have human and monetary resources that few academics can claim."

Washington is full of nonprofit headquarters with marble lobbies, rooftop helipads, and offices with private showers. In that context, the Center for Voting and Democracy must be called a shoestring operation. It occupies a maze of Dilbert cubicles in a cookie-cutter suburban office building. They now have a staff of about seven, augmented by college interns during the summer months. It doesn't look like much featherbedding is going on. Richie admits he can't pay some staffers what they deserve.

Warren Smith's computer simulations imply that IRV, while not the best system, is better than what we've got now (provided there are any sincere voters at all). It is easier yet to like IRV when a single IRV election replaces two plurality elections, as has been the case in most of the communities recently adopting it. There IRV saves money and en-sures maximum voter turnout. What's not to like?

"I was just on the range voting website this weekend," Richie said, "and there are mathematical zealots out there. They can just be vastly overstating their belief of what some certain flaw means—like 'non-monotonicity.'"

Ask a theorist what's wrong with IRV, and you can expect a one-word answer. It just won't be a word that means anything to average folks. The word is *nonmonotonicity*. This describes the winner-turns-loser paradox and similar odd behavior. When voters raise their estimation of a candidate by ranking him higher, it should help his chances of win-ning (or at very least, it should not *hurt* his chances). This reasonable demand is called *monotonicity*. Even plain old plurality voting offers monotonicity. Voting for Roosevelt can never cause Roosevelt to lose.

The opposite is nonmonotonicity. With IRV, there are cases where a candidate can lose because too many people voted for him, or win only because some of his supporters decided to stay home and not vote. It is important to understand that this doesn't happen in all IRV elections. When there are two major candidates and a few minor ones—a typical American election, in other words—there's no problem whatsoever. Paradoxes happen only when there are three or more strong candidates in the running. Then the order in which the candi-dates are eliminated is all-important, and strange things can happen.

"Some people, it really freaks them out," said Richie. "Freaks them out" may be putting it mildly. Warren Smith's range voting website fea-tures an IRV "Myths and Lies" page. It warns that the Center for Vot-ing and Democracy is a "font of falsities about IRV" and that its website is full of "undefined meaningless hogwash." A main target of Smith's ire is nonmonotonicity.

Of all the problems with voting systems, nonmonotonicity may be the hardest to stomach—provided you understand what it is. The Cen-ter does not seem to dispute that nonmonotonicity is a bad thing. Its position is that such paradoxes are too rare to worry about. "We've had thousands of elections and it's not an issue," Richie says. Steven Hill, a senior analyst with the Center, dismisses "these mathematical 'paradoxes' that, while in theory are interesting for mathematicians to doodle around with on their sketch pads, in fact have no basis in reality . . . It's also possible that a meteorite will strike the Earth and wipe out life as we know it—though not probably likely for a few more million years."

Who's afraid of the big bad nonmonotonicity? Like voting cycles, nonmonotonicity is truly disturbing *when you think about it* but (ironically) could well go unnoticed. Had at least one in six of David Duke's supporters switched their vote to Edwin Edwards in the 1991 Louisiana open primary, Edwards would have lost. This is a classic winner-turns-loser paradox. As far as I can tell, none of the media hand-wringing over the election made quite that point. Everyone knew something had gone awry. They weren't sure what to blame. It was indeed nonmonotonicity that deprived voters of a choice they would have preferred to the Wizard or the Lizard.

Another example: In 2006, Peru held a primary plus runoff for president (not using IRV, either, but the outcome likely would have been the same). At least seven preelection polls claimed that Lourdes Flores Nano could have beaten or tied any of the other candidates in a runoff. But Flores came in third in the primary and never made it to the runoff. The final vote was between Ollanta Humala Tasso (who came in first in the primary) and Alan García Pérez. Garcia beat Humala and was elected president.

Had 834,979 or more Humala Tasso supporters switched their votes to García Pérez in the primary, that would have shut Humala out of the primary. Then Garcia would have gone up against Flores and lost, according to polls. Consequently, García won *only* because he didn't get those 834,979 extra votes.

Is this a pointless game of "would have, should have, could have"? Not really. The familiar argument that vote splitting is unfair takes the same subjunctive tense. *Had only* the Republicans united behind Roosevelt or Taft, their man would have won instead of Wilson. *Had only the Nader supporters voted for Gore* . . . We want elections where everyone can play Monday morning quarterback and agree that the right candidate won. Whenever it occurs, IRV's winner-turns-loser paradox is going to leave a lot of voters feeling that the wrong candidate won.

"No System Is Perfect," concedes the FairVote website, citing Arrow and his Nobel Prize. "This means that for any system one can come up with an example that makes that system look bad. The question, therefore, is not whether one can come up with an example, but rather how realistic that example is. A second question is whether one has any real examples of absurd outcomes, instead of invented ones."

The point is well taken. (It is followed by invented examples of what can go wrong with approval, Condorcet, and Borda voting.) You might well argue that the kind of elections that give IRV trouble are unrealistic in the American context. We have a two-party system. We should worry about spoilers, not about those rare races with three or more real contenders. IRV does just fine with spoilers.

The catch is that we have two-way races because the plurality vote encourages parties to produce them. Under IRV—or under *any* system that truly addresses vote splitting—we would find that the support for "minor" candidates is greater than today's vote counts indicate. There are millions of people who might have voted for Nader, Buchanan, Perot, Anderson, and so forth, but who *didn't* because they knew they'd be throwing away their votes. IRV would encourage supporters of such candidates to rank them first. IRV would also encourage more independent runs by spurned major-party candidates—more Teddy Roosevelts and Joe Liebermans. No longer would they have to feel like traitors to their party. All of this would presumably produce more three-way races than there are now.

This effect would probably be amplified if proportional representation were also adopted, as FairVote advocates. Everywhere it's been used, proportional representation has increased the number and diversity of political parties. In America, that would probably mean that the Greens and Libertarians could expect to win a few seats in Congress and state legislatures. This would give those parties greater visibility and enable them to raise more money. The enhanced credibility would spill over into races for a single seat. A Green or Libertarian candidate for mayor would not automatically be marginalized. Sometimes they would give the Republican and Democrat a run for their money.

That's fine. If you believe in the American value of freedom of choice, it's better than fine. It does, however, mean that there will be more of the multicandidate races where IRV is subject to the winner-turns-loser paradox. Many of the academic critics of IRV support proportional representation, FairVote's original focus. They object only to the notion that you're locked into using IRV for single-office races if you want single transferable vote proportional representation for legislatures. Not many tools are optimal for two different tasks. You can use a hammer to pound a nail and also to open a can of beer. It's not likely to be equally good at both.

Richie is not a mathematician, he readily admits. He is, however, amply aware of one mathematical fact. Two centuries and counting of erudite debate have failed to produce a consensus on what method of voting is best. Richie brings different talents and attitudes to the cause of better voting. This has led to incomprehension among the academics about what he is doing and why. Political activism means cultivating personal relationships. It demands a keen sensitivity to what others feel (even when they are misinformed). It is hard to imagine a sharper contrast to mathematics, one of the few fields where it doesn't matter what other people think.

It is not so much that the Center "grabbed onto" IRV, Richie said, as that the communities of activists, politicians, and voters did. "IRV seems to be something they're more readily able to support, than a proportional system. I think they can see what it means clearly. In some ways it's less transformative."

Richie is not so close-minded about other systems as some think. "I just wish the advocates of various voting systems would get out there and get their system before people and try to persuade people it's a good idea. I have said over the years, 'Okay, your voting equipment can't do instant-runoff voting, let's try approval voting.' Look how easy it is."

But he says he's found that approval voting is a "non-starter. The issues that I'll raise about it, that it seems like a Steve Brams or someone just doesn't accept, a politician will get almost immediately. Isn't it weird that someone can actually get 51 percent in our current system and lose in approval voting?"

This is an argument presented on the Center's website. It applies to range as well as to approval voting. Either "could cause the defeat of a candidate who was the favorite candidate of 51% of voters. If this result were to happen the system would likely be repealed."

The scenario sounds alarming. When you consider how and why it could happen, it makes sense. In order for the 51 percent–favored candidate, Kennedy, to lose, there must be another candidate, Nixon, who is approved by more than 51 percent of the voters. That means that at least 2 percent of the voters have to be approving *both* Kennedy and Nixon. That's like seeing a car with both Kennedy and Nixon bumper stickers. It's possible, but it doesn't make much political sense.

The only halfway credible situations are when a few of Kennedy's supporters believe Nixon is almost as good and unstrategically approve him, too—but none of Nixon's supporters approve Kennedy. Warren Smith provides his own example. Fifty-one percent of the voters are for candidate Hitler, and 49 percent are for candidate Gandhi. The candidates and their platforms are nearly identical, with one exception. If elected, Hitler has vowed to kill everyone who didn't vote for him. (Gandhi will kill no one.)

Notice that Hitler must win with *any* ranked voting system. He's got 51 percent of the vote. Yet Gandhi is clearly better for society as a whole. Nearly half the voters are dead unless Gandhi wins. Smith sees this as a fundamental fault of ranked voting. Ranked systems look at *how many* people prefer A to B without looking at *how strongly* A is preferred to B. With approval or range voting, it is at least possible for Gandhi to win, by having some people ignore strategy and cast completely honest ballots.

Logically and ethically, this "flaw" is no flaw at all. Richie nonetheless has an important point. He is talking about *politicians'* reactions to this paradox. Every working politician and strategist today was schooled on the notion of "minimal coalitions," a term coined by William Riker in *The Theory of Political Coalitions* (1962). Riker challenged the then-prevalent idea that politicians must appeal to as many voters as possible. They don't *have* to do that to win, Riker said, and they *don't* do that. Votes are expensive, for one thing. There is no point in raising additional millions for a race you are already likely to win. Costs can be ideological as well. Every big campaign contribution is a marker that will one day be called in. The fewer people you "owe one," the better.

Candidates therefore strive to win by the smallest comfortable margin possible. With the plurality vote, minimal coalitions are particularly simple. Anyone who secures 50 percent support plus one vote is guaranteed to win. Oh, in practice you throw in another percent or two for margin of error. Much of today's political strategizing consists of slicing and dicing the electorate to identify the 51 percent who can be persuaded to vote for a candidate.

A system that changes that rule—that forces politicians to look at a broader public good—may well be a tough sell to those whose skill set is so finely optimized to the status quo.

The feud between Richie's Center and the arrogant, pushy scientists began to get messy in 2005. Warren Smith started his own Center for Range Voting (motto: "Get Real Democracy"). Despite the soundalike name, this "Center" is basically just a website (www.rangevoting.org). Most of the content is written by Smith, who makes a multifaceted case for the superiority of range voting while savaging every other voting system out there.

In the 2006 IRV campaigns, Richie found himself battling letter-writing campaigns from range voting "zealots." These were mostly people who learned about range voting from Smith's site. "What zealots basically do is follow real political opportunities we've created and try to jump into the debate and say our system's wrong," Richie said. "We've got this IRV campaign in Pierce County now, and these range voting people are sending letters to the editor. That's not helping them, it's just making us irritated."

The referenda were about adopting IRV, yes or no. Thus reasoned attacks on IRV didn't directly help range voting, certainly annoyed IRV's supporters and Richie, and mainly went over the head of most civilians. "I must admit it's hard for me to be as rational as I'd like to be about range voting because of the ongoing antics of Warren Smith and especially his rather crazed missionary Clay Shentrup," said Richie. Shentrup, a Seattle grunge rock musician who performs under the name "Broken Ladder," must qualify as one of the most militant figures in voting reform. "FOR ANYONE WHO DOESN'T KNOW, I HAVE BEEN OBSESSING OVER VOTING METHODS THIS SUMMER," Shentrup reported on his blog in 2006. "I HAVE RECENTLY BEEN MAKING A LOT OF PHONE CALLS TO PEOPLE IN THE GREEN PARTY AND LIBERTARIAN PARTY, AND OTHER VOTING REFORM ADVOCATES, TRYING TO CONVINCE THEM TO PUSH FOR RANGE VOTING, INSTEAD OF THIS HORRIBLE INSTANT RUNOFF VOTING THING THEY ARE PUSHING FOR . . ."

Richie's side of the story is that "Clay calls IRV advocates up late at night to rant at them . . . Seems like a bright guy in a certain way, but I suspect someone's going to need a restraining order from him in some part of his life."

Richie finds the range voting crowd politically naïve. He believes their behavior ends up supporting the status quo. In the short run, this is undeniably true. Range voting was not on the ballot in 2006 and has not been on the ballot *anywhere*.

The vast majority of the voters who approved IRV in San Francisco, North Carolina, Minneapolis, and elsewhere probably would be hard put to explain exactly how IRV differs from other ranked voting systems. What they have bought into is simple: a way of voting that lets people express their feelings about candidates more precisely *and* the promise that the system will prevent spoilers. Smith contends that range voting delivers on that promise better than IRV does.

One does not have to be much of a cynic to see that politics is not just about what the voters want. Political parties have become a battleground in the war between IRV and range voting. Both groups are courting the Greens and Libertarians (whose money and organizational ability far exceeds that of either "Center"). So far, IRV is way ahead with third-party endorsements. Smith claims that range voting is better for small parties.

He cites evidence from Ireland and Australia, nations that use IRV for single-office seats. Both nations have a long-entrenched two-party system. Smith conjectures that range voting will be better for growing third parties because of what he calls the "nursery effect."

This is best explained with an example. Smith has said that, in the 2004 presidential election, he would have cast this range vote (on a scale of zero to one hundred):

Ralph Nader, John Kerry, and David Cobb (Green Party): one hundred points each.

George W. Bush, Michael Peroutka (Constitution Party): zero points each.

Michael Badaranik (Libertarian), Roger Calero (Socialist Workers): twenty points each.

Smith maximized the difference between front runners Bush and Kerry. He liked Nader and Cobb as much or more than Kerry, so they also got one hundred. He liked Peroutka as little or less than Bush, forcing a zero score. This left two other third-party candidates (Badaranik and Calero) that Smith judged to be between Bush and Kerry in appeal. Smith rated them candidly. His point is, it's ridiculous to play a strategy game with candidates who have such remote chances of winning. (Calero *couldn't* have taken office, even had he won. He was born in Nicaragua.) By giving Badaranik and Calero twenty points, Smith expresses the fact that he finds them preferable to one of the major candidates in the race.

This is the "nursery effect." A minor candidate who convinces range voters that he offers a superior alternative to one of the two major candidates will encourage voters to score him honestly. "Small third parties are like infants," Smith wrote. "They cannot survive in the jungle . . . Range voting gives them that nurturing so that they can grow up instead of being stomped on by an elephant." But "once they grow up and get big and tough," range voting "throws them out of the nursery."

If it looked as if Badaranik or Calero might actually win, you'd probably want to vote strategically. They'd no longer need the nursery effect, and they wouldn't get it.

Had this been an approval ballot, Smith would *not* have approved Badaranik and Calero. Had this been an IRV ballot, Smith would have ranked Badaranik and Calero fourth and fifth (or left them off entirely). Smith therefore believes that range voting makes it easier to gauge the true support of minor candidates. This, in turn, is good for any party looking to broaden its appeal and challenge the major parties.

The elephant (and donkey) in the room *is* those major parties. What's in it for them? Richie is the pragmatist, collecting endorsements from prominent Democrats and Republicans and trying to reassure all that IRV is nothing to fear. Smith is no fan of the major parties. He faults IRV for not hastening their decline quickly enough.

One too-little-acknowledged fact is that *any* voting method that solves the problem of vote splitting will make changes in party politics. It is vote splitting that enforces the two-party system. Eliminate vote splitting, and things will be different—how different, no one knows.

"The party structure is not a given," Kenneth Arrow said. "It's a consequence of the electoral structure. So it's pretty hard to disentangle."

Plurality voting is the only system that pays no attention at all to how many people *dislike* a candidate. The result is a bias in favor of relatively extreme, out-of-the-mainstream candidates. "Moderates" find it harder to get elected. I put "moderate" in quotes because it means here only a candidate who happens to lie between two others ideologically. The in-between candidate might actually be far right or far left, as long as someone else is even farther out there.

Democratic systems strive to achieve a good fit between the electorate and the winning candidate. This generally means electing a so-called "moderate." The point is not to endorse political moderation but to advocate political reality. Everyone can't get exactly what he wants. When you look at the unruly spectrum of voter opinion and try to identify the candidate who will achieve the greatest overall satisfaction, it will usually be someone near the political center of gravity, *not* an "extremist." This has implications for leadership. A leader has to make hard decisions that won't please everyone. Those decisions become all the harder when the leader is battling the perception that she represents only half (or less) of the voters. Moderates have the best mandates.

How easy should it be for a "moderate" to win? I suppose most people's gut reaction is that a moderate should have neither a special advantage nor a special disadvantage. There are moderates who aren't qualified ("President Perot"). There have been elections where the moderate was the *only* sane choice (Roemer v. Edwards v. Duke). It all depends. Character, competence, experience, and charisma count as much as ideology. Voters, rather than the arbitrary bias of the voting system, should decide which candidate offers the best overall package.

This is roughly what all the brave new voting systems attempt to offer. But as Richie says, there is a perception that IRV is less transformative. In practice, of the popular systems it is probably the closest to a plurality vote. IRV allows candidates to continue microtargeting their 51 percent of the vote, heedless of the other 49 percent. Warren Smith damns IRV for being a glass half full. The incompleteness of IRV's reform may in fact be why Richie has been able to achieve as much as he has.

Not that IRV has always been an easy sell. In the San Francisco IRV campaign, "There were two communities that were really against it," Richie said. "One was political consultants, who had been used to doing two campaigns [for a primary and a runoff] and now might only be doing one. The political consultants' role became particularly important when it was narrowed down to two, because then it's zero sum. It's wedge issues, polarization, punishing negative ads. The downtown business community liked the lower turnout in the December runoff because they thought it helped their candidate. They liked being able to pummel the person they didn't like."

The power structure in San Francisco is not so different from that anywhere else. (America's mobile consultant caste ensures that different regions' politics are now as similar as their Wal-Marts.) The near-universal political fantasy is that, *if only my party could get in power* and run this city, state, or country a few years, things would be so much better. Those dopes in the other party would have to admit how wrong they were. Has this ever happened? Is it going to happen? Not in this world. Partisans will not be dissuaded by pragmatic arguments, not even by the object lesson of a happy, well-functioning society achieved in some way alien to their own philosophy.

The plurality vote plays to the fantasy. It offers proportional representation in time. We have a left-of-center party in power about half the time and a right-of-center party in power the other half of the time. Once a party gets voted in, it makes some changes, and the winners think things are going great. Problems are blamed on the foot-dragging opposition. The other half of the country nitpicks the new political era, delights in its failings, and schemes to recover power.

Eventually the pendulum does swing the other way. And even that's not so bad. Ralph Nader was candid enough to admit what many on the left and right must feel inside. When you're on a mission from God, it sometimes helps to have the "bad guys" in power.

We would like to think only genuine changes in voters' minds and hearts ought to change the way the country is run. Parties that want power have a responsibility to persuade, to compete in the marketplace of political ideas. The reality is that parties and candidates are managed by ideologues who believe they know what's best for the country better than the voters do. They also know that persuading the voters (in any deep sense) is glacially slow compared to what is possible with our back-and-forth plurality vote. For those who run the political show, the present system's mood swings may be more satisfying than the prospect of a system that fairly reflects what the voters want.

SEVENTEEN

Blue Man Coup

Rick Santorum lost his big bet on Green. Despite the infusion of Republican money, Pennsylvania Green candidate Carl Romanelli fell a few thousand valid signatures short of making the 2006 ballot. That development was bad news for Santorum and good news for his true challenger, Democrat Bob Casey, Jr. "It's 14:59 and Romanelli's 15 minutes of fame are up," gloated Casey press secretary Larry Smar. "The question is whether Rick Santorum will ask Romanelli for his money back."

He didn't, and Santorum wasn't giving up on Romanelli all that fast. He insisted on including Romanelli in the televised debate of Senate candidates. Casey insisted he would debate Santorum alone or not at all. The debate ended up being between Santorum, Romanelli, and an empty chair.

Probably nothing could have saved Santorum's neck in the Republican rout of 2006. Call it karma, or irrelevant alternatives. Some key Democratic gains in Congress were due to the spoiler effect, much as had been George W. Bush's presidential victory six years earlier.

In Arizona, Democrat Gabrielle Giffords beat Randy Graf for the seat representing the Eighth Congressional District. No Democrat had won that conservative district in a generation. The money that Giffords's supporters spent on ads in behalf of Graf in the Republican primary may well have bought the Democratic Party a House seat.

There were a couple of Senate races where the Republican Party must regret not paying more attention to spoilers. In Virginia, Republican incumbent George Allen spent more than twelve million dollars. Like Santorum, Allen had been considered a shoo-in for reelection and possible presidential material for 2008. His troubles began when he called a campaign tracker "macaca." The video went up on YouTube, and the media reported the word to be an obscure ethnic slur. YouTube's range voters gave the "macaca" video four stars out of five. That's more impressive than Allen's showing in the real election, where he trailed Democrat Jim Webb by 7,217 votes. Independent Green Party candidate Glenda Parker got about 26,000 votes.

Most of Parker's votes might otherwise have gone to Webb. Allen had the presence of mind to promote having Parker in his debate with Webb. Predictably, Webb wasn't keen on that. (The League of Women Voters kept Parker out of the debate, citing a rule requiring participants to be polling 15 percent support.) Had Parker gotten just a little more publicity—from the debate, ads, *anything*—she undoubtedly could have wrested 7,218 more votes from Webb. Allen then would have won *and* prevented a Democratic takeover of the Senate. Guess how much Parker spent on her campaign? "Less than $600" in contributions, she told a reporter, plus several years' worth of her own vacation money.

Then there's the Blue Man from Bozeman. In 1999, Stan Jones began drinking colloidal silver, a supposed "natural" antibiotic. He feared that Y2K computer crashes would lead to societal collapse. That, in turn, would mean no antibiotics for the marauding bands of postapocalyptic survivors. The silver potion has the side effect of turning the skin a slatey blue. When Jones first ran for U.S. Senate in 2002, his complexion was a hue that might otherwise signal a dinner companion's desperate need for the Heimlich maneuver. "People ask me if it's permanent and if I'm dead," Jones said. "It's my fault I overdosed, but I still believe it's the best antibiotic in the world."

Unlike most third-party candidates, Jones had no trouble getting media coverage. Much of it was along the lines of "News of the Weird: Smurf Runs for Senate." Jones was not the ideal advertisement for libertarian philosophies. It is tough to argue that we don't need nanny-government agencies to regulate drug safety when your listeners' first question is going to be "Dude, why are you blue?"

By 2006, Jones had stopped taking his miracle elixir. His complexion reverted to something a few shades less cadaverous. Without the blue-man gimmick to fall back on, he had to earn attention with sound bites alone. Fortunately, he was "batshit crazy," one blogger reported. During a debate with his major-party opponents, he "launched into a tirade about emerging 'world communist government' forged by 'secret meetings between Bush and other leaders'" and "also about 'little microchips inserted in our brains' (I am not making this up . . .)"

In interviews, Jones has admitted not paying income taxes. He believes that the United States government was "either complacent or involved" in 9-11 and that one-world government nasties are plotting to replace the United States with a "North American Union" using a currency called the "Amero" and a constitution based on "that of Communist Russia."

Think that's a wacko conspiracy theory? Well, try this one on for size: on Election Day 2006, a mystery man most Americans had never heard of controlled the balance of power in the mightiest nation on Earth. That man was Stan Jones.

In order to gain a majority in the U.S. Senate, the Democratic Party needed to add six seats to the forty-five they controlled, without losing any. The party won Santorum's seat in Pennsylvania, Allen's in Virginia, and others' in Rhode Island, Ohio, and Missouri. That left only Montana. There, the Big Sky State's scandal-plagued Republican senator Conrad Burns lost to Democrat Jon Tester by only 2,847 votes. Stan

Jones got 10,324. It's a safe bet that Jones pulled votes mainly from Burns and that he cost a conservative Republican reelection in what remained a very conservative state. Montana gave the Democrats a fifty-one-seat Senate majority. Minority leader Harry Reid thereby became majority leader (and, yes, Reid had been elected to the Senate in 1998 only because of another Libertarian spoiler).

There are some big differences between science and politics. Kenneth Arrow remarked on them in my conversation with him. "As a scientist, you can say, 'Oh boy, what I said last year is wrong!'" he explained. "That's broad-minded, up to date, intellectually progressive. In politics, it's a pretty bad idea."

It is nearly impossible to champion political change without adopting a pretense of certainty. Reality is rarely so black and white. Nothing is certain . . . except maybe mathematics.

Warren Smith's case for range voting is about as compelling as a purely mathematical case can be. The question is how it will play out in political practice. I suspect that no one on this planet is capable of predicting all the consequences of a voting system.

For what it's worth, range voting has more of a track record than most systems. It's all over the Internet, and its approval-voting form worked well enough for Renaissance Venice and still does for the United Nations. That tends to dispel fears of any truly terrible unintended consequences.

America has become Condorcet's "experiment" in democracy. The nation has been tinkering with its ways of voting ever since the Revolution. Relatively obscure systems such as cumulative voting and Bucklin voting (a ranked system with approval-like features) once found homes in towns of the plains and Western states. Today IRV is getting a real trial in the American context. That is sure to tell us things we won't learn any other way. The theoretical case for range (and approval) voting is more compelling yet. A real-world trial is overdue. I imagine that even the system's critics would endorse this. If range voting is as bad as they think, they would have the empirical data to support this. (And the community could go back to plurality voting or try IRV or something else.) If range voting is as good as its proponents think, we'd have learned something more valuable yet. "There are few ways we as individuals can work effectively against the widespread evils of the modern world," Guy Ottewell wrote. "Helping to bring about really sound elections could be the most powerful."

Surely there are a few American communities willing to volunteer?

Glossary

Approval Voting

☒ Adams

☐ Bush

☒ Clay

☐ DeWitt

It's like the familiar **plurality vote** except that you're allowed to vote for more than one candidate. As usual, the candidate getting the most votes wins. Approval voting is simple and solves the problems of **spoilers** and **vote splitting**. See pages 191–92.

Borda Count

2 Adams

3 Bush

1 Clay

4 DeWitt

Voters rank the candidates from most to least preferred: 1, 2, 3, etc. The rankings are then converted into points. In an election with four candidates, every first-place ranking is worth three points, second place is worth two points, third place is one point, and fourth (last) place is worth nothing. The points are added, and the candidate with the most points wins. Named for French mathematician Jean-Charles de Borda (1733–1799), the Borda count is easy to manipulate. It is used mainly in sports polls—and has led to scandals there. See pages 140–41.

Glossary

Clones

Similar candidates who appeal to the same group of voters. With a **plurality vote**, two popular clones can split the vote, leading to the election of someone less popular. See page 189.

Condorcet Cycle

A puzzling situation described by the Marquis de Condorcet. It is possible for two-way majority votes to produce a circular outcome: Candidate A may beat B, B may beat C, *and* C may beat A. Who then should win? This intriguing paradox has spurred the development of voting theory. In strictly practical terms, it may be an overrated concept. Condorcet cycles are rare to nonexistent in real elections. See pages 38–39 and 144.

Condorcet Voting

2   Adams

3   Bush

1   Clay

4   DeWitt

The basic idea is that the proper winner of an election should be able to beat every other candidate in two-way votes. Proposed by the Marquis de Condorcet (1743–1794), this method is most easily realized by having voters fill out ballots ranking the candidates and letting computers determine the winner. The commonsense rationale has made Condorcet voting popular with some online communities, but there are cases where the Condorcet winner is clearly not the best choice. See pages 142–43.

Condorcet Winner

A candidate who is the majority favorite in two-way votes with each of the other candidates. The goal of **Condorcet voting** is to elect the Condorcet winner—if there is one. See page 142.

Cumulative Voting

40	Adams
20	Bush
40	Clay
0	DeWitt

Each voter gets a fixed number of votes (say one hundred) to allocate among the candidates as desired. The number of votes cast by each voter must add up to the correct total. The candidates with the greatest number of votes are elected. Cumulative voting is a **proportional representation** system used to elect legislatures. Casting the most effective cumulative ballot requires accurate knowledge of party strength. In practice, political parties tell followers how to vote in order to secure the greatest possible number of seats for the party.

Impossibility Theorem

The foundation of modern voting theory. Economist Kenneth Arrow (b. 1921) demonstrated that no ranked-choice voting system can meet a set of commonsense conditions; therefore all such ways of voting are defective. The impossibility theorem has led some scholars to conclude that democracy is fatally flawed. Scoring systems (such as **approval** and **range voting**) fall outside the scope of the impossibility theorem. See pages 43–44 and 47–52.

Instant-Runoff Voting (IRV)

2	Adams
3	Bush
1	Clay
4	DeWitt

Each voter ranks the candidates in order of preference. If one candidate gets a majority of first-place votes, that candidate wins. Otherwise, the least popular candidate (by number of first-place votes) is eliminated, and all the ballots ranking him number one are redistributed to the ballots' second-place choices. The process of elimination and redistribution continues until one candidate has a majority of the vote. This simulates a series of runoffs in which the least popular candidate of each round is eliminated. In a typical American election, "third-party" votes ultimately count toward the major-party candidate each voter judges more acceptable. When there are three or more strong candidates, IRV can produce quirky results. See pages 166–67.

Glossary

Plurality Voting

☐ Adams

☐ Bush

☒ Clay

☐ DeWitt

This is the method used in nearly all American elections: "one man, one vote." It is prone to **vote splitting**. See page 47.

Proportional Representation

The doctrine that political parties (or other groups) should be represented in a legislature in proportion to their size in the electorate. Neither the **plurality vote** nor its many rival systems can guarantee this. Achieving proportional representation requires a voting method devised for that purpose, such as the **single transferable vote** or **cumulative voting**. See pages 163–65.

Range Voting

[9] Adams

[1] Bush

[10] Clay

[0] DeWitt

Voters rate the candidates on a scale of zero to ten (or any other numerical range specified). The candidate with the highest average rating wins. Range voting can be confused with **cumulative voting** (where the numbers awarded to candidates must add up to a fixed total). Range voting is used widely in Internet polls and not at all in public elections. Yet computer studies suggest that it may be the best voting system of all. See pages 233–36.

Single Transferable Vote (STV)

[2] Adams

[3] Bush

[1] Clay

[4] DeWitt

The most popular system for **proportional representation**, used globally. Voters rank the candidates in order of preference. Unpopular candidates are successively eliminated and their supporters' votes are transferred to other candidates, ensuring that no vote is "wasted." STV is easier for voters than another proportional system, **cumulative voting**. When STV is used to elect a single candidate, it is called **instant-runoff voting** (IRV). See pages 164–65.

Glossary

Spoilers

Minor candidates who draw enough votes from a would-be winner to cause him to lose. In a two-party system, spoilers are the most familiar form of **vote splitting**. See page 20.

Vote Splitting

The central flaw of **plurality voting**. A group of like-minded voters may split their votes among two or more similar candidates rather than rallying behind one. Vote splitting diminishes the chances that any of the affected candidates will win. Most of the voting methods in this book were devised to prevent vote splitting. See page 20.

Voting Cycle (see *Condorcet Cycle*)

Addresses

There are many excellent websites on voting reform. The two most readable and comprehensive (and mutually antagonistic) are those of FairVote: The Center for Voting and Democracy (www.fairvote.org) and the Center for Range Voting (www.rangevoting.org).

Approval voting has two sites, one for Citizens for Approval Voting (www.approval voting.org), and another for the affiliated PAC, Americans for Approval Voting (www .approvalvoting.com).

The Electoral Reform Society, which can trace its roots back to Charles Dodgson, covers proportional representation and related topics at www.electoral-reform.org.uk.

Electowiki (www.wiki.electorama.com/wiki/Main_Page) has a detailed discussion of scores of voting methods and their properties. It is more technically oriented than the above sites.

Highly recommended is Ka-Ping Yee's webpage on voting at www.zesty.ca/voting. Yee has devised a brilliant way of presenting the results of voting systems as colorful maps. This is probably the best way of appreciating the fine points of IRV's "winner-turns-loser" paradox or the Borda anti-spoiler effect.

Writing politicians is a quixotic task. A reasonable place to start is with those who have spoken in favor of IRV. They are ahead of the curve. They know there's a problem with plurality voting and are willing to promote change. Tell them you care about voting reform; someone in their office will read it, and letters help to set priorities. Three of IRV's most influential supporters are:

Addresses

Governor Howard Dean

Chairman, Democratic National Committee

430 S. Capitol St. SE

Washington, DC 20003

www.democrats.org/page/petition/chairman

The Honorable John McCain

United States Senate

241 Russell Senate Office Building

Washington, DC 20510-0303

mccain.senate.gov/index.cfm?fuseaction=Contact.Home

The Honorable Barack Obama

United States Senate

713 Hart Senate Office Building

Washington, DC 20510

obama.senate.gov/contact/index.php

Notes

Prologue: The Wizard and the Lizard

3   "outstanding leadership potential": Maginnis 1992, 18.

4   "WHEN WAS THE LAST TIME WHITEY": Rider 1991, 41.

4   "We had to get David out": Ibid.

5   Raised nineteen thousand dollars to pay a fifty-five-dollar fine: *Newsweek*, Nov. 18, 1991, 27, 28; also Maginnis 1992, 26, which gives slightly different figures.

5   "plays the system like a violin": Bridges 2001, 33.

6   "Two out of ten women": Maginnis 1992, 7.

6   "is granted up to $200,000": New Orleans *Times-Picayune*, Aug. 2, 1992.

6   "I like to gamble": Bridges 2001, 35.

6   "It was illegal for them to give": Ibid., 32.

6   "What's wrong with making money?": Ibid., 35.

7   Louisiana Democrats outnumbered Republicans twenty to one: Maginnis 1992, 106.

8   Analysis of 1979 race: Maginnis 1992, 107.

8   "so slow it takes him an hour and a half": Bridges 2001, 34.

8   "in bed with a dead girl or a live boy": Ibid.

8   "You are happy with the open primary now": Maginnis 1992, 104.

9   "Give me a wheel barrow for my money": Bridges 2001, 34.

9   "He's the strongest sonofabitchin' governor": Maginnis 1992, 37.

9   Hospital bribes, casino debt: Bridges 2001, 35.

10   "A $100,000 contribution to Edwards": Ibid., 38.

10   33 percent versus 28 percent: Ibid., 39.

10   "The only way Edwards can ever be reelected": Maginnis 1992, 12.

10   "The choice is between Edwin Edwards": Bridges 2001, 39.

10   "I was representing them both": DuBos 2003.

11   "Cancel, cancel": Maginnis 1992, 52.

11   "I felt the Republicans almost had to put up somebody": Ibid., 110.

11   Analysis of presidential chances: Ibid., 111.

12   "If Clyde runs": Ibid., 115.

12   "Dan Quayle helped me make up my mind": quoted in ibid., 114.

13   "I was too intolerant": Ibid., 276.

13   "Do you believe blacks are genetically inferior": Ibid., 99–100.

14   "probably deserve to go into the ash bin": *Newsweek*, Nov. 18, 1991, 25.

14   Evangelical Bible Church didn't exist: Maginnis 1992, 320.

14   "After a rally, the women would": Ibid., 77.

14   Citizen warned Duke to stay away from daughter: Ibid.

14   "out till three or four o'clock": Rider 1991, 41.

14   "Duke is not a womanizer": Maginnis 1992, 330.

14   Picou twenty-six years old: Ibid., 2.

15   "That settled us down some": Ibid., 78.

15   Teeter poll results: Ibid., 160.

15   August, September polls: Ibid., 197.

15   24 percent undecided: Ibid.

16   Avoid being seen with large crowds of black people: Ibid., 269.

16   "David Duke thinks he hates Jews now": Ibid., 264.

16   Bush would vote for Edwards: *Newsweek*, Nov. 18, 1991, 25.

16   "I have sat at my desk and cried": Maginnis 1992, 289.

17   "I'll tell you what happened": Ibid., 289–90.

17   "Mr. Duke, can you name": Ibid., 311.

17   "As spokesman for the Cajuns": Ibid., 303.

18   Bob Hawks claims: *Newsweek*, Nov. 25, 1991, 19.

18   "There were many smart, well-intentioned people": blogger at www.mootlife.com, homepage.mac.com/elliotjscott/iblog/B1924247129/C941640382/E1805629854/.

18   "I'm going to hold my nose": *Newsweek*, Nov. 18, 1991, 28.

18   Runoff election results: Maginnis 1992, 342.

18   "for twenty years created a hunger": Ibid., 344.

18   Harvey's appointment to levee board, corruption charges: Braun and Vartabedian 2005.

19   "We have some frozen sperm": Baughman 2002.

19   "I will be a model prisoner": Ibid.

21   "everywhere except where": Hillinger 2006, 9.

21   Campaign spending figures: www.opensecrets.org.

Notes

I. Game Theory

27 Gödel's wife forbade him from driving: Dawson 1997, 179.

27 "Well, are you ready": Ibid., 180.

27 "Do you think a dictatorship": Ibid.

27 "I know how that can happen!": Suber 1990.

27 Gödel moved by Forman's talk: Dawson 1997, 180.

27 Enjoyed *Bambi, Snow White*: Ibid., 181.

29 "We're beaten; terrible outlook": www.fff.org/freedom/fd0403a.asp.

31 Morgenstern presented himself as a man of the world: Steve Brams, interview, New York, Aug. 30, 2005.

31 Claimed relation to Kaiser Friedrich: In Kenneth Arrow's recollection, Morgenstern claimed descent from an illegitimate daughter of Friedrich. See also Sylvia Nasar's *A Beautiful Mind* (1998), 84.

31 Morgenstern's faults: Shubik 1978.

32 Von Neumann attended talk: Morgenstern 1976, 807.

32 Morgenstern insisted von Neumann's name go first: Ibid., 813.

32 "The skepticism concerning Morgenstern's contribution": Shubik 1978, 132.

33 "We would have all been happier": Ibid., 133.

33 "Without Oskar, I would have never written": Ibid., 132.

33 "I never knew how well": Arrow, interview, Palo Alto, Calif., Dec. 16, 2005.

34 Forced to go out and play as punishment: Feiwel 1987b, 3–4.

34 "There was a very famous logician": Arrow, interview.

35 "I never thought of this": Ibid.

35 "places of business": Hotelling 1929, 45.

36 "tendency of the outermost entrepreneurs": Ibid., 56.

36 "Buyers are confronted": Ibid., 54, 57.

37 "Each candidate 'pussyfoots'": Ibid., 54.

38 "What bothered me": Arrow, interview.

39 "Instead of seeing this as an intellectual opportunity": Ibid.

39 "I thought I had heard": Feiwel 1987a, 191.

40 "There was a third episode": Arrow, interview.

40 "It had been brought to my attention": Black 1996, xvii.

41 "Acting apparently at random": Ibid.

41 "forty-seven-year-old wife": quoted in Klein 2006, 80.

42 "This Air Force thing": Feiwel 1987b, 647.

42 "The idea was that because of the new nature of warfare": Arrow, interview.

42 "Everyone sat up": Feiwel 1987b, 647.

42   Studied placement of U.S. submarines: Oppenheimer 2004, 2.

42   "People were *trying* to be helpful": Arrow, interview.

43   "Oh! That is nothing": Feiwel 1987a, 193.

43   "I just started playing around": Arrow, interview.

44   "Ted, would you look at this?": Feiwel 1987a, 667.

2. The Big Bang

46   1997 skating judging: Loosemore 1997.

46   "something that adds significantly to the suspense": Ibid.

46   "If you are in front of me": Landsburg 1999.

49   "If a man says he likes Republicans better than Democrats": Riker 1982, 17.

51   "when I used that term": Arrow, interview.

51   Compared to Gödel's proof: See Samuelson 1997, 938; Brams and Fishburn 2002, 178 (which also poses a parallel to Heisenberg's uncertainty principle).

51   "The search of the great minds": Samuelson 1977, 938.

52   "for their pioneering contributions": www.almaz.com/nobel/economics/1972b.html.

52   "perhaps the most": www.nobelprize.org/nobel_prizes/economics/laureates/1972/press.html.

52   "Obviously, he was a little miffed": Arrow, interview.

52   Arrow cost Bergson a Nobel Prize: This is Paul Samuelson's view in Samuelson 2004, 25. Samuelson maintains that Bergson's work on social welfare functions was more distinct from Arrow's than the Nobel judges appreciated.

52   "Whatever the merits": Black 1996, xviii.

53   "the activities of the Rand Corporation": Ibid.

53   "During the 1930s and 1940s": Amadae 2003, 2.

54   "it is no exaggeration": Ibid., 10–11.

54   "part of the campaign": Ibid.

54   "I gave a talk on this": Arrow, interview.

55   "Many forms of Government have been tried": House of Commons, Nov. 11, 1947 (quoted in Baker 1990).

55   "Those who cast the votes": Though this quote appears widely on the web and in some printed sources, I suspect it's a fake. I was unable to find it in any Stalin biography. Google Book Search lists ten books containing the quote, but none are primarily about Stalin, and all date from 2002 or later. See also urbanlegends.about.com/od/dubiousquotes/a/stalin_quote.htm.

55   "What Kenneth Arrow proved": Hillinger 2004, 3.

56   *Congressional Government*: Wilson 1885.

57   "the big bang": Sen 1986, 1074.

3. A Short History of Vote Splitting

59 "a beautiful example": Klarreich 2002.

60 Polk owned slaves: Riker 1982, 224.

61 "the agitation of the slavery question is mischievous": Polk 1910, vol. 4, 251. The entry is dated December 22, 1848.

66 Theory that Breckinridge meant to pull out: Davis 1974 and Tabarrok and Spector 1999, 283.

67 "open ally of the saloon": quoted in Gustafson 2001.

67 "We want the Democratic Party to bite the dust": minutes of the 1885 annual meeting of the Woman's Christian Temperance Union, quoted in ibid.

71 "fathead . . . dumber than a guinea pig": see www.elections.harpweek.com/1912/cartoon-1912-Medium.asp?UniqueID=18&Year=1912.

72 "Where but to the Socialist Party": Shulte 2004.

74 Measured hem lengths with tape measure: Sifry 2002, 102.

74 "In the final analysis": Cohn 2000.

74 Dole claimed 57 percent against Clinton: Saari 1995, 11.

74 "never saw my presidency as legitimate": Morris 1997, 31.

75 Pomper survey: Pomper 1993 and Brams and Merrill 1994.

75 POWs, Perot grudge against Bush, assassination claim: Posner 1977; www.realchange.org/perot.htm.

76 Perot believed Rollins was a CIA spy for Bush: Klein 2006, 164.

78 "Nader's own Lewis Carroll alternate reality": Levine 2004.

78 Nader was backer of *Roger and Me*: Martin 2002, 250.

78 "We're going to do it": Levine 2004.

78 "Moore instantly turned and looked hard": Ibid.

79 Quarter of public would vote for McCain as third-party candidate: Sifry 2002, 214.

79 "At the end of the day": Moore and Slater 2003, 240.

79 "If you are the establishment": Ibid.

80 "We're going to": C-SPAN coverage quoted in ibid., 256.

80 "had chosen to sire children without marriage": Davis 2004.

80 "the fag candidate": RussBLib in blog at www.bartcopnation.com/dc/dcboard.php?az=show_topic&forum=8&topic_id=522.

81 "Wait a minute, that's a universal negative": Davis 2004.

81 "We had no idea": Ibid.

81 "Don't give me that shit": Moore and Slater 2003, 257. Slightly different versions of this exchange have appeared elsewhere. See Kelley 2004, 598.

82 "We are not going to do that": Levine 2004.

83 Vidal thought Nader an ideal candidate: Martin 2002, 150.

83 Nader feared being a spoiler, helping Nixon: Ibid., 151.

83 "The vice president has no time": Ibid., 227.

83 Gore was one of top ten senators sympathetic to Nader: Ibid., 226.

84 "Well, I'll see": Ibid., 227.

84 "George Ronald Clinton": Nader interview, by Wesley J. Smith, in *Mother Jones*, July/ August 1996.

84 "none of the above" pitch to New Hampshire voters: Martin 2002, 229.

84 "If I really wanted to beat Clinton": quoted in Levine 2004.

84 "Since you're planning to raise $5 million": quoted in ibid.

84 Nader's views on Bush, Gore: see for instance Martin 2002, 253.

85 "Ralph, this is shaping up": Ibid., 245.

85 "had a personal animus": Ibid., 254.

85 "We opposed it": Ibid., 263.

85 Bill Jones letter: Raskin 2004.

86 "engaging in a self-indulgent exercise": quoted in Sifry 2002, 200.

86 "I respect what you have to say": Ibid.

86 "I have never said": Ibid., 207.

86 "I will not speak his name": Martin 2002, 268.

86 "That Bastard" and "Grim Reaper": Ibid., 265.

87 "responded like I'd joined": Ibid., 264.

87 "the object being to *deny* them": Sifry 2002, 299.

88 Campaigned in swing states: Martin 2002, 263; ibid., 342–43.

88 "went into the swing states": Martin 2002, 264.

88 "I wouldn't vote for Al Gore": www.workingforchange.com/printitem.cfm?itemid=9670.

89 "I want to kill him": Sifry 2002, 224.

89 "I'll strangle the guy": Ibid.

89 "Screw the corporate media": Martin 2002, 266.

89 Watched returns on black-and-white TV: Ibid., 267.

89 "Fearless leader!": www.workingforchange.com/printitem.cfm?itemid=9670.

90 *ABC News* poll: released Nov. 8, 2000, and cited in Sifry 2002, 311.

4. The Most Evil Man in America

92 John Beckley: Strother 2003, xiii, calls Beckley an "ace political consultant" probably responsible for getting Jefferson elected president.

93 Mail to 1896 voters; Yiddish publication: Moore and Slater 2003, 159.

93 Napolitan worked for JFK and Johnson, heads of state: www.sourcewatch.org/index .php?title=Joseph_Napolitan.

93   "Campaigns are like arms races": Hill 2002, 149.

94   Seven thousand political consultants: Moore and Slater 2003, 9.

94   Number of consultants reputedly tripled in the 1990s: Hill 2002, 146.

94   Atwater birthdate: Brady 1997, 4.

94   "He's not mean enough": Ibid., 12.

94   "Lee Atwater is the probably the most evil man": Ibid., 195.

94   "If I've done an innovative thing": Ibid., 104.

95   "While I didn't invent 'negative politics'": Atwater and Brewster 1991, 62.

95   Negative campaigning stories: Kopel 2000 and Geer 2006.

95   "Go out there and tell 'em Coke was caught": Farren 2004.

96   JFK lovers in White House pool: Collins 1998.

96   Finkelstein made *liberal* a dirty word; gay marriage: Klein 2006, 72.

97   "Choose from the following characteristics": Brady 1997, 72.

97   Atwater passed poll results to Sprouse: Ibid., 71–73. This is Marvin Chernoff's recollection of Atwater's 1985 account. As Brady notes, Atwater tended to embellish "dirty tricks" stories.

99   "I'm not going to respond to that guy": Ibid., 84.

99   "Lee, this man said the most terrible things about you on TV": Ibid.

99   "If there's a hand grenade rolling around": Ibid., 138.

100   Dukakis opposition research staff, budget: Ibid., 171–72.

100   "The only group I was very interested in": Ibid., 171.

100   "They're going to try to tear you": Ibid., 177.

100   "I felt that keeping it positive": Ibid.

101   Raped woman twice, slashed man twenty-two times: Klein 2006, 103.

101   Focus group; played tapes for Bush: Brady 1997, 177–79.

101   "Obviously, I am for Dukakis": Ibid., 192.

101   "Did you hear about Willie's endorsement?": Ibid.

102   "Governor, if Kitty Dukakis": www.en.wikipedia.org/wiki/Michael_Dukakis.

102   "'We can't afford to alienate white voters'": Brady 1997, 213.

102   "Hey, don't pay any attention": Ibid., 188.

103   "But they sure do": Klein 2006, 208.

103   "I'm fed up with it": Simon 2004.

103   Atwater womanizing; story about Secret Service: Brady 1997, 126.

104   Deal between Atwater and Democrats over infidelity rumors: Brodie and Mack 1990, 88.

104   Question about "adulterous" affair: LeBoutillier 2001.

104   "The answer to the 'A' question": Ibid.

104   "I'm just as Republican as Lee Atwater": Brady 1997, 236.

104   Seizure, vision, tumor diagnosis: Ibid., 268–69.

104   "I can't imagine me getting back": Ibid., 278.

105   Confessed affairs to wife, friends: Ibid., 313.

105   "My illness helped me to see what was missing in society": quoted in ibid., 314.

105   West study of negative ads: Klein 2006, 106.

105   "the most toxic midterm": Nagourney 2006.

105   "extra-chromosome crowd": Brady 1997, 103.

106   Nine-dot puzzle: Ibid., 144.

106   Answer to puzzle:

5. Run, Ralph, Run!

107   "We're not alike": Moore and Slater 2003, 138.

108   "would be the first to go": Malchow 2003, 247.

108   "There is no middle": Lemann 2003.

109   Gompers's charges, list of fifteen thousand donors: Shulte 2004.

110   "more than $100,000": CNN transcript, aired July 12, 2002.

110   "We disavow and condemn": Ibid.

110   Rumor of Rove's involvement: Moore and Slater 2003, 69.

110   "They pretty much admitted": Ibid.

110   "There's no evidence that Rove": Ibid., 69–70.

112   "I thought it would be bad for us": Blumenthal 2004a.

112   "should be given all the fair-labor standards": Buchanan and Nader 2004.

112   Major contractor of RNC: Miller and Irmas 2005, which reports 2004 RNC payments of $8.4 million to Sproul.

113   "pretty mad": Knapp 2004.

113   "clearly nonplussed": Blumenthal 2004a.

113   "Confronted with the accusation": Blumenthal 2004b.

113   "I'm not being paid": quoted in Blumenthal 2004a.

114   Democratic e-mail: Cohen 2004.

115   "opposed to Congressional pay raises": Ibid.

115   "perhaps the one issue out of a thousand": Ibid.

115 "pull some very crucial votes": Ibid.

115 "apparently embarrassed at how many will be shown": Ibid.

115 "It's a free country": Ibid.

115 "it is my fervent hope": Brewer 2004.

115 "We won't take any signatures from them": Cohen 2004.

116 "We have to get on the ballot": Ibid.

116 "We don't want that money": Ibid.

116 "It is conceivable that pro-Bush, pro-Republicans": Ibid.

116 "Republicans are human beings too": Ibid.

116 Moore biography: Walley 2003 and Wikipedia entry, www.en.wikipedia.org/wiki/ Roy_Moore.

117 "If the feds want this plaque": Walley 2003.

117 "call out the State Police": Ibid.

117 Third-largest party: Clarkson 2004, which says the Constitution Party had 320,000 members.

118 "Why Christians Should Not Vote": www.intellectualconservative.com/article3114 .html.

118 "The possibility that Roy Moore": Clarkson 2004.

118 "the Supreme Court shall not have jurisdiction": HR 3799.

118 "there's nothing to keep three men": Clarkson 2004, quoting a *New York Times* piece.

118 "Some judge would probably let a man": Ibid.

118 "I personally like Judge Roy Moore": Ibid.

119 "After you have divided up the secure Bush states": Ibid.

119 Sifry on Colorado and Oregon: Ibid.

119 "It's time for Democrats": Noah 2004.

119 "But, if Alabamians have learned anything": quoted in Clarkson 2004.

6. Year of the Spoiler

120 "a congressman we can be proud of": www.en.wikipedia.org/wiki/Duke_Cunningham.

121 "Tijuana sewage": *The Hill*, May 18, 2006, www.hillnews.com/thehill/export/TheHill/ News/Campaign/051806_airwar.html.

121 Griffith spent two thousand dollars: Jenkins 2006.

121 "most assuredly NOT conservative": www.williamgriffith.us/index.html.

121 "I am grateful for the enthusiasm": Jenkins 2006.

121 "Think lobbyist Brian Bilbray's": radio ad quoted on the Daily Kos blog, www.dailykos .com/storyonly/2006/6/1/131354/2296.

122 "unheard of": Kaplan and O'Connor 2006.

122 "turned his back": "The Mailzilla," 2006.

122   45 versus 44 percent: Ibid.

123   "the year of the 'Spoiler'": www.fairvote.org.

123   Poll found Santorum least popular senator: www.surveyusa.com/50State2006/100USSenatorApproval060523Net.htm.

123   Claim that Iraq weapons of mass destruction had been found: "Rick Santorum," Wikipedia entry, which dates this claim to June 2006.

124   All but thirty dollars came from conservatives: Kiel 2006.

124   "This is politics": Jackson 2006.

125   Nonviolence is fourth of ten values: see Romanelli's campaign website, www.romanelli2006.com/node/6.

125   "I thought he was just": Smith 2006.

125   Poll showing Romanelli getting 5 percent: Hefling 2006.

126   More than $200,000 spent: Archibold 2006.

126   "We don't comment on strategy": Brodesky 2006.

126   Polls showing Giffords would beat Graf; race with Huffman too close to call: Archibold 2006.

126   "When it came time to secure": U.S. News and World Report, Sept. 7, 2006.

126   Huffman held Dean responsible: Kamman 2006.

126   "They're idiots": U.S. News and World Report, Sept. 7, 2006.

126   "Gabby Giffords wanted me": Scarpinato 2006.

127   Friedman biography: O'Keefe 2005.

127   "Thank God for bars": www.news.yahoo.com/s/ap/20060511/ap_on_el_gu/governor_kinky_1.

128   "more than half of her largest": Slater 2006.

128   "This is a never-before-seen": Slater 2005.

128   "I would be pleased": Blumenthal 2006.

129   "Some people I've talked with": Cain 2006.

129   "sexual contact without consent": Stanford 2006.

129   Clark's criminal past; Goldschmidt pedophile: Ibid.

129   "Talk about pennies from heaven" . . . "We're getting money": Cain 2006.

7. Trouble in Kiribati

133   Two Native American houseboys: Darnton 1997, 27.

133   "America offers the prospect": Darnton 1997, quoting Condorcet in A. O'Connor and M. F. Arago, Oeuvres de Condorcet (Paris: Firmin Didot Frères, 1847–49).

134   "America for Condorcet": Darnton 1997, 29.

134   Condorcet's influence, Jefferson translation of anti-slavery essay: Williams 2004, 139–40.

135 "How many eggs in your omelet?": Carlyle, quoted in 1911 *Encyclopaedia Britannica*, vol. 6, 852.

136 "Condorcet himself perished a victim": Todhunter 1931, 352.

136 "what they call 'a good Academician'": Letter, Condorcet to Jacques Turgot, translated by Iain McLean in McLean 2003, 3.

138 "It is an opinion generally held": De Grazia 1953, 43.

138 "One may compare them exactly": Ibid., 44.

138 "Perhaps the truth really is": Reuters 2006.

139 "no way of knowing": Brams and Hager 2002.

140 Heisman trophy: Cabrera 2006.

141 *Essay on the Application*: The original title is *Essai sur l'Application de l'Analyse à la Probabilité des Décisions Rendues à la Pluralité des Voix*.

141 "We must state at once": Todhunter 1931, 352.

142 "A famous mathematician": Iain McLean's translation in McLean 2003, 4.

143 1788 publication: *On the Constitution and Functions of Provincial Assemblies*. See ibid., 7.

144 "As long as it relies": quoted in McLean 2003, 10.

144 "stated so briefly as to be hardly intelligible": quoted in Black 1958, 175.

146 "My scheme is intended": Black 1958, 182.

146 "abused . . . deliberately ranking": McLean 2003, 11.

146 AP poll rigged: Kislanko 2005.

146 "I was at NEC Research Institute": Smith, interview (phone), Oct. 26, 2006, and www.rangevoting.org/rangeVborda.html. I have blended two of Smith's tellings of this tale. Smith adds that parent company NEC survives "thanks to a bailout by the Japanese government." Just for the record, NEC Research Institute merged with NEC USA's Computers and Communication Research Laboratory in 2002 to form NEC Labs (which is still in operation).

147 "good elections are greatly needed": McLean 1990, 103.

147 "In fact no method of election": A. Murray's translation, quoted in ibid., 106.

147 "something akin to finding": Reilly 2002, 361.

148 "It remains to be seen": H. Van Trease, quoted in ibid., 368.

148 Jefferson and Madison owned *Essay*: www.rangevoting.org/ConstVt.html.

148 "Had every Athenian citizen": For this reference I am indebted to Warren D. Smith in Smith 2005a.

8. The New Belfry

149 "A little bit of realism": Cohen 1995, 291. The quoted letter, to actor Wilson Barrett, is dated May 12, 1884.

149 Description of speech impediment: Cohen 1995, 290.

150 "dull as ditchwater": Cohen 1995, quoting a fellow Oxonian.

150 Political affiliations of Liddell, Dodgson: Ibid., 389.

150 "'Early Debased'": Ibid., 387.

151 Attended House of Commons debate: Ibid., 423.

151 "The following paper has been written": reprinted in Black 1958, 222.

151 "whether new or not I cannot say": Ibid., 215.

151 Black found pages uncut: Ibid., 193–94.

152 "we partly used my method": Ibid., 201.

152 "in the immediate prospect": Ibid., 222.

152 Pages of *Essay* uncut: Ibid., 193–94.

153 Sent book to Alice; gift not acknowledged: Cohen 1995, 211.

154 "we will simply state what appears to us": Black 1958, 199–200.

154 "Frankly I think": Black 1996, xx.

154 "God help me to lead a new and better life": Cohen 1995, 208.

155 "Gracious Lord, send Thy Holy Spirit": Ibid., 203.

156 "(As I hope to investigate . . .)": Black 1958, 224.

156 "What responses he got": Ibid., 212.

156 "marked out a race-course": Carroll 1992, 34–35.

156 Committees going around in circles: See de Rooy 2005.

157 "The majorities may be 'cyclical'": Black 1958, 226.

157 "persistent," "no election": Ibid., 230.

157 Dodsgon objected to picture of Snark: Carroll 2006, xxx.

160 Intended to publish book on voting theory: Black 1958, 190, 207.

160 "A really scientific method": Ibid., 234.

160 "But oh my dear I am tired": Lyall 2001.

9. Instant Runoff

163 "Predominant power should not be turned over": Horwill 1925, 18.

164 Conservative politics: See a letter Ware wrote to Booker T. Washington in which he likens trade-unionism to slavery. The letter, dated June 2, 1913, is housed with Washington's papers at the Library of Congress, container 932. See also vol. 12, p. 197, in the Booker T. Washington Papers website at www.historycooperative.org/btw/Vol.12/html/197.html.

165 "How I wish the enclosed": Cohen 1995, 426.

165 "however Conservative the object": Ibid., 426.

165 "Please don't call my scheme": Ibid., 427.

167 "IRV elects candidates": "Instant Runoff Voting," www.fairvote.org/library/brochure/
newirvrunoffbrochure.pdf.

169 "winner-turns-loser paradox": Doron and Kronick 1977.

169 Voting for Edwards caused him to lose: This discussion is indebted to an untitled
flyer comparing IRV and approval voting, www.zesty.ca/approval/approval.pdf.

170 "In IRV, every time": www.rangevoting.org/rangeVirv.

IO. Who's Afraid of the Big Bad Cycle?

172 Story about Robert Lincoln, Equinox House: Ward 1992.

173 A score (twenty-three) cities used STV: Cabrera 2006.

174 "I consider PR [proportional representation] the most un-American": www.nyu.edu/
gsas/dept/history/public_history/PR.

174 Figures for city council seats: Ibid.

174 "complicated, trying the voters' patience": Ibid.

174 "there is among the PR groups": Ibid.

175 Staller biography: www.rotten.com/library/bio/entertainers/actors/cicciolina/.

175 "'Stalin Frankenstein' Project": www.nyu.edu/gsas/dept/history/public_history/PR.

175 "By 1960 there was only Cambridge": Richie, interview, Tacoma Park, Md., Oct. 9, 2006.

176 "I am quite prepared to be told": Black 1958, 230.

177 "Suppose A to be the candidate": Ibid., 232.

177 "This principle of voting": Ibid., 233.

177 Decision to use Gingrich in TV ad: Morris 1997, 184.

178 Falwell on Clinton and Lucifer: Potter 2006.

178 Riker biography: Bueno De Mesquita and Shepsle 2001.

179 Riker interpreted Powell amendment as Condorcet cycle: Riker 1958 and 1965.

180 "has been seized upon": Riker 1982, 154.

180 "The main thrust of Arrow's theorem": Ibid., 136.

181 "consigns democratic outcomes—and hence the democratic method": Ibid., 119.

181 "I don't care": www.en.wikiquote.org/wiki/William_Marcy_Tweed.

181 "For a price, I will come to your organization": Saari 2001, 100.

181 "I don't want to identify who": Saari, interview, Irvine, Calif., Mar. 21, 2006.

182 "Stop them damned pictures": www2.truman.edu/parker/research/cartoons.html.

183 Riker manipulated U.S. News list: McLean 2003, 17.

183 Riker claims cyclical majority: Riker 1982, 228–29.

184 Only a few ways cycles can occur: See Miller 2001.

185 "We have not exorcised": Feld and Grofman 1992, 235.

185 "Can you direct me": McQuaig 2001.

II. Buckley and the Clones

186 Morgenstern upset at learning other salaries: Steven Brams, interview, New York, Aug. 30, 2005.

186 Morgenstern charmed by Austrian wife; deathbed visit: Ibid.

190 "the worst candidate can win" paradox: Hillinger 2005.

190 "Why shouldn't supporters": personal e-mail, Weber, Apr. 25, 2006.

191 Vote for as many candidates as they like; most votes wins: This two-sentence description of approval voting is indebted to Ka-Ping Yee.

194 Presidential primaries article: Kellett and Mott 1977.

194 "This form of voting": Ottewell 2004.

195 Strategic approval voting: Myerson and Weber 1993; Smith 2000.

198 "created this kind of aura": Smith, interview (phone), Oct. 26, 2006.

199 "The patrician republic gave Venice": Finlay 1980, quoted in Lines 1986, 170–71.

199 Use for electing popes: Colmer and McLean 1998.

199 Use in Soviet Union, United Nations: See references in Brams and Fishburn 2003, 4.

199 Does not violate constitutions, requires only statute: Brams and Fishburn 1983, 9.

200 "I was at a conference": Saari, interview, Irvine, Calif., Mar. 21, 2006.

I2. Bad Santa

202 "Oh, isn't that *funny*!": Saari, interview, Irvine, Calif., Mar. 21, 2006.

202 "a hobby, looked at on weekends": Ibid.

202 "was telling me about Arrow's theorem": Ibid.

202 "Like an addiction": Ibid.

202 "They asked me what voting method": Ibid.

203 "I'll leave it to your imagination": Ibid.

203 "Well, now there's a quandary": Ibid.

203 "Brams and Fishburn objected to the paper": Ibid.

203 "We began our analysis": Saari and Van Newenhizen 1988a, 103.

203 "bizarre cases": Brams, Fishburn, and Merrill 1988a, 124.

204 "AV [approval voting] is much worse": Saari and Van Newenhizen 1988b, 133–34.

204 "A more accurate title for AV": Ibid., 142.

204 "It may make good sense": Ibid.

204 "'Dad, did you ever write a paper'": Saari, interview.

204 "'Steve's a good person'": Ibid.

207 "While the behavioral assumptions": Ibid.

208 "Although excellence is the clear choice": Saari and Van Newenhizen 1988b, 139.

208 "Indeed, these problems": Ibid., 1988b, 146–47.

208 "Let me give you": Saari, interview.

210 Article on Perot and approval voting: Brams and Merrill 1994.

210 "authoritarian and conspiratorial": Ibid., 40.

210 "*Clinton could have come*": Tabarrok 2001, 288.

210 "Indeterminacy, like inconsistency": Brams, Fishburn, Merrill 1988a, 129.

213 "The primary challenge": Weber, personal e-mail, Apr. 25, 2006.

213 Humphrey's advisors wanted Ventura in debates: Sifry 2002, 22.

214 Similar to a 'prisoner's dilemma': In a true prisoner's dilemma, the worst outcome is to cooperate while your partner(s) betray you. In the approval voting case, the worst scenario is for everyone (Goodell's and Ottinger's supporters) to betray each other. This results in the election of Buckley, the "worst" candidate to liberals.

214 "This is the paper": Weber, personal e-mail, Apr. 25, 2006.

217 "The great weakness": Letter, Terry Sanford to Donald Saari, April 19, 1985, reported in Saari and Van Newenhizen 1988b, 141–45.

217 "They had three excellent candidates": Saari, interview, Irvine, Calif., Mar. 21, 2006.

I3. Last Man Standing

219 "That's the Condorcet winner!": Saari, interview, Irvine, Calif., Mar. 21, 2006.

220 "I find the Condorcet winner": Saari 1995, 46.

220 "Pairwise voting is a mess!": Ibid., 70.

221 "1. Yes. As a matter": see comments and vote results at www.en.wikipedia.org/wiki/Wikipedia:Manual_of_Style_%28biographies%29/Survey_on_Style-Prefixed_Honorary_Titles.

222 "Forgive me for having": www.en.wikipedia.org/wiki/Wikipedia_talk:How_to_hold_a_consensus_vote.

222 "This is not the purpose": Ibid.

223 "true majority voting": Dasgupta and Maskin 2004.

223 "suspicious numbers": Yee, interview (phone), July 21, 2006.

224 "suggests to me that it is": www.en.wikipedia.org/wiki/Wikipedia_talk:How_to_hold_a_consensus_vote.

225 The Condorcet winner doesn't necessarily deserve to win: See Saari 1995.

227 "Manipulative behavior is important": Ibid., 12–13.

227 Saari's talk to fourth-graders: Saari 1991.

227 "Kids wanted to write Congress": Saari, interview.

227 "I think the field": Ibid.

228 "I thought for sure [this idea] was correct": Ibid.

228 "The Borda count, because of its symmetry": Ibid.

228 "the easiest to manipulate": McLean 2003, 16.

228 "wide-spread prior knowledge": Saari 1995, 235–36.

229 "You start getting into these debates": Smith, interview (phone), Oct. 26, 2006.

230 "There are *billions* of properties": Saari, interview.

230 "Academics probably are not": Brams and Fishburn 2003, 5.

14. Hot or Not?

231 "Ever hang out with your friends": www.hotornot.com/pages/about.html.

232 NetNielson rating: en.wikipedia.org/wiki/Hot_or_Not.

233 Loiseau suicide over downgrade: www.en.wikipedia.org/wiki/Bernard_Loiseau.

236 "Arrow's Nobel-winning 1951 'impossibility theorem'": Smith 2006, 1.

236 "Arrow's theorem is not nearly": Smith 2005b, 2.

237 "expected avoidable human unhappiness": www.math.temple.edu/~wds/homepage/
bayregdum.txt.

238 Early studies inconclusive: Smith, interview (phone), Oct. 26, 2006.

238 Smith's simulations: Full data is at www.math.temple.edu/~wds/homepage/voFdata/.

240 Robust superiority: In three simulations with near-complete voter ignorance, honest
Borda did slightly better than honest range for five candidates only. See ibid.

242 "trained from birth to rule": www.math.temple.edu/~wds/homepage/rvcritreply.

242 "switching to range voting": Ibid.

242 Honeybee "range voting": Smith 2006.

244 10 percent honesty: Smith 2000, 26.

245 "There is no machine": www.fairvote.org/blog/index.php/2006/06/27/there-are-
solutions-to-the-voting-machine-conundrum/.

246 "unnecessarily complicated": "curmudgeon [web name]"on www.thenewstribune.com.

247 Voters don't know vice president: Smith, interview.

247 "a wisdom of crowds thing": Hong, interview (phone), Nov. 10, 2006.

247 "people will look at the pictures": Ibid.

247 "Sometimes people can't even express": Ibid.

248 "Before we started": Smith, Quintal, Greene 2005, 10.

248 "evaluative voting": Felsenthal 1989, Hillinger 2004. For Ossipoff's discussion, see
www.rangevoting.org/OssipoffEnd.html.

249 "Everything should be made": www.rangevoting.org/Complexity.html.

15. Present but Not Voting

250 "Does that mean it's louder?": *This Is Spinal Tap*, Embassy Pictures, 1984.

250 Special Marshall amplifier models: www.spinaltapfan.com/atozed/TAP00160.HTM.

252 "present but not voting": www.en.wikipedia.org/wiki/Jeremy_Bentham.

252 "No approach to welfare economics": Sen 1984, 1073.

252 "The viewpoint will be taken": Arrow 1963, 9.

252 Controversy, Lionel Robbins: This discussion is greatly indebted to Hillinger 2004 and 2005.

253 "a kind of bible on methodology": Hillinger 2004, 15.

254 "assigning the utility 1": Arrow 1963, 32.

254 "It is hard not to see": Ibid.

255 Passage discouraged generations of theorists: See for instance Riker 1982, 110–12, which dismisses "utilitarian voting" for much the same reason as Arrow.

255 "a fundamental blind spot": Hillinger 2005, 6.

255 "the above result appears": Arrow 1963, 33.

256 Samuelson said Arrow-style proof possible for range voting: Hook 1967.

256 "Harsanyi's axioms": Hillinger 2006, 9.

257 "conditions satisfied comfortably": Sen 1986, 1074.

257 "To admit a simple solution": Hillinger 2006, 56.

257 "always cuts me down": Smith, interview.

257 "Saari kind of lives": Ibid.

257 "At first I tried to publish": Hillinger, personal e-mail, Jan. 12, 2007.

258 "The Case for Utilitarian Voting": Hillinger 2005.

258 Ossipoff, Simmons endorsements: see "Endorsements" link at www.rangevoting.org.

258 "I can see that Range Voting": www.rangevoting.org/OttewellEndorse.html.

258 "The profession dealing with collective choice": Hillinger, personal e-mail.

258 "There is an open door": Hillinger 2006, 48.

16. The Way Democracy Will Be

261 "In a way, I secretly hope": Guterman 2000.

261 "People are happy with plurality voting": Weber personal e-mail, Apr. 25, 2006.

262 "We received immediate answers": Flanigan e-mail, quoted in personal e-mail from Ottewell, Apr. 22, 2006.

263 "quota queen": Bolick 1993.

263 "Unbelievably, the woman": quoted in Richie and Naureckas 1993.

263 "we had to change the name": Richie, interview, Tacoma Park, Md., Oct. 9, 2006.

263 "IRV was sort of there": Ibid.

264 "I thought that Al Gore": Ibid.

264 "I think it's helped us": Ibid.

264 Muppets use IRV: www.fairvote.org/media/irv/Muppets/muppets/muppets.htm.

265 "I'm in favor of trying it": *Time*, "Notebook," April 15, 2002.

265 "the biggest year yet for IRV": Voting and Democracy Review 15, June 2002, on Center website, www.fairvote.org/e_news/annivnwsltr.htm.

266 "They grabbed onto something": Saari, interview, Irvine, Calif., Mar. 21, 2006.

266 "I find it disturbing": Hillinger 2004, 14.

266 "I'm trying to get money": Smith, interview (phone), Oct. 26, 2006.

267 "I was just on the range voting": Richie, interview.

267 "Some people, it really": Ibid.

267 "font of falsities about IRV": www.rangevoting.org/Irvtalk.html.

268 "We've had thousands of elections": Richie, interview.

268 "these mathematical 'paradoxes'": www.rangevoting.org/DebateHillIRV1.html.

268 Peru election: www.rangevoting.org/Peru06.html.

269 "No System Is Perfect": www.fairvote.org/?page=1686.

269 "This means that for any system": www.fairvote.org/?page=1688.

270 "IRV seems to be something": Richie, interview.

271 "I just wish the advocates": Ibid.

271 "non-starter": Ibid.

271 "could cause the defeat": www.fairvote.org/irv/approval.htm.

271 Hitler-versus-Gandhi example: www.rangevoting.org/Maskin.html.

272 "Get Real Democracy": www.rangevoting.org.

273 "What zealots basically do": Richie, interview.

273 "I must admit it's hard": Richie, personal e-mail.

273 "FOR ANYONE WHO DOESN'T KNOW": "Broken Living: The Life and Times of Clay Shentrup," brokenliving.blogspot.com, Sep. 30, 2006.

273 "Clay calls IRV advocates up": Richie, personal e-mail.

274 Range voting people as supporters of the status quo: Richie, personal e-mail.

274 Range voting better for third parties: www.rangevoting.org/NurseryEffect.html.

275 "Small third parties": Ibid.

276 "The party structure is not a given": Arrow, interview, Palo Alto, Calif., Dec. 16, 2005.

277 IRV is closest to plurality: A good visual illustration of this is on Ka-Ping Yee's webpage at www.zesty.ca/voting.

277 "There were two communities": Richie, interview.

17. Blue Man Coup

279 "It's 14:59": O'Toole 2006.

280 "macaca" video, rating: www.youtube.com/watch?v=r90z0PMnKwI.

280 "Less than $600": Champion 2006.

Notes

281   "People ask me if it's permanent": CNN.com, "Senate Candidate Blue—Literally," Oct. 3, 2002.

281   "It's my fault I overdosed": www.rotten.com/library/medicine/quackery/argyria/.

281   "batshit crazy": www.hensleigh.net, Oct. 6, 2006.

281   "launched into a tirade": Ibid.

281   "either complacent or involved": Duganz 2006.

282   "As a scientist, you can say": Arrow, interview, Palo Alto, Calif., Dec. 16, 2005.

283   "There are few ways": www.rangevoting.org/OttewellEndorse.html.

Sources

Adams, James R., and Ernest W. Adams (2000). "The Geometry of Voting Cycles." *Journal of Theoretical Politics* 12: 131–53.

Amadae, S. M. (2003). *Rationalizing Capitalist Democracy: The Cold War Origins of Rational Choice Liberalism*. Chicago: University of Chicago Press.

Archibold, Randal C. (2006). "In Cost and Vitriol, Race in Arizona Draws Notice." *The New York Times*, Sept. 11, 2006.

Arrow, Kenneth J. (1963). *Social Choice and Individual Values* (second edition). New Haven and London: Yale University Press. Originally published 1951. The 1963 edition includes a new chapter appraising subsequent work.

Atwater, Lee, and Todd Brewster (1991). "Lee Atwater's Last Campaign." *Life*, Feb. 1991, 58–67.

Baker, Daniel B., ed. (1990). *Political Quotations*. Detroit: Gale Research.

Baughman, Christopher (2002). "Edwin Edwards Preparing for Next Stage of His Life: Federal Prison." *Baton Rouge Advocate*, Oct. 20, 2002.

Bender, Steve, James T. Black, and Dianne Young (1997). "Crusader Cartoonists." *Southern Living*, April 1997.

Bergson, Abram (Burk) (1938). "A Reformulation of Certain Aspects of Welfare Economics." *Quarterly Journal of Economics*, 310–34.

Black, Duncan (1948). "On the Rationale of Group Decision-making." *Journal of Political Economy* 56: 23–34.

——— (1958). *The Theory of Committees and Elections*. Cambridge: Cambridge University Press.

Sources

Black, Duncan, ed. by Iain McLean, Alistair McMillan, and Burt L. Monroe (1996). *A Mathematical Approach to Proportional Representation: Duncan Black on Lewis Carroll*. Boston/Dordrecht/London: Kluver Academic Publishers.

Blumenthal, Max (2004a). "Nader's Dubious Raiders." AlterNet, June 25, 2004.

——— (2004b). "Republican Dirty Tricks." AlterNet, Oct. 15, 2004.

Blumenthal, Ralph (2006). "Clear-Cut Race Shifting into Texas-Size Free-for-All." *The New York Times*, Sept. 22, 2006.

Blumenthal, Sidney (1980). *The Permanent Campaign: Inside the World of Elite Political Operatives*. Boston: Beacon Press.

Boehm, George A. W. (1976). "One Fervent Vote Against Wintergreen." Privately circulated mimeograph.

Bolick, Clint (1993). "Clinton's Quota Queens." *The Wall Street Journal*, Apr. 30, 1993.

Bowen, Howard (1943). "The Interpretation of Voting in the Allocation of Economic Resources." *Quarterly Journal of Economics* 58: 27–49.

Brady, John Joseph (1997). *Bad Boy: The Life and Politics of Lee Atwater*. Reading, Mass.: Addison Wesley.

Brams, Steven J. (2006). "Approval Voting: A Better Way to Select a Winner." MIT Alumni Association website, alum.mit.edu/ne/whatmatters/200211/index.html.

Brams, Steven J., and Peter C. Fishburn (1978). "Approval Voting." *American Political Science Review*, Sept. 1978, 831–47.

——— (1983). *Approval Voting*. Boston: Birkhauser.

——— (2002). "Voting Procedures." In *Handbook of Social Choice and Welfare, Vol. 1*. Edited by K. J. Arrow, A. K. Sen, and K. Suzumura. Boston: North Holland/Elsevier.

——— (2003). "Going from Theory to Practice: The Mixed Success of Approval Voting." Delivered at 2003 meeting of American Political Science Association, Philadelphia, Aug. 28–31.

Brams, Steven J., Peter C. Fishburn, and Samuel Merrill III (1988a). "The Responsiveness of Approval Voting: Comments on Saari and Van Newenhizen." *Public Choice* 59, 121–31.

Brams, Steven J., Peter C. Fishburn, and Samuel Merrill III (1988b). "Rejoinder to Saari and Van Newenhizen." *Public Choice* 59, 149.

Brams, Steven J., and Paul Hager (2002). "Why the Academy Awards May Fail to Pick the 'Best Picture' Again." www.cs.indiana.edu/~hagerp/ampas_nyu.htm.

Brams, Steven J., and Samuel Merrill III (1994). "Would Ross Perot Have Won the 1992 Presidential Election Under Approval Voting?" *PS: Political Science and Politics* 27: 39–44.

Brams, Steven J., and M. Remzi Sanver (2006). "Voting Systems That Combine Approval and Preference." www.nyu.edu/gsas/dept/politics/faculty/brams/approval_preference.pdf.

Braun, Stephen, and Ralph Vartabedian (2005). "Levees Weakened as New Orleans Board, Federal Engineers Feuded." *Los Angeles Times*, Dec. 25, 2005.

Brewer, Mark (2004). "Mich. GOP Rips Ballot by Backing Nader's Bid." *The Detroit News*, Oct. 1, 2004.

Bridges, Tyler (2001). *Bad Bet on the Bayou: The Rise of Gambling in Louisiana and the Fall of Governor Edwin Edwards*. New York: Farrar, Straus and Giroux.

Brodesky, Josh (2006). "Huffman's Foes in Primary Blast National GOP Support." *Arizona Daily Star*, Sept. 6, 2006.

Brodie, John, and Bob Mack (1990). "Up Close and Personal with Lee Atwater, Homebody." *Spy*, May 1990, 88–89.

Budoff, Carrie (2006). "Santorum Calls Casey a 'Thug' in Residency Flap." *Philadelphia Daily News*, May 20, 2006.

Buchanan, Pat, and Ralph Nader (2004). "Ralph Nader: Conservatively Speaking." *The American Conservative*, June 21, 2004.

Bueno De Mesquita, Bruce, and Kenneth Shepsle (2001). "William Harrison Riker. "Washington, D.C.: National Academy Press, newton.nap.edu/html/biomems/wriker.html.

Cabrera, Marisa (2006). "Oscars Insight: Proportional Voting System Makes for Wide-open Nomination Pick." FairVote research report.

Cain, Brad (2006). "Starrett Doesn't Mind 'Spoiler' Tag in Oregon Governor's Race." Associated Press, Aug. 20, 2006.

Carroll, Lewis (1992). *Alice's Adventures in Wonderland and Through the Looking Glass*. New York: Knopf. Reprints the 1865 and 1871 books.

——— (ed. by Martin Gardner) (2006). *The Annotated Hunting of the Snark*. New York: Norton.

Casti, John L., and Werner DePauli (2000). *Gödel: A Life of Logic*. Cambridge, Mass.: Perseus.

Champion, Allison Brophy (2006). "Glenda Parker a Third Wheel to Allen, Webb." *The Culpepper Star Exponent*, Sept. 8, 2006.

Clarkson, Fred (2004). "Will Roy Moore Crack the Bush Base?" *Salon*, May 4, 2004.

Cohen, Jeff (2004). "Nader's 'Grassroots' Campaign . . . Courtesy of GOP." CommonDreams.org, July 20, 2004.

Cohen, Morton N. (1995). *Lewis Carroll: A Biography*. New York: Knopf.

Cohn, Edward (2000). "Perot, Revised." *The American Prospect*, Jan. 3, 2000.

Collins, Gail (1998). *Scorpion Tongues: Gossip, Celebrity, and American Politics*. New York: William Morrow.

Colmer, Josep M., and Iain McLean (1998). "Electing Popes: Approval Balloting and Qualified-majority Rule." *The Journal of Interdisciplinary History* 29: 1–22.

Sources

Cox, Gary W. (1987). *The Cabinet and the Development of Political Parties in Victorian England*. New York: Cambridge University Press.

Darnton, Robert (1997). "Condorcet and the Craze for America in France." In *Franklin and Condorcet: Two Portraits from the American Philosophical Society*. Philadelphia: American Philosophical Society.

Dasgupta, Partha, and Eric Maskin (2004). "The Fairest Vote of All." *Scientific American*, March 2004, 92–97.

Davis, Richard H. (2004). "The Anatomy of a Smear Campaign." *Boston Globe*, March 21, 2004.

Davis, William C. (1974). *Breckinridge: Statesman, Soldier, Symbol*. Baton Rouge: Louisiana State University Press.

Dawson, John W. (1997). *Logical Dilemmas: The Life and Work of Kurt Gödel*. Wellesley, Mass.: A. K. Peters.

De Grazia, Alfred (1953). "Mathematical Derivation of an Election System" (translation of Jean-Charles de Borda's 1781 "Memoir on Elections by Ballot" with commentary). *Isis*, June 1953, 42–51.

De Rooy, Lenny (2005). "Lenny's Alice in Wonderland Site." www.alice-in-wonderland.net.

DeMeyer, Frank, and Charles Plott (1970). "The Probability of a Cyclic Majority." *Econometrica* 38: 345–54.

Doherty, Joseph W. (2006). "The Hidden Network: Political Consultants form Party Infrastructure." *Campaigns and Elections*, Aug. 2006, 39–42.

Doron, Gideon, and Richard Kronick (1977). "Single Transferable Vote: An Example of a Perverse Social Choice Function." *American Journal of Political Science* 21: 303–311.

Dotson, Chad (2006). "From the Right: The Voter Vault Victory?" *Campaigns and Elections*, May 2006.

DuBos, Clancy (2003). "Getting Down with Raymond Strother." *Gambit Weekly*, May 20, 2003.

Duganz, Pat (2006). "Jones Not Blue About Odds of Winning Senate Seat." *Montana Kaimin*, Nov. 8, 2006.

Edsall, Thomas B. (2006). *Building Red America: The New Conservative Coalition and the Drive for Permanent Power*. New York: Basic Books.

Estrich, Susan (1989). "Willie Horton and Me: The Hidden Politics of Race." *Washington Post Magazine*, Apr. 23, 1989.

Farren, Mick (2004). "The Dark Art of Elections." *Los Angeles City Beat*, Oct. 21, 2004.

Feiwel, George R., ed. (1987a). *Arrow and the Ascent of Modern Economic Theory*. Basingstoke: Macmillan Press.

——— (1987b). *Arrow and the Foundations of the Theory of Economic Policy*. Basingstoke: Macmillan Press.

Sources

Feld, Scott L., and Bernard Grofman (1992). "Who's Afraid of the Big Bad Cycle?: Evidence from Thirty-six Elections." *Journal of Theoretical Politics* 4: 231–37.

Felsenthal, D. S. (1989). "On Combining Approval with Disapproval Voting." *Behavioral Science* 34: 53–60.

Finlay, Robert (1980). *Politics in Renaissance Venice*. New Brunswick, N.J.: Rutgers University Press.

Fishburn, Peter C., and Steven J. Brams (1983). "Paradoxes of Preferential Voting." *Mathematics Magazine* 56: 207–14.

Gavin, Patrick W. (2006). "American Democracy: Can It Be Repaired?" *Washington Examiner*, Aug. 3, 2006.

Geer, John G. (2006). "Nasty, Brutish and Short." *Los Angeles Times*, Apr. 23, 2006.

Gertner, Jon (2004). "The Very Personal Is the Political." *The New York Times*, Feb. 15, 2004.

Gibbard, Allan (1973). "Manipulation of Voting Schemes: A General Result." *Econometrica* 41: 587–601.

Gorman, Mark, and Morton Kamien (1968). "The Paradox of Voting: Probability Calculations." *Behavioral Science* 13 (July 1968): 306–16.

Green, Joshua (2004). "Karl Rove in a Corner." *The Atlantic Monthly*, Nov. 2004.

Guinier, Lani (1993). "Lani Guinier's Challenge to the Press." *Extra!*, Nov./Dec. 1993.

Gustafson, Melanie Susan (2001). *Women and the Republican Party, 1854–1924*. Champaign: University of Illinois Press.

Guterman, Lila (2000). "When Votes Don't Add Up." *The Chronicle of Higher Education*, Nov. 3, 2000.

Harsanyi, John C. (1953). "Cardinal Utility in Welfare Economics and the Theory of Risk-taking. *Journal of Political Economy* 61: 434–35.

Hefling, Kimberly (2006). "Poll: Casey Leads Santorum Despite Third Candidate; Race Tightens." Associated Press, Aug. 15, 2006.

Herbert, Bob (2005). "Impossible, Ridiculous, Repugnant." *The New York Times*, Oct. 6, 2005.

Hill, Steven (2002). *Fixing Elections: The Failure of America's Winner Take All Politics*. New York and London: Routledge.

Hillinger, Claude (2004). "On the Possibility of Democracy and Rational Collective Choice." University of Munich, Department of Economics discussion paper 2004–21. ssrn.com/abstract=608821.

——— (2005). "The Case for Utilitarian Voting." *Homo Oeconomicus* 23: 295–321. Also, University of Munich, Department of Economics discussion paper 2005–11. epub. ub.uni-muenchem.de.

——— (2006). "Science and Ideology in Economic, Political and Social Thought." SEMECON, University of Munich. ssrn.com/abstract=945947.

Sources

Hoag, Clarence Gilbert, and George Hervey Hallet, Jr. (1926). *Proportional Representation*. New York: Macmillan.

Hook, S., ed. (1967). *Human Values and Economic Policy: A Symposium*. New York: New York University Press.

Horwill, George (1925). *Proportional Representation: Its Dangers and Defects*. London: G. Allen and Unwin.

Hotelling, Harold (1929). "Stability in Competition." *The Economic Journal* 39: 41–57.

Humbert, Marc (2006). "Hillary Clinton Using Harsher Rhetoric." *Washington Post*, Jan. 19, 2006.

Jackson, Peter (2006). "In Potential Boost for Santorum, GOP Aids Green Candidate." Associated Press, Aug. 1, 2006.

Jenkins, Logan (2006). "Griffith Could Make 50th District Race More Interesting." *San Diego Union-Tribune*, May 29, 2006.

Johnson, Dennis W. (2001). *No Place for Amateurs: How Political Consultants Are Reshaping American Democracy*. New York: Routledge.

Kamman, Jon (2006). "Republican Candidates Lash Out at GOP Tactics." *The Arizona Republic*, Sept. 6, 2006.

Kaplan, Jonathan E., and Patrick O'Connor (2006). "All Eyes on California-50." *The Hill*, June 8, 2006.

Kellett, John, and Kenneth Mott (1977). "Presidential Primaries: Measuring Popular Choice." *Polity* 9: 528–37.

Kelley, Kitty (2004). *The Family: The Real Story of the Bush Dynasty*. New York: Doubleday.

Kiel, Paul (2006). "GOP Donors Funded Entire PA Green Party Drive." TPM Muckraker.com, Aug. 2, 2006.

Kislanko, Paul (2005). "Building a Glass House." football.kislanko.com/BCSglass.html.

Klarreich, Erica (2002). "Election Selection: Are We Using the Worst Voting Procedure?" *Science News*, Nov. 2, 2002, 280ff.

Klein, Joe (2006). *Politics Lost: How American Democracy Was Trivialized by People Who Think You're Stupid*. New York: Doubleday.

Knapp, George (2004). "Investigation into Trashed Voter Registrations." Oct. 13, 2004. www.klas-tv.com/Global/story.asp?S=2421595&nav=168XRvNe.

Kopel, Dave (2000). "The Veep's Underwear." *NRO Weekend*, Sept. 20–Oct. 1, 2000. www.davekopel.com/Misc/OpEds/VPunderwear.htm.

Lamis, Alexander P., ed. (1999). *Southern Politics in the 1990s*. Baton Rouge: Louisiana State University Press.

Landsburg, Steven E. (1999). "Win, Place, and No!" *Slate*, Feb. 6, 1999. www.slate.com/id/18581/.

Leach, Karoline (1996). "Ina in Wonderland." *Times Literary Supplement*, May 3, 1996.

———— (1999). *In the Shadow of the Dreamchild*. London: Peter Owen.

LeBoutillier, John (2001). "Why the Bushes Will Never Hire Linda Tripp." NewsMax.com, Feb. 12, 2001.

Lemann, Nicholas (2003). "The Controller." *The New Yorker*, May 12, 2003.

Leonard, Robert J. (1995). "From Parlor Games to Social Science: von Neumann, Morgenstern, and the Creation of Game Theory 1928–1944." *Journal of Economic Literature* 33: 730–61.

Leonhardt, David (2007). "What $1.2 Trillion Can Buy." *The New York Times*, Jan. 17, 2007.

Levin, J., and Barry Nalebuff, (1995). "An Introduction to Vote-counting Schemes." *Journal of Economic Perspectives* 9, no. 1: 3–26.

Levine, Harry G. (2004). "Ralph Nader as Mad Bomber." www.hereinstead.com/Ralph-Nader-As-Mad-Bomber.html.

Lines, Marjorie (1986). "Approval Voting and Strategy Analysis: A Venetian Example." *Theory and Decision* 20: 155–72.

Lizza, Ryan (2006). "George Allen's Race Problem: Pin Prick." *New Republic*, May 8, 2006.

Loosemore, Sandra (1997). "If It Ain't Broke, Don't Fix It: An Analysis of the Figure Skating Scoring System." www.frogsonice.com/skateweb/obo/score-tech.shtml.

Luce, R. Duncan, and Howard Raiffa (1957). *Games and Decisions*. New York: Wiley.

Lyall, Sarah (2001). "Granddaughter of Lewis Carroll's Muse Puts Collection Up for Sale." *The New York Times*, April 19, 2001.

Mackenzie, Dana (2000). "May the Best Man Lose." *Discover*, Nov. 2000, 84ff.

Maginnis, John (1992). *Cross to Bear*. Baton Rouge, La.: Darkhorse Press.

"The Mailzilla: Attack of the Monster Direct Mail Mistakes." *Campaigns and Elections*, May 2006.

Maisel, L. Sandy, ed. (1991). *Political Parties and Elections in the United States: An Encyclopedia*, vol. 1. New York: Garland.

Malchow, Hal (2003). *The New Political Targeting*. Washington, D.C.: Campaigns and Elections.

Martin, Barry (1999). "Flag Waving in the Palmetto State." The Southerner Journal, www.southerner.net.

Martin, Justin (2002). *Nader: Crusader, Spoiler, Icon*. New York: Basic Books.

McCoy, John (1997). "The Ether Monument, Boston Public Gardens." mccoy.pair.com/personal/ether.html.

McGivern, Tim (2004). "Register and Support Ralph?" *Weekly Alibi*, www.alibi.com, Aug. 20, 2004.

McKelvey, Richard (1979). "General Conditions for Global Intransitivities in Formal Voting Models." *Econometrica* 47: 1085–112.

Sources

McLean, Iain (1990). "The Borda and Condorcet Principles: Three Medieval Applications." *Social Choice and Welfare* 7: 99–108.

——— (2002). "Australian Electoral Reform and Two Concepts of Representation." Paper for APSA Jubilee Conference, Canberra, Oct. 2002.

——— (2003). "The Reasonableness of Independence." Nuffield College Politics Working Paper 2003-W6. Oxford: University of Oxford.

McLean, Iain, and Fiona Hewitt (trans. and eds.) (1994). *Condorcet, Foundations of Social Choice and Political Theory*. Aldershot, UK: Edward Elgar.

McQuaig, Linda (2001). *All You Can Eat: Greed, Lust and the New Capitalism*. New York: Penguin.

Merrill, Samuel (1988). *Making Multicandidate Elections More Democratic*. Princeton, N.J.: Princeton University Press.

Miller, John J., and Ramesh Ponnuru (2001). "The GOP's Libertarian Problem." *National Review Online*, March 19, 2001.

Miller, Mark Crispin, and Jared Irmas (2005). "Team Bush Paid Millions to Nathan Sproul—and Tried to Hide It." *Baltimore Chronicle*, July 5, 2005.

Miller, Nicholas R. (2001). "The Geometry of Voting Cycles: Theoretical Developments." Presented at 2001 meeting of the Public Choice Society, San Antonio, Mar. 9–11.

Mooney, Chris (2003). "W.'s Christian Nation." *The American Prospect*, June 1, 2003.

Moore, Glover (1953). *The Missouri Controversy, 1819–1821*. Lexington: University of Kentucky Press.

Moore, James, and Wayne Slater (2003). *Bush's Brain: How Karl Rove Made George W. Bush Presidential*. New York: Wiley.

Morgenstern, Oskar (1976). "The Collaboration Between Oskar Morgenstern and John von Neumann on the Theory of Games." *Journal of Economic Literature* 14: 805–16.

Morris, Dick (1997). *Behind the Oval Office: Winning the Presidency in the Nineties*. New York: Random House.

Myerson, Roger B., and Robert J. Weber (1993). "A Theory of Voting Equilibria." *American Political Science Review* 87: 102–14.

Nagourney, Adam (2006). "New Campaign Ads Have a Theme: Don't Be Nice." *The New York Times*, Sept. 27, 2006.

Nanson, E. J. (1882). "Methods of Election." *Transactions and Proceedings of the Royal Society of Victoria* 19: 197–240.

Nasar, Sylvia (1998). *A Beautiful Mind*. New York: Simon & Schuster.

Niemi, Richard, and Herbert Weisberg (1968). "A Mathematical Solution for the Probability of the Paradox of Voting." *Behavioral Science* 13: 317–23.

Noah, Timothy (2004). "Judge Roy Moore Speaks!" *Slate*, March 11, 2004.

Sources

O'Keefe, Eric (2005). "Lone Star Long Shot." *Cigar Aficionado*, Nov. 28, 2005.

Oppenheimer, Joe (2004). "Democracy and Justice: A Review of Gerry Mackie's Democracy Defended." Review essay submitted for publication in *Social Justice Research*.

O'Toole, James (2006). "Green Party Hopeful Is Out; Win for Casey." *Pittsburgh Post-Gazette*, Oct. 4, 2006.

Ottewell, Guy (2004). "The Arithmetic of Voting." Written 1968, published 1977 and revised several times. www.universalworkshop.com/pages/ArithmeticOfVoting.htm.

Pescatore, Brittney (2006). "The Greatest Opposition Research of All Time." *Campaigns and Elections*, Sept. 2006, 13.

Polk, James K., (ed. by Milo M. Quaife) (1910). *Diary*. Chicago: McClurg.

Pomper, Gerald M. (1993). "The Presidential Election." In *The Election of 1992* (Gerald M. Pomper, ed.). Chatham, N.J.: Chatham House.

Pooley, Eric (1996). "Who Is Dick Morris?" *Time*, Sept. 2, 1996.

Posner, Gerald (1977). *Citizen Perot*. New York: Random House.

Potter, Dena (2006). "Falwell Defends Clinton-Satan Remark." *Chicago Sun-Times*, Sept. 26, 2006.

Poundstone, William (1992). *Prisoner's Dilemma*. New York: Doubleday.

Public Broadcasting Service (2005). "Karl Rove—the Architect." TV show, video and transcripts at www.pbs.org/wgbh/pages/frontline/shows/architect.

Purnick, Joyce (2004). "Data Crunchers Try to Pinpoint Voters' Politics." *The New York Times*, Apr. 7, 2004.

Raskin, Jamin (2004). "The Return of Vote-Pairing." *Slate*, Oct. 25, 2004. slate.com/id/2108641/.

Regis, Ed (1987). *Who Got Einstein's Office?* Reading, Mass.: Addison-Wesley.

Reilly, Benjamin (2002). "Social Choice in the South Seas: Electoral Innovation and the Borda Count in the Pacific Island Countries." *International Political Science Review* 23, 355–72.

Reuters (2006). "The Post-Oscars Debate: Why *Brokeback* Lost." May 6, 2006.

Richie, Rob, and Jim Naureckas (1993). "Lani Guinier: 'Quota Queen' or Misquoted Queen?" *Extra!*, July/Aug. 1993.

Rider, Andrea (1991). "Conduct Unbecoming a Racist." *Spy*, Sept. 1991.

Riker, William H. (1958). "The Paradox of Voting and Congressional Rules for Voting on Amendments." *American Political Science Review* 52: 349–66.

——— (1962). *The Theory of Political Coalitions*. New Haven: Yale University Press.

——— (1965). "Arrow's Theorem and Some Examples of the Paradox of Voting." In *Mathematical Applications in Political Science*, vol. 1. Edited by John Claunch. Dallas: Arnold Foundation, Southern Methodist University, 41, 69.

Sources

———— (1982). *Liberalism Against Populism: A Confrontation Between the Theory of Democracy and the Theory of Social Choice*. San Francisco: Freeman, 1982.

———— (1986). *The Art of Political Manipulation*. New Haven and London: Yale University Press, 1986.

Roddy, Dennis B. (2004). "Campaign 2004: Voter Registration Workers Cry Foul." *Pittsburgh Post-Gazette*, Oct. 20, 2004.

Ryerson, James (2004). "Sidewalk Socrates." *The New York Times Magazine*, Dec. 26, 2004.

Saar, John (1973). "GOP Probes Official as Teacher of 'Tricks.'" *Washington Post*, Aug. 10, 1973.

Saari, Donald G. (1991). "A Fourth Grade Experience." www.math.uci.edu/~dsaari/fourthgrade.pdf.

———— (1995). *Basic Geometry of Voting*. Berlin/Heidelberg/New York: Springer.

———— (2001). *Chaotic Elections!* American Mathematical Society.

Saari, Donald G., and Jill Van Newenhizen (1988a). "The Problem of Indeterminacy in Approval, Multiple, and Truncated Voting Systems." *Public Choice* 59: 101–20.

Saari, Donald G., and Jill Van Newenhizen (1988b). "Is Approval Voting an Unmitigated Evil? A Response to Brams, Fishburn, and Merrill." *Public Choice* 59: 133–47.

Samuelson, Paul (1977). *The Collected Scientific Papers of Paul A. Samuelson*, vol. IV. Cambridge, Mass.: MIT Press.

Samuelson, Paul (2004). "Abram Bergson." In *Biographical Memoirs* 83: 23–34. Washington: National Academy of Sciences.

Satterthwaite, Mark (1975). "Strategyproofness and Arrow's Conditions." *Journal of Economic Theory* 10: 187–217.

Scarpinato, Daniel (2006). "Graf Leads GOP; 'Gabby Wanted Me, Has Me,' Front Runner Says." *Arizona Daily Star*, Sept. 13, 2006.

Sen, Amartya K. (1966). "A Possibility Theorem on Majority Decisions." *Econometrica* 34: 491–99.

———— (1970a). *Collective Choice and Social Welfare*. San Francisco: Holden-Day.

———— (1970b). "The Impossibility of a Paretian Liberal." *Journal of Political Economy* 78: 152–57.

———— (1986). "Social Choice Theory." Chapter in *Handbook of Mathematical Economics*, vol. 3 (ed. by Kenneth J. Arrow and Michael D. Intriligator). Amsterdam: North-Holland, 1986.

Sen, Amartya K., and Prasanta Pattanaik (1969). "Necessary and Sufficient Conditions for Rational Choice Under Majority Decisions." *Journal of Economic Theory* 1: 18–202.

Shubik, Martin (1978). "Oskar Morgenstern: Mentor and Friend." *International Journal of Game Theory*, 131–35.

Sources

Shulte, Elizabeth (2004). "When 1 Million Voted for Socialism." *Socialist Worker*, Oct. 1, 2004, 8.

Sifry, Micah L. (2002). *Spoiling for a Fight: Third-Party Politics in America*. New York: Routledge.

Simon, Roger (2004). "Willie Horton Redux?" *Jewish World Review*, Mar. 18, 2004.

Slackman, Michael (2005). "Watch Your Mouths, Candidates. The Voters Certainly Do." *The New York Times*, April 13, 2005.

Slater, Wayne (2005). "Strayhorn Gambles on Democrat Donors." *The Dallas Morning News*, July 29, 2005.

——— (2006). "Strayhorn Gets Democratic Cash." *The Dallas Morning News*, Jan. 27, 2006.

Smith, Sharon (2006). "Battle Over Ballot Spot Leads to Capitol Brouhaha." *The Patriot-News*, Aug. 19, 2006.

Smith, Warren D. (2000). "Range Voting." Paper No. 56 at math.temple.edu/~wds/homepage/works.html.

——— (2005a). "Direct Democracy." Paper No. 81 at math.temple.edu/~wds/homepage/works.html.

——— (2005b). "The Voting Impossibilities of Arrow, Gibbard & Satterthwaite, and Young." Paper No. 79 at math.temple.edu/~wds/homepage/works.html.

——— (2006). "Ants, Bees, and Computers Agree Range Voting Is Best Single-Winner System." Paper No. 96 at math.temple.edu/~wds/homepage/works.html.

Smith, Warren D., Jacqueline N. Quintal, and Douglas S. Greene (2005). "What If the 2004 U.S. Presidential Election Had Been Held Using Range or Approval Voting?" Paper No. 82 at math.temple.edu/~wds/homepage/works.html.

Solgard, Paul, and Paul Landskroener (2002). "Municipal Voting System Reform: Overcoming the Legal Obstacles." *Bench and Bar of Minnesota*, Oct. 2002.

Sperling, David L. (2003). "Booting Up for Safety." *Wisconsin Resources Magazine*, Dec. 2003.

Stanford, Phil (2006). "Finally, a Dash of Drama in Guv's Race." *The Portland Tribune*, Aug. 28, 2006.

Strother, Raymond (2003). *Falling Up: How a Redneck Helped Invent Political Consulting*. Baton Rouge: Louisiana State University Press.

Suber, Peter (1990). *The Paradox of Self-Amendment: A Study of Logic, Law, Omnipotence, and Change*. New York: Lang. www.earlham.edu/~peters/writing/psa.

Tabarrok, Alexander (2001). "President Perot or Fundamentals of Voting Theory Illustrated with the 1992 Election." *Public Choice* 106: 275–97.

Tabarrok, Alexander, and Lee Spector (1999). "Would the Borda Count Have Avoided the Civil War?" *Journal of Theoretical Politics* 11: 261–88.

Sources

Todhunter, Isaac. (1931). *A History of the Mathematical Theory of Probability from the Time of Pascal to That of Laplace*. New York: G. E. Stechert. Reprint of 1865 book.

Turnipseed, Tom (1991). "What Lee Atwater Learned and the Lesson for His Protégés." *The Washington Post*, April 16, 1991.

Walley, J. Zane (2003). "Judge Roy Moore: Captain America." Worldnetdaily.com, Aug. 21, 2003.

Ward, Geoffrey C. (1992). "Adam Powell and Malcolm X." *American Heritage*, July/Aug. 1992.

Weber, Robert J. (1977). "Comparison of Voting Systems." *Cowles Foundation Discussion Paper No. 498*. New Haven: Yale University.

——— (1995). "Approval Voting." *Journal of Economic Perspectives*, Winter 1995, 39–49.

Williams, David (2004). *Condorcet and Modernity*. Cambridge: Cambridge University Press.

Wilson, Woodrow (1885). *Congressional Government*. Boston: Houghton, Mifflin. Reissued 1956 and 1981.

Acknowledgments

Books are finite, and arguments are endless. At least they appear to be in the science of voting. As author, I have had to play moderator. In so doing, I've tried to be aware of the delicate politics of who gets the last word. I apologize in advance to anyone who feels that I cut off an argument at an inopportune point.

I'm grateful to everyone who took time to speak with me, to direct me to other people and resources, or to read the manuscript for comment. Especial thanks are due to Kenneth J. Arrow, Steven J. Brams, the contributors at ElectoWiki, Terry Fonville, Paul Hager, James Hong, Lawrence Hussar, Pete Kelly, Thomas LeBien, Guy Ottewell, Janet Phelps, Gerald M. Pomper, Rob Richie, Donald Saari, Arthur Flannigan Saint-Aubin, Warren D. Smith, Pauline Testerman, Robert J. Weber, Joseph Wisnovsky, and Ka-Ping Yee.

My research on spoilers in American presidential elections would have been vastly more laborious had it not been for Dave Liep's invaluable *Atlas of U.S. Presidential Elections* (www.uselectionatlas.org).

Index

Index

Index

Index